FREE Study Skills DVD Offer

Dear Customer,

Thank you for your purchase from Mometrix! We consider it an honor and a privilege that you have purchased our product and we want to ensure your satisfaction.

As a way of showing our appreciation and to help us better serve you, we have developed a Study Skills DVD that we would like to give you for FREE. This DVD covers our *best practices* for getting ready for your exam, from how to use our study materials to how to best prepare for the day of the test.

All that we ask is that you email us with feedback that would describe your experience so far with our product. Good, bad, or indifferent, we want to know what you think!

To get your FREE Study Skills DVD, email freedvd@mometrix.com with *FREE STUDY SKILLS DVD* in the subject line and the following information in the body of the email:

- The name of the product you purchased.
- Your product rating on a scale of 1-5, with 5 being the highest rating.
- Your feedback. It can be long, short, or anything in between. We just want to know your impressions and experience so far with our product. (Good feedback might include how our study material met your needs and ways we might be able to make it even better. You could highlight features that you found helpful or features that you think we should add.)
- Your full name and shipping address where you would like us to send your free DVD.

If you have any questions or concerns, please don't hesitate to contact me directly.

Thanks again!

Sincerely,

Jay Willis
Vice President
jay.willis@mometrix.com
1-800-673-8175

Mometrix
TEST PREPARATION
The World's #1 Test Preparation Company

Mometrix
TEST PREPARATION
SAT
Subject Test US History 2019 & 2020

SAT US History Subject Test
Secrets Study Guide

Full-Length Practice Test

Step-by-Step Review
Video Tutorials

Written and edited by the Mometrix Texas Teacher Certification Test Team

Printed in the United States of America

This paper meets the requirements of ANSI/NISO Z39.48-1992 (Permanence of Paper).

Mometrix offers volume discount pricing to institutions. For more information or a price quote, please contact our sales department at sales@mometrix.com or 888-248-1219.

Mometrix Media LLC is not affiliated with or endorsed by any official testing organization. All organizational and test names are trademarks of their respective owners.

Paperback
ISBN 13: 978-1-5167-1170-3
ISBN 10: 1-5167-1170-X

DEAR FUTURE EXAM SUCCESS STORY

First of all, **THANK YOU** for purchasing Mometrix study materials!

Second, congratulations! You are one of the few determined test-takers who are committed to doing whatever it takes to excel on your exam. **You have come to the right place.** We developed these study materials with one goal in mind: to deliver you the information you need in a format that's concise and easy to use.

In addition to optimizing your guide for the content of the test, we've outlined our recommended steps for breaking down the preparation process into small, attainable goals so you can make sure you stay on track.

We've also analyzed the entire test-taking process, identifying the most common pitfalls and showing how you can overcome them and be ready for any curveball the test throws you.

Standardized testing is one of the biggest obstacles on your road to success, which only increases the importance of doing well in the high-pressure, high-stakes environment of test day. Your results on this test could have a significant impact on your future, and this guide provides the information and practical advice to help you achieve your full potential on test day.

Your success is our success

We would love to hear from you! If you would like to share the story of your exam success or if you have any questions or comments in regard to our products, please contact us at **800-673-8175** or **support@mometrix.com**.

Thanks again for your business and we wish you continued success!

Sincerely,
The Mometrix Test Preparation Team

Need more help? Check out our flashcards at:
http://mometrixflashcards.com/SATII

TABLE OF CONTENTS

Introduction

Thank you for purchasing this resource! You have made the choice to prepare yourself for a test that could have a huge impact on your future, and this guide is designed to help you be fully ready for test day. Obviously, it's important to have a solid understanding of the test material, but you also need to be prepared for the unique environment and stressors of the test, so that you can perform to the best of your abilities.

For this purpose, the first section that appears in this guide is the **Secret Keys**. We've devoted countless hours to meticulously researching what works and what doesn't, and we've boiled down our findings to the five most impactful steps you can take to improve your performance on the test. We start at the beginning with study planning and move through the preparation process, all the way to the testing strategies that will help you get the most out of what you know when you're finally sitting in front of the test.

We recommend that you start preparing for your test as far in advance as possible. However, if you've bought this guide as a last-minute study resource and only have a few days before your test, we recommend that you skip over the first two Secret Keys since they address a long-term study plan.

If you struggle with **test anxiety**, we strongly encourage you to check out our recommendations for how you can overcome it. Test anxiety is a formidable foe, but it can be beaten, and we want to make sure you have the tools you need to defeat it.

Secret Key #1 – Plan Big, Study Small

There's a lot riding on your performance. If you want to ace this test, you're going to need to keep your skills sharp and the material fresh in your mind. You need a plan that lets you review everything you need to know while still fitting in your schedule. We'll break this strategy down into three categories.

Information Organization

Start with the information you already have: the official test outline. From this, you can make a complete list of all the concepts you need to cover before the test. Organize these concepts into groups that can be studied together, and create a list of any related vocabulary you need to learn so you can brush up on any difficult terms. You'll want to keep this vocabulary list handy once you actually start studying since you may need to add to it along the way.

Time Management

Once you have your set of study concepts, decide how to spread them out over the time you have left before the test. Break your study plan into small, clear goals so you have a manageable task for each day and know exactly what you're doing. Then just focus on one small step at a time. When you manage your time this way, you don't need to spend hours at a time studying. Studying a small block of content for a short period each day helps you retain information better and avoid stressing over how much you have left to do. You can relax knowing that you have a plan to cover everything in time. In order for this strategy to be effective though, you have to start studying early and stick to your schedule. Avoid the exhaustion and futility that comes from last-minute cramming!

Study Environment

The environment you study in has a big impact on your learning. Studying in a coffee shop, while probably more enjoyable, is not likely to be as fruitful as studying in a quiet room. It's important to keep distractions to a minimum. You're only planning to study for a short block of time, so make the most of it. Don't pause to check your phone or get up to find a snack. It's also important to **avoid multitasking**. Research has consistently shown that multitasking will make your studying dramatically less effective. Your study area should also be comfortable and well-lit so you don't have the distraction of straining your eyes or sitting on an uncomfortable chair.

The time of day you study is also important. You want to be rested and alert. Don't wait until just before bedtime. Study when you'll be most likely to comprehend and remember. Even better, if you know what time of day your test will be, set that time aside for study. That way your brain will be used to working on that subject at that specific time and you'll have a better chance of recalling information.

Finally, it can be helpful to team up with others who are studying for the same test. Your actual studying should be done in as isolated an environment as possible, but the work of organizing the information and setting up the study plan can be divided up. In between study sessions, you can discuss with your teammates the concepts that you're all studying and quiz each other on the details. Just be sure that your teammates are as serious about the test as you are. If you find that your study time is being replaced with social time, you might need to find a new team.

Secret Key #2 – Make Your Studying Count

You're devoting a lot of time and effort to preparing for this test, so you want to be absolutely certain it will pay off. This means doing more than just reading the content and hoping you can remember it on test day. It's important to make every minute of study count. There are two main areas you can focus on to make your studying count:

Retention

It doesn't matter how much time you study if you can't remember the material. You need to make sure you are retaining the concepts. To check your retention of the information you're learning, try recalling it at later times with minimal prompting. Try carrying around flashcards and glance at one or two from time to time or ask a friend who's also studying for the test to quiz you.

To enhance your retention, look for ways to put the information into practice so that you can apply it rather than simply recalling it. If you're using the information in practical ways, it will be much easier to remember. Similarly, it helps to solidify a concept in your mind if you're not only reading it to yourself but also explaining it to someone else. Ask a friend to let you teach them about a concept you're a little shaky on (or speak aloud to an imaginary audience if necessary). As you try to summarize, define, give examples, and answer your friend's questions, you'll understand the concepts better and they will stay with you longer. Finally, step back for a big picture view and ask yourself how each piece of information fits with the whole subject. When you link the different concepts together and see them working together as a whole, it's easier to remember the individual components.

Finally, practice showing your work on any multi-step problems, even if you're just studying. Writing out each step you take to solve a problem will help solidify the process in your mind, and you'll be more likely to remember it during the test.

Modality

Modality simply refers to the means or method by which you study. Choosing a study modality that fits your own individual learning style is crucial. No two people learn best in exactly the same way, so it's important to know your strengths and use them to your advantage.

For example, if you learn best by visualization, focus on visualizing a concept in your mind and draw an image or a diagram. Try color-coding your notes, illustrating them, or creating symbols that will trigger your mind to recall a learned concept. If you learn best by hearing or discussing information, find a study partner who learns the same way or read aloud to yourself. Think about how to put the information in your own words. Imagine that you are giving a lecture on the topic and record yourself so you can listen to it later.

For any learning style, flashcards can be helpful. Organize the information so you can take advantage of spare moments to review. Underline key words or phrases. Use different colors for different categories. Mnemonic devices (such as creating a short list in which every item starts with the same letter) can also help with retention. Find what works best for you and use it to store the information in your mind most effectively and easily.

Secret Key #3 – Practice the Right Way

Your success on test day depends not only on how many hours you put into preparing, but also on whether you prepared the right way. It's good to check along the way to see if your studying is paying off. One of the most effective ways to do this is by taking practice tests to evaluate your progress. Practice tests are useful because they show exactly where you need to improve. Every time you take a practice test, pay special attention to these three groups of questions:

- The questions you got wrong
- The questions you had to guess on, even if you guessed right
- The questions you found difficult or slow to work through

This will show you exactly what your weak areas are, and where you need to devote more study time. Ask yourself why each of these questions gave you trouble. Was it because you didn't understand the material? Was it because you didn't remember the vocabulary? Do you need more repetitions on this type of question to build speed and confidence? Dig into those questions and figure out how you can strengthen your weak areas as you go back to review the material.

Additionally, many practice tests have a section explaining the answer choices. It can be tempting to read the explanation and think that you now have a good understanding of the concept. However, an explanation likely only covers part of the question's broader context. Even if the explanation makes sense, **go back and investigate** every concept related to the question until you're positive you have a thorough understanding.

As you go along, keep in mind that the practice test is just that: practice. Memorizing these questions and answers will not be very helpful on the actual test because it is unlikely to have any of the same exact questions. If you only know the right answers to the sample questions, you won't be prepared for the real thing. **Study the concepts** until you understand them fully, and then you'll be able to answer any question that shows up on the test.

It's important to wait on the practice tests until you're ready. If you take a test on your first day of study, you may be overwhelmed by the amount of material covered and how much you need to learn. Work up to it gradually.

On test day, you'll need to be prepared for answering questions, managing your time, and using the test-taking strategies you've learned. It's a lot to balance, like a mental marathon that will have a big impact on your future. Like training for a marathon, you'll need to start slowly and work your way up. When test day arrives, you'll be ready.

Start with the strategies you've read in the first two Secret Keys—plan your course and study in the way that works best for you. If you have time, consider using multiple study resources to get different approaches to the same concepts. It can be helpful to see difficult concepts from more than one angle. Then find a good source for practice tests. Many times, the test website will suggest potential study resources or provide sample tests.

Practice Test Strategy

If you're able to find at least three practice tests, we recommend this strategy:

UNTIMED AND OPEN-BOOK PRACTICE

Take the first test with no time constraints and with your notes and study guide handy. Take your time and focus on applying the strategies you've learned.

TIMED AND OPEN-BOOK PRACTICE

Take the second practice test open-book as well, but set a timer and practice pacing yourself to finish in time.

TIMED AND CLOSED-BOOK PRACTICE

Take any other practice tests as if it were test day. Set a timer and put away your study materials. Sit at a table or desk in a quiet room, imagine yourself at the testing center, and answer questions as quickly and accurately as possible.

Keep repeating timed and closed-book tests on a regular basis until you run out of practice tests or it's time for the actual test. Your mind will be ready for the schedule and stress of test day, and you'll be able to focus on recalling the material you've learned.

Secret Key #4 – Pace Yourself

Once you're fully prepared for the material on the test, your biggest challenge on test day will be managing your time. Just knowing that the clock is ticking can make you panic even if you have plenty of time left. Work on pacing yourself so you can build confidence against the time constraints of the exam. Pacing is a difficult skill to master, especially in a high-pressure environment, so **practice is vital**.

Set time expectations for your pace based on how much time is available. For example, if a section has 60 questions and the time limit is 30 minutes, you know you have to average 30 seconds or less per question in order to answer them all. Although 30 seconds is the hard limit, set 25 seconds per question as your goal, so you reserve extra time to spend on harder questions. When you budget extra time for the harder questions, you no longer have any reason to stress when those questions take longer to answer.

Don't let this time expectation distract you from working through the test at a calm, steady pace, but keep it in mind so you don't spend too much time on any one question. Recognize that taking extra time on one question you don't understand may keep you from answering two that you do understand later in the test. If your time limit for a question is up and you're still not sure of the answer, mark it and move on, and come back to it later if the time and the test format allow. If the testing format doesn't allow you to return to earlier questions, just make an educated guess; then put it out of your mind and move on.

On the easier questions, be careful not to rush. It may seem wise to hurry through them so you have more time for the challenging ones, but it's not worth missing one if you know the concept and just didn't take the time to read the question fully. Work efficiently but make sure you understand the question and have looked at all of the answer choices, since more than one may seem right at first.

Even if you're paying attention to the time, you may find yourself a little behind at some point. You should speed up to get back on track, but do so wisely. Don't panic; just take a few seconds less on each question until you're caught up. Don't guess without thinking, but do look through the answer choices and eliminate any you know are wrong. If you can get down to two choices, it is often worthwhile to guess from those. Once you've chosen an answer, move on and don't dwell on any that you skipped or had to hurry through. If a question was taking too long, chances are it was one of the harder ones, so you weren't as likely to get it right anyway.

On the other hand, if you find yourself getting ahead of schedule, it may be beneficial to slow down a little. The more quickly you work, the more likely you are to make a careless mistake that will affect your score. You've budgeted time for each question, so don't be afraid to spend that time. Practice an efficient but careful pace to get the most out of the time you have.

Secret Key #5 – Have a Plan for Guessing

When you're taking the test, you may find yourself stuck on a question. Some of the answer choices seem better than others, but you don't see the one answer choice that is obviously correct. What do you do?

The scenario described above is very common, yet most test takers have not effectively prepared for it. Developing and practicing a plan for guessing may be one of the single most effective uses of your time as you get ready for the exam.

In developing your plan for guessing, there are three questions to address:

- When should you start the guessing process?
- How should you narrow down the choices?
- Which answer should you choose?

When to Start the Guessing Process

Unless your plan for guessing is to select C every time (which, despite its merits, is not what we recommend), you need to leave yourself enough time to apply your answer elimination strategies. Since you have a limited amount of time for each question, that means that if you're going to give yourself the best shot at guessing correctly, you have to decide quickly whether or not you will guess.

Of course, the best-case scenario is that you don't have to guess at all, so first, see if you can answer the question based on your knowledge of the subject and basic reasoning skills. Focus on the key words in the question and try to jog your memory of related topics. Give yourself a chance to bring the knowledge to mind, but once you realize that you don't have (or you can't access) the knowledge you need to answer the question, it's time to start the guessing process.

It's almost always better to start the guessing process too early than too late. It only takes a few seconds to remember something and answer the question from knowledge. Carefully eliminating wrong answer choices takes longer. Plus, going through the process of eliminating answer choices can actually help jog your memory.

Summary: Start the guessing process as soon as you decide that you can't answer the question based on your knowledge.

How to Narrow Down the Choices

The next chapter in this book (**Test-Taking Strategies**) includes a wide range of strategies for how to approach questions and how to look for answer choices to eliminate. You will definitely want to read those carefully, practice them, and figure out which ones work best for you. Here though, we're going to address a mindset rather than a particular strategy.

Your chances of guessing an answer correctly depend on how many options you are choosing from.

How many choices you have	How likely you are to guess correctly
5	20%
4	25%
3	33%
2	50%
1	100%

You can see from this chart just how valuable it is to be able to eliminate incorrect answers and make an educated guess, but there are two things that many test takers do that cause them to miss out on the benefits of guessing:

- Accidentally eliminating the correct answer
- Selecting an answer based on an impression

We'll look at the first one here, and the second one in the next section.

To avoid accidentally eliminating the correct answer, we recommend a thought exercise called **the $5 challenge**. In this challenge, you only eliminate an answer choice from contention if you are willing to bet $5 on it being wrong. Why $5? Five dollars is a small but not insignificant amount of money. It's an amount you could afford to lose but wouldn't want to throw away. And while losing $5 once might not hurt too much, doing it twenty times will set you back $100. In the same way, each small decision you make—eliminating a choice here, guessing on a question there—won't by itself impact your score very much, but when you put them all together, they can make a big difference. By holding each answer choice elimination decision to a higher standard, you can reduce the risk of accidentally eliminating the correct answer.

The $5 challenge can also be applied in a positive sense: If you are willing to bet $5 that an answer choice *is* correct, go ahead and mark it as correct.

Summary: Only eliminate an answer choice if you are willing to bet $5 that it is wrong.

8

Which Answer to Choose

You're taking the test. You've run into a hard question and decided you'll have to guess. You've eliminated all the answer choices you're willing to bet $5 on. Now you have to pick an answer. Why do we even need to talk about this? Why can't you just pick whichever one you feel like when the time comes?

The answer to these questions is that if you don't come into the test with a plan, you'll rely on your impression to select an answer choice, and if you do that, you risk falling into a trap. The test writers know that everyone who takes their test will be guessing on some of the questions, so they intentionally write wrong answer choices to seem plausible. You still have to pick an answer though, and if the wrong answer choices are designed to look right, how can you ever be sure that you're not falling for their trap? The best solution we've found to this dilemma is to take the decision out of your hands entirely. Here is the process we recommend:

Once you've eliminated any choices that you are confident (willing to bet $5) are wrong, select the first remaining choice as your answer.

Whether you choose to select the first remaining choice, the second, or the last, the important thing is that you use some preselected standard. Using this approach guarantees that you will not be enticed into selecting an answer choice that looks right, because you are not basing your decision on how the answer choices look.

This is not meant to make you question your knowledge. Instead, it is to help you recognize the difference between your knowledge and your impressions. There's a huge difference between thinking an answer is right because of what you know, and thinking an answer is right because it looks or sounds like it should be right.

Summary: To ensure that your selection is appropriately random, make a predetermined selection from among all answer choices you have not eliminated.

Test-Taking Strategies

This section contains a list of test-taking strategies that you may find helpful as you work through the test. By taking what you know and applying logical thought, you can maximize your chances of answering any question correctly!

It is very important to realize that every question is different and every person is different: no single strategy will work on every question, and no single strategy will work for every person. That's why we've included all of them here, so you can try them out and determine which ones work best for different types of questions and which ones work best for you.

Question Strategies

READ CAREFULLY

Read the question and answer choices carefully. Don't miss the question because you misread the terms. You have plenty of time to read each question thoroughly and make sure you understand what is being asked. Yet a happy medium must be attained, so don't waste too much time. You must read carefully, but efficiently.

CONTEXTUAL CLUES

Look for contextual clues. If the question includes a word you are not familiar with, look at the immediate context for some indication of what the word might mean. Contextual clues can often give you all the information you need to decipher the meaning of an unfamiliar word. Even if you can't determine the meaning, you may be able to narrow down the possibilities enough to make a solid guess at the answer to the question.

PREFIXES

If you're having trouble with a word in the question or answer choices, try dissecting it. Take advantage of every clue that the word might include. Prefixes and suffixes can be a huge help. Usually they allow you to determine a basic meaning. Pre- means before, post- means after, pro - is positive, de- is negative. From prefixes and suffixes, you can get an idea of the general meaning of the word and try to put it into context.

HEDGE WORDS

Watch out for critical hedge words, such as *likely, may, can, sometimes, often, almost, mostly, usually, generally, rarely,* and *sometimes.* Question writers insert these hedge phrases to cover every possibility. Often an answer choice will be wrong simply because it leaves no room for exception. Be on guard for answer choices that have definitive words such as *exactly* and *always.*

SWITCHBACK WORDS

Stay alert for *switchbacks.* These are the words and phrases frequently used to alert you to shifts in thought. The most common switchback words are *but, although,* and *however.* Others include *nevertheless, on the other hand, even though, while, in spite of, despite, regardless of.* Switchback words are important to catch because they can change the direction of the question or an answer choice.

Copyright © Mometrix Media. You have been licensed one copy of this document for personal use only. Any other reproduction or redistribution is strictly prohibited. All rights reserved.

FACE VALUE

When in doubt, use common sense. Accept the situation in the problem at face value. Don't read too much into it. These problems will not require you to make wild assumptions. If you have to go beyond creativity and warp time or space in order to have an answer choice fit the question, then you should move on and consider the other answer choices. These are normal problems rooted in reality. The applicable relationship or explanation may not be readily apparent, but it is there for you to figure out. Use your common sense to interpret anything that isn't clear.

Answer Choice Strategies

ANSWER SELECTION

The most thorough way to pick an answer choice is to identify and eliminate wrong answers until only one is left, then confirm it is the correct answer. Sometimes an answer choice may immediately seem right, but be careful. The test writers will usually put more than one reasonable answer choice on each question, so take a second to read all of them and make sure that the other choices are not equally obvious. As long as you have time left, it is better to read every answer choice than to pick the first one that looks right without checking the others.

ANSWER CHOICE FAMILIES

An answer choice family consists of two (in rare cases, three) answer choices that are very similar in construction and cannot all be true at the same time. If you see two answer choices that are direct opposites or parallels, one of them is usually the correct answer. For instance, if one answer choice says that quantity x increases and another either says that quantity x decreases (opposite) or says that quantity y increases (parallel), then those answer choices would fall into the same family. An answer choice that doesn't match the construction of the answer choice family is more likely to be incorrect. Most questions will not have answer choice families, but when they do appear, you should be prepared to recognize them.

ELIMINATE ANSWERS

Eliminate answer choices as soon as you realize they are wrong, but make sure you consider all possibilities. If you are eliminating answer choices and realize that the last one you are left with is also wrong, don't panic. Start over and consider each choice again. There may be something you missed the first time that you will realize on the second pass.

AVOID FACT TRAPS

Don't be distracted by an answer choice that is factually true but doesn't answer the question. You are looking for the choice that answers the question. Stay focused on what the question is asking for so you don't accidentally pick an answer that is true but incorrect. Always go back to the question and make sure the answer choice you've selected actually answers the question and is not merely a true statement.

EXTREME STATEMENTS

In general, you should avoid answers that put forth extreme actions as standard practice or proclaim controversial ideas as established fact. An answer choice that states the "process should be used in certain situations, if…" is much more likely to be correct than one that states the "process should be discontinued completely." The first is a calm rational statement and doesn't even make a definitive, uncompromising stance, using a hedge word *if* to provide wiggle room, whereas the second choice is a radical idea and far more extreme.

11

BENCHMARK

As you read through the answer choices and you come across one that seems to answer the question well, mentally select that answer choice. This is not your final answer, but it's the one that will help you evaluate the other answer choices. The one that you selected is your benchmark or standard for judging each of the other answer choices. Every other answer choice must be compared to your benchmark. That choice is correct until proven otherwise by another answer choice beating it. If you find a better answer, then that one becomes your new benchmark. Once you've decided that no other choice answers the question as well as your benchmark, you have your final answer.

PREDICT THE ANSWER

Before you even start looking at the answer choices, it is often best to try to predict the answer. When you come up with the answer on your own, it is easier to avoid distractions and traps because you will know exactly what to look for. The right answer choice is unlikely to be word-for-word what you came up with, but it should be a close match. Even if you are confident that you have the right answer, you should still take the time to read each option before moving on.

General Strategies

TOUGH QUESTIONS

If you are stumped on a problem or it appears too hard or too difficult, don't waste time. Move on! Remember though, if you can quickly check for obviously incorrect answer choices, your chances of guessing correctly are greatly improved. Before you completely give up, at least try to knock out a couple of possible answers. Eliminate what you can and then guess at the remaining answer choices before moving on.

CHECK YOUR WORK

Since you will probably not know every term listed and the answer to every question, it is important that you get credit for the ones that you do know. Don't miss any questions through careless mistakes. If at all possible, try to take a second to look back over your answer selection and make sure you've selected the correct answer choice and haven't made a costly careless mistake (such as marking an answer choice that you didn't mean to mark). This quick double check should more than pay for itself in caught mistakes for the time it costs.

PACE YOURSELF

It's easy to be overwhelmed when you're looking at a page full of questions; your mind is confused and full of random thoughts, and the clock is ticking down faster than you would like. Calm down and maintain the pace that you have set for yourself. Especially as you get down to the last few minutes of the test, don't let the small numbers on the clock make you panic. As long as you are on track by monitoring your pace, you are guaranteed to have time for each question.

DON'T RUSH

It is very easy to make errors when you are in a hurry. Maintaining a fast pace in answering questions is pointless if it makes you miss questions that you would have gotten right otherwise. Test writers like to include distracting information and wrong answers that seem right. Taking a little extra time to avoid careless mistakes can make all the difference in your test score. Find a pace that allows you to be confident in the answers that you select.

KEEP MOVING

Panicking will not help you pass the test, so do your best to stay calm and keep moving. Taking deep breaths and going through the answer elimination steps you practiced can help to break through a stress barrier and keep your pace.

Final Notes

The combination of a solid foundation of content knowledge and the confidence that comes from practicing your plan for applying that knowledge is the key to maximizing your performance on test day. As your foundation of content knowledge is built up and strengthened, you'll find that the strategies included in this chapter become more and more effective in helping you quickly sift through the distractions and traps of the test to isolate the correct answer.

Now it's time to move on to the test content chapters of this book, but be sure to keep your goal in mind. As you read, think about how you will be able to apply this information on the test. If you've already seen sample questions for the test and you have an idea of the question format and style, try to come up with questions of your own that you can answer based on what you're reading. This will give you valuable practice applying your knowledge in the same ways you can expect to on test day.

Good luck and good studying!

Pre-Columbian History to 1789

FIRST EUROPEAN EXPLORERS IN AMERICA

Although **Christopher Columbus**, in 1492, frequently gets credit for "discovering" America (notwithstanding the fact that people were already living on the continent), **Vikings** from Scandinavia actually arrived in about A.D. 1000. These explorers constructed no permanent settlements, however, and did not remain for long. It was not until economic expansion in Europe made exploration worthwhile that explorers would return. Columbus, and the explorers who would come later, were looking for the **Northwest Passage** that would take them directly to Asia and were actually annoyed by the new land that kept getting in the way. Columbus actually died believing that he had landed in some outpost of India (hence, "Indians").

ENGLISH INTEREST IN THE NEW WORLD

The English lagged somewhat behind other European nations in exploration of the New World. Finally, however, a combination of economic and social incentives convinced them to look west. For one thing, the **enclosure movement** in England had made land very scarce, and the practice of **primogeniture** meant that only the eldest son could inherit the land. For these reasons, many Englishmen moved to the New World for the promise of cheap land. England also had a large population at this time and thus the government viewed the New World as a good place to send criminals and beggars. Another reason for the increase in interest in America was the **Protestant Reformation**. Many English Catholics and Protestants felt alienated by the new Church of England, and wanted to find somewhere in which they could worship more freely.

SETTLING OF NORTH AMERICA BY THE ENGLISH

The first English attempt to found a colony in the New World was made by Sir Humphrey Gilbert in **Newfoundland** in 1583, and was a complete failure. Sir Walter Raleigh would lead two more failed attempts at founding a colony on **Roanoke Island** in 1586 and 1588. The second of these colonies is known as the **Lost Colony**, because it disappeared without a trace while Raleigh was gone. Finally, the British were able to establish a permanent colony at **Jamestown**, Virginia in 1607. The settlers in Jamestown came for gold and to convert the Natives to Christianity. One of the important events of the early years of Jamestown was the issuing of the Virginia Charter, which declared that English settlers in the New World would be treated as Englishmen with full English rights.

VIRGINIA COLONY

BEGINNINGS

The English colony of **Virginia**, which began at Jamestown, was at first plagued by a poor location and a paucity of skilled laborers. Captain **John Smith** was elected leader in 1608, and he proved to be the strict leader the colony needed to survive. A large proportion of the settlers would die during the winter of 1609-10. What finally saved the Virginia colony was the wild popularity of **tobacco**. In 1619, the **House of Burgesses** met, becoming the first legislative body to be formed in the New World. King James I of England correctly predicted that this would only lead to trouble for

his nation. Also, in 1619, 20 African indentured servants arrived on a Dutch warship; Virginia would become the first colony to legalize **slavery**, in 1660.

ROYAL COLONY

Virginia officially became a **Royal Colony** in 1624. This was in part because the Virginia Company (the joint-stock company that had previously administered affairs) had gone bankrupt, and partly because King James I wanted to exercise more control. After the English Civil War of the 1640s, many of the supporters of the king, known as **cavaliers**, settled in Virginia. During this period, the wealthy colonists began claiming the coastal land and pushing the poor people farther inland, where they were prey to Indian attacks and were underrepresented in the House of Burgesses. Frustrated, a group of settlers led by **Nathaniel Bacon** burned Jamestown to the ground. **Bacon's Rebellion**, as it came to be known, is thought of by some as a harbinger of things to come.

BEGINNINGS OF ENGLISH COLONIES OF MARYLAND, THE CAROLINAS, AND GEORGIA

Maryland was established in 1634 as a **proprietary colony**, meaning it was exclusively owned by one person. The owner, Lord Baltimore, ran his colony like a feudal estate. Maryland prospered because of tobacco and became a haven for persecuted Catholics. **North Carolina** was originally settled by Virginians, and quickly acquired a reputation as independent and democratic. Many English colonists avoided North Carolina because they felt it was overrun by pirates. **South Carolina**, meanwhile, was a proprietary colony established in 1670. South Carolina hosted a large number of religious groups. **Georgia**, meanwhile, was a proprietary colony established in 1733. Its namesake, George II, hoped that it would be a buffer zone between the colonists and the Indians, and populated it almost exclusively with criminals and debtors.

SOUTHERN COLONIES
ECONOMIC LIFE

In the early days of the Southern colonies, most people lived on **small farms**. Although they made up a tiny part of the population, the owners of the **coastal plantations** wielded enormous power. These aristocrats typically grew a single crop on their lands: in North Carolina, Virginia, and Maryland, **tobacco** was the cash crop, while the large growers in South Carolina and Georgia favored **rice** and **indigo**. Plantations, like the feudal manors of the past, were almost totally self-sufficient units, although the owners imported most of their luxury items from England. The Southern colonies had the closest ties with England, mainly because England provided the market for their tobacco; crops grown in the colonies were sold back in England by agents (known as factors).

SOCIAL LIFE

The social lives of the Southern colonists were filled with dancing, card-playing, cotillions, hunts, and large community dinners. Southerners were considered to be very optimistic in temperament, in contrast to their more dour Northern counterparts. It was extremely difficult to move up in the **social hierarchy** in the South; the richer colonists generally took the best land and thus were able to maintain their position in the economy and in the government, as the poor had to move away from the towns to find farmland. Because farming was the only available occupation, there were

not any venues for ambitious men to distinguish themselves. North Carolina was generally considered to be the state with the least **social stratification**.

LIFE EXPECTANCY AND EDUCATION

The average man in the Southern colonies could expect to live **35 years**. This was in part due to disease; stagnant water and unfamiliar heat helped the spread of many contagions throughout the population, and malaria was a constant danger. Because of the high mortality rate, most families were very large. Also, **education** was not a high priority in the colonies in those days. One problem was that the population was too scattered for a central public school to be possible. Wealthy plantation owners would hire a **tutor** for their children, who might later be sent off to William and Mary or one of the new schools up North: Harvard, Yale, or Princeton. For the less affluent, however, it was more likely that any education would be received as an **apprentice** of an experienced craftsman.

> **Review Video: <u>Southern Colonies: Family Life and Education</u>**
> Visit mometrix.com/academy and enter code: 881049

RELIGIOUS AND POLITICAL LIFE

In all of the Southern colonies, the **Anglican Church** was supported by taxes. Anyone who wanted to enter politics would have to be a member of the Church, though the majority of the colonists were not. In general, the Southern colonies had the greatest degree of **religious toleration**. Politics during this period were largely controlled by the planter aristocracy. Each Southern colony had a **governor** (chosen by the colony's English sponsor), a **governor's council**, and an **assembly** to represent the people. During the 1700s, these assemblies took more and more power away from the governors. In order to run for office, a man had to be a member of the Anglican Church; many people, including Thomas Jefferson, would acquire membership in the Church and then never set foot inside it again.

> **Review Video: <u>Southern Colonies: Religion and Politics</u>**
> Visit mometrix.com/academy and enter code: 515423

BEGINNING OF SLAVE TRADE

After periods in which Native Americans or indentured servants from England were used as laborers, most of the labor in the Southern British North American colonies was performed by **African slaves**. These slaves were taken in wars between African chieftains, and then sold to European traders. Oftentimes, the African leaders would trade slaves for guns in order to protect themselves from other slave traders. Several African states, most notably the Yoruba and the Dahomey, became wealthy from this trade. The journey from West Africa to the West Indies was dangerous and depressing, and many slaves died en route. Before they were sold into the American colonies, slaves first worked in the brutal heat of the sugar plantations of the British West Indies. Only about half would survive long enough to see America.

LEGALIZATION OF SLAVERY

Between 1640 and 1660, the Southern colonies slowly evolved from a system of servitude to one of **slavery**. In 1661, Virginia became the first colony to legalize **chattel slavery for life**, and made it such that the children of slaves would be slaves as well. The number of slaves increased dramatically in the 1680s after the **Royal African Company** lost its monopoly and the industry was thrown open to anyone. Virginia established **slave codes** to keep revolts down: slaves could not be taught to read, could not gather together, could not have weapons, and could not leave the

plantation without written permission. Naturally, slaves often rebelled against their treatment, but they were outnumbered and overpowered.

EARLY RESISTANCE TO SLAVERY

Many slaves resisted submission, and many died as a result. For any serious offense, a slave would be executed in front of his or her peers as a deterrent. From its inception, there was **resistance** to slavery. In 1688, the **Quakers** declared that slavery was inhuman and a violation of the Bible. Many felt that slavery degraded both master and slave. In order to justify the hateful institution, slave-owners declared that blacks were less than human, or that, as descendants of the Biblical figure Ham, they were ordered by God to serve whites. The hymn "Amazing Grace" was written by guilt-wracked former slave trader **John Newton**. Slaves could only become free by proving mulatto (half white) status, or by buying their freedom (some masters would allow their slaves to work for pay on the weekends).

PURITANISM AND THE PILGRIMS IN MASSACHUSETTS COLONY

Puritans believe in the idea of predestination, meaning that God has already chosen which people will get into heaven. In order to suggest to others (and to themselves) that they were among the elect, **Puritans** were obsessed with maintaining proper decorum in public. Those Puritans who wanted to fully separate from the Church of England were known as **Pilgrims** (or Separatists). The Pilgrims originally went to Holland, but after determining that they would be unable to make a good life there, they got permission from the Virginia Company to settle in the northern part of the Virginia colony in 1620. The **Plymouth Company** was commissioned, and the **Mayflower** set sail. Because of storms and poor navigation, however, they ended up in the area that would come to be known as Massachusetts. One of the early moves of the group was to agree to the **Mayflower Compact**, whereby all members of the group would be bound to the will of the majority.

PURITANS

The Puritans established the colony of **Massachusetts Bay** in 1630. They hoped to purify the **Church of England** and then return to Europe with a new and improved religion. The Massachusetts Bay Puritans were more immediately successful than other fledgling colonies because they brought enough supplies, arrived in the springtime, and had good leadership (including **John Winthrop**). Puritans fished, cut timber for ships, and trapped fur. The local government was inextricably bound with the church; only church members were allowed to vote for the **General Court** (similar to the House of Burgesses), although everyone was required to pay taxes. The Puritans established a **Bible Commonwealth** that would last 50 years. During this time, Old Testament law was the law of the community.

POLITICAL AND SOCIAL LIFE IN THE EARLY MASSACHUSETTS COLONIES

The **Massachusetts Bay Puritans** were known for religious intolerance and a general suspicion of democracy. Even though they had left England because of religious persecution, they did not set up their colony as a safe haven for others. One of the people who was kicked out of the colony for

blasphemy was **Roger Williams**, who went on to found a colony at **Providence**. Williams taught that the colonists should be fair to the Indians, and that political leaders should stay out of religion. Roger Williams eventually founded the **Baptist Church**. The Puritans generally felt that the common people were incapable of governing themselves and should be looked after by their government. Also, many Puritans objected to democracy because they felt it was inefficient.

ENGLISH CIVIL WAR AND THE NEW ENGLAND CONFEDERATION

During the English Civil War, the Puritans tried to separate from the Church of England; they issued the **Body of Liberties**, which stated that the Massachusetts Bay was independent of England and was therefore no longer bound by English Civil Law, that there could be no arbitrary governors appointed to dissolve a local legislature, and that town meetings of qualified voters would be held to discuss local issues. Later, in 1643, a **New England Confederation** was formed, consisting of Massachusetts Bay, New Plymouth, Connecticut River Valley, and New Haven. The goals of this confederation were to protect the colonists from the French (in Canada) and the Indians; to safeguard their commercial interests from the Dutch in New Netherlands (later New York); and to return runaway slaves.

> **Review Video: The New England Confederation**
> Visit mometrix.com/academy and enter code: 745315

DOMINION OF NEW ENGLAND

The impertinence of the **Massachusetts Bay colony** was a constant annoyance to **King Charles II** and he thus punished them by granting charters to rival colonies in Connecticut and Rhode Island and by creating the **Dominion of New England**. The purpose of this organization was to boost trade by enforcing the **Navigation Acts** of 1660 and 1663, which stated that all trade had to be done on English ships and had to pass through England before it could go anywhere else. The English, of course, made the colonists pay a tax on any exports that were not bound for England. The colonists loathed the Dominion government, not only because of its economic penalties, but because it tried to promote the Anglican Church in America. A rebellion against the Dominion probably would have occurred if the **Glorious Revolution** in England had not ended it prematurely.

> **Review Video: Life in New England**
> Visit mometrix.com/academy and enter code: 551857
>
> **Review Video: The Puritans: Massachusetts Bay Colony**
> Visit mometrix.com/academy and enter code: 407058

LAND, DEMOGRAPHY, CLIMATE, ECONOMICS, AND SLAVERY IN PURITAN LIFE

The **land** settled by the Puritans was rocky and bare, and it took tremendous labor to subsist off of its products. Massachusetts had an extremely homogenous **population**, mainly because there was little reason to stay there other than to be among people of the same faith. Non-Puritan immigrants usually moved south, where the soil was better and the population was more tolerant. Because agriculture was so tricky, a more diverse **economy** developed in New England than existed in the South. Puritans engaged in fishing and trapping, and there were a number of craftsmen in each town. There were **slaves** in New England, though not nearly as many as in the South. Furthermore, slaves in New England were more commonly used as household servants than hard laborers.

SOCIAL AND RELIGIOUS LIFE OF THE PURITANS

There was more chance for **social mobility** in Massachusetts than in any other colony in America. This was mainly due to the diverse economy. As for religion, it dominated every area of an individual's life. The Puritan Church was known as the **Congregational Church**; at first, this was an exclusive group, but it gradually became easier to become a member. Indeed, by the mid-1600s religious fervor seemed to be waning in Massachusetts. A group called the **Jeremiads** warned the people that they were in danger of lapsing into atheism, but many people did not mind. Around this time, ministers began to offer **half-way covenants**, which gave church members partial privileges.

SALEM WITCH TRIALS

During the 1690s in New England, there was still a strong belief in **Christian mysticism**. Many people were paranoid about spiritualists and mediums. This, combined with perhaps some local feuds, led to 19 women and one man being executed for **witchcraft** in 1692. Most likely, however, the accused individuals were only suffering from delusions caused by a kind of hallucinogenic bread mold (ergot). The witch trials only stopped when people in high places began being accused. The **Salem witch trials** tarnished the image of the clergy for a long time, and further contributed to a general relaxation of religious fervor in this period.

THE GREAT AWAKENING

The Great Awakening was a religious revival in New England in the 1730s and 40s. It began in response to the growing secularism and was aided by the recent migrations into the cities, where it was easier for large crowds to form. **Jonathan Edwards** was one of the most famous preachers of this time. The **Great Awakening** was the first mass movement in America; it helped break down the divides between the various regions of the British colonies and led to the formation of some new Protestant denominations. Though the Revivalists did not directly advocate the abolition of slavery, they did suggest that there was divinity in all creation, and that therefore blacks were worthy of being converted to Christianity.

BIBLE COMMONWEALTH AND POLITICAL AND INTELLECTUAL LIFE IN NEW ENGLAND

The New England colonies started out as **Bible Commonwealths**, where Biblical law was local law, and a man's standing in the church determined his political power. Over time, however, New England became more liberal, and politics came to be dominated by the **wealthy men** rather than by the church leaders. Life expectancy in the New England colonies became roughly what it is today. **Education** was valued greatly in New England, and the fact that most people lived close to a town made it possible for more people to receive an inexpensive training. Puritans believed that ignorance of God's word could lead one to be tricked by the devil, and thus they made sure that all of their children learned to read.

NEW NETHERLANDS COLONY

The Dutch East India Company hired the English explorer **Henry Hudson** to search for the Northwest Passage to Asia. Instead, he journeyed up the Hudson River and claimed the area now known as **New York** for the Dutch. The Dutch purchased **Manhattan Island** from the Manhattan Indians for $24, and established a town called **New Amsterdam** there, an aristocratic town, in which everyone had to be a member of the Dutch Reform Church. Eventually, in 1664, this Dutch settlement would be overwhelmed by the British colonies surrounding it. King Charles II gave the area to his successor, James, Duke of York, who quickly gave the town and colony the name it bears today.

PENNSYLVANIA COLONY, QUAKERS, AND THE CHARTER OF LIBERTIES

The Pennsylvania (literally "Penn's woods") colony was established by **William Penn** in 1681. Penn declared that the colony would provide religious and political freedom for all. The main religious group to settle in the area was the **Society of Friends** (Quakers). Quakers believed that every person could communicate with the divine, that the church should not be supported by tax dollars, and that all men are equal. The Quakers have always been pacifists, and they were the first group to oppose slavery. In Pennsylvania, voting rights were extended only to land holders or large taxpayers. The **Charter of Liberties** (1701) established a unicameral legislature working alongside a governor.

MIDDLE COLONIES

ECONOMIC LIFE, SLAVERY, AND SOCIETY

The **Middle Colonies** (New York, Pennsylvania, Delaware, East and West New Jersey) shared characteristics with both New England and the Southern colonies. The **economy** was diverse, though less so than in New England. Shipping and commerce would gradually become crucial in the port cities of Philadelphia and New York. There were plenty of **slaves** in the Middle Colonies, most of whom served as laborers on ships. The Dutch treated their slaves well; the English did not. People in these colonies tended to have a healthier lifestyle than their neighbors to the south, and therefore they tended to live longer. The diverse economy made **social mobility** possible, though large landowners were for the most part entrenched in positions of power.

EDUCATION, RELIGION, AND POLITICS

Most education in the Middle Colonies was received as an **apprentice** to a successful craftsman. Often, local churches would maintain schools during the week. The two main religious organizations in this region were the **Anglican Church** and the **Dutch Reform Church**, often at each other's throat because they were competing for members and tax dollars. A typical government in the Middle Colonies had a **governor**, a governor's council, and a **representative assembly**. Men were only allowed to vote if they owned property. The Middle Colonies had the most diverse population, mainly because they had available land and promised religious freedom (at least in Pennsylvania).

GEORGE GRENVILLE AND THE PROCLAMATION OF 1763

George Grenville became the prime minister of Britain in 1763, and immediately abandoned the policy of "salutary neglect" that had been upheld by Walpole. On the contrary, he asserted that the American colonists should have to pay for British military protection, even though the Americans claimed not to need it. According to the **Proclamation of 1763**, all American colonists were to stay east of the Appalachian Mountains. This policy was ostensibly created in order to protect the colonists in the wake of **Chief Pontiac's Rebellion** in 1763, in which Indians attacked colonists and were subsequently slaughtered by the British. Many colonists, however, felt that the Proclamation was a transparent attempt to maintain British control of the fur trade.

SUGAR (REVENUE) ACT, CURRENCY ACT, AND THE QUARTERING ACT

The Sugar (Revenue) Act of 1764 established a duty on basically any products that were not British in origin: for instance, molasses, indigo, and sugar. Unlike the Molasses Act, the **Sugar Act** was fully enforced. Most colonists resented this taxation, which they felt was used to fund the French and Indian War. The **Currency Act of 1764** forbade colonists from issuing paper money, and stated that all taxes paid to England must be paid in gold and silver rather than paper. This act eliminated the worthless Continental Dollar. The **Quartering Act of 1765** required colonists to provide bedding and food to the regiments of British soldiers in America. This regulation increased paranoia amongst the colonists, who began to wonder exactly why the British soldiers were there in the first place.

STAMP ACT OF 1765

The Stamp Act of 1765 was levied without the consent of the colonists. It specified that a stamp must be applied to all legal documents (there was considerable debate over the definition of this phrase) indicating that a tax had been paid for the defense of the colonies. This act was extremely unpopular, perhaps most because its presence was so visible; its implementation generated loud cries of "**taxation without representation**." The British responded by claiming that the colonists had "virtual representation" by members of Parliament. The colonists continued to claim that they needed direct and actual representation, although many feared that even if they were to get it, they would probably lose most votes anyway.

STAMP ACT CONGRESS, THE SONS OF LIBERTY, AND THE DECLARATORY ACT

In 1765, the colonists created the Stamp Act Congress in New York in order to peacefully resolve the conflicts created by the Stamp Act. This group established the **Non-importation Agreements**, which amounted to a boycott of English products. At the same time, the **Sons of Liberty** in Boston were running amok: vandalizing British goods, tarring and feathering stamp collectors, and erecting so-called "liberty poles," from which collectors would be hung by their pants. In 1766, the new British prime minister **Rockingham** repealed the Stamp Act because the boycotts were damaging the British economy. In part to punish the colonists for their insubordination, in 1766 the British Parliament issued the **Declaratory Act**, which asserted that they had the right to legislate on behalf of the colonists at any time.

TOWNSHEND ACTS

The Townshend Acts, named after Charles "Champagne Charlie" Townshend, the prime minister of Britain from 1766-1772, placed an indirect tax on household items coming into the colonies, and tightened the custom duties. The Acts also called for stricter vice-admiralty courts and established the **Writs of Assistance**, which were essentially blank search warrants. The colonists' response to the Townshend Acts was twofold: a **pamphlet war** was waged by men like John Dickinson, James Otis, and Samuel Adams; and there were also more violent protests, as for instance the **Boston Massacre**, in which a mob in the Boston Commons was fired on by the British, perhaps accidentally. Colonists used the "Massacre" as a rallying cry, and the Townshend Acts were repealed (with the notable exception of the tax on tea).

LORD NORTH, THE GASPEE, THE COMMITTEES OF CORRESPONDENCE, AND JOHN WILKES

Lord North succeeded Townshend as British prime minister in 1772. In this year, the Sons of Liberty set fire to the **Gaspee**, a British revenue ship, off the coast of Rhode Island. The Sons of Liberty were driven to further violence by Massachusetts governor Tom Hutchinson's announcement that his salary would be paid by the British. The **Committees of Correspondence** were subsequently formed to organize the protest against the British, and to keep colonists informed on British matters. At around this time, the British MP **John Wilkes** became a folk hero in the colonies because of his impassioned speeches in defense of liberty. Although Wilkes never spoke directly on behalf of the colonists, he was jailed for his speeches.

COERCIVE (INTOLERABLE) ACTS

The Coercive Acts, known as the **Intolerable Acts** in America, were issued in response to the Boston Tea Party, and had several parts. The **Boston Port Act** closed the port down, supposedly until such time as the destroyed tea was paid for, although this never happened. The **Massachusetts Government Act** put the colony under martial law. A military governor, Thomas Gage, was placed in charge of the colony. The **Administration of Justice Act** required that all judges, soldiers, and tax agents be English, and that all crimes be tried in England. The **New Quartering Act** asserted that British soldiers were allowed to enter private homes and demand lodging. The **Quebec Act of 1774** declared that everything west of the Appalachians was Quebec; although this was basically done so that Britain could govern more effectively, it caused speculation among the colonists that the British were going to sell America to the French.

FIRST CONTINENTAL CONGRESS

The First Continental Congress was held September 5, 1774, and was attended by a representative of every colony except Georgia. This Congress issued the **Suffolk Resolves**, stating that they would give Boston aid in the form of food and clothing, but would not take up arms on behalf of Boston. The **Continental Association**, an agreement not to buy or sell English goods, was formed. A conservative named Joseph Galloway advocated the creation of a **Council of All Colonies**, a legislative body which would share power with Parliament. The **Galloway Plan** was nixed by Massachusetts, however, because that colony refused to share power with any British authority. Massachusetts at this time was in a highly volatile state.

THOMAS GAGE AND PAUL REVERE

Thomas Gage, the military governor of Massachusetts, was under increasing duress at the beginning of 1775 and asked the British government for either 20,000 more troops or a repeal of the Coercive Acts. Instead, Britain sent 2,000 troops, which **Gage** used to collect guns, gunpowder, and shot. On April 18 of 1775, the British troops sailed across Boston Harbor toward the large stockpile at Concord. **Paul Revere** then took his famous ride to warn the other colonists about the approach of the British. Although Revere was captured, his ride was finished by Samuel Prescott and William Dawes. On the way to Concord, in Lexington, shots were fired and 8 colonial militiamen were killed. The British then moved on to Concord, where the real fighting began.

SECOND CONTINENTAL CONGRESS

The Second Continental Congress was held May 10, 1775 in Philadelphia. **George Washington** became the commander of the Americans, mainly because it was felt that he would be able to bring the Southern colonies into the fold. This Congress also drew up the **Olive Branch petition**, a peace offering made to the King of England. The **Articles of Confederation** were drawn up here; their emphasis on states' rights proved to be a poor setup for organizing a comprehensive military strategy. This Congress created the **Committees of Safety**, a system for training community militias. This Congress created a bureaucracy for the purpose of organizing a navy and raising money. Finally, it was here that the colonists formally declared **independence**.

Review Video: The First and Second Continental Congress
Visit mometrix.com/academy and enter code: 835211

REASONS FOR DECLARING INDEPENDENCE

At the time that the Declaration of Independence was issued, many colonists were opposed to complete separation from England. Many of them still considered themselves Englishmen and were afraid to be branded as traitors. They also realized that they were in uncharted waters: no revolt had ever been successful in winning independence. Finally, many colonists feared that even if they were successful in winning independence, the result would be chaos in America. The minds of many of these reluctant colonists were changed, however, by the **Battle of Bunker Hill**, which was won by the British. After this battle, King George II declared that the colonists were in a state of rebellion. Furthermore, the British labeled the members of the **Second Continental Congress** as traitors and ignored the **Olive Branch petition**. Confused colonists were further flamed by the British use of Hessian mercenary soldiers. The writings of **Thomas Paine** also converted many colonists to the revolutionary cause.

DECLARATION OF INDEPENDENCE

The Declaration of Independence was proposed at the **Second Continental Congress** by Richard Henry Lee, and was composed by a committee of Franklin, Jefferson, John Adams, Robert Livingston, and Roger Sherman. The document has three parts: a **preamble** and reasons for separation; a **theory of government**; and a formal **declaration of war**. Jefferson attempted to have it include a condemnation of slavery, but was rebuffed. The Declaration had many aims: to enlist help from other British colonies; to create a cause for which to fight; to motivate reluctant colonists; to ensure that captured Americans would be treated as prisoners of war; and to establish an American theory of government. In fulfilling this last purpose, Jefferson borrowed heavily from Enlightenment thinkers like Montesquieu, Rousseau, and Locke, asserting famously that "all men are created equal."

SIGNIFICANCE

The issuing of the Declaration of Independence had effects both on the Revolutionary War and on world history at large. As far as its immediate effects, it changed the war in America from a war for liberty to a war for independence, by rhetorically **emancipating** America from Britain. It also opened a path for the **French Revolution** a few years later, one motivated by the principles expressed in the Declaration. Revolutions in South America, Africa, and Asia have also used the Declaration of Independence as inspiration. In the subsequent history of the United States, the document would be used by **abolitionists** as an argument against slavery, and by **suffragists** as an argument for the right of women to vote.

> **Review Video: Declaration of Independence**
> Visit mometrix.com/academy and enter code: 256838

SARATOGA CAMPAIGN

The British military plan during the early stages of the Revolutionary War was known as the **Saratoga campaign** (or the German Plan). It called for a three-pronged attack aimed at capturing New York and thus separating the Northeast from the Southern colonies. This plan broke down because of the following reasons: One of the generals, Howe, was supposed to go up the Hudson River to Albany, but instead decided to go after Philadelphia. Another general, Burgoyne, was able to conquer Fort Ticonderoga, but then languished without supplies for months, and eventually had to surrender to colonial troops. The third general, St. Ledger, made considerable progress across New York from Lake Ontario, but lost steam after a series of small battles.

BATTLE OF SARATOGA

The colonial General Gates defeated the British General Burgoyne at the **Battle of Saratoga** in 1777. This defeat confirmed the failure of the British Saratoga Campaign. More importantly, perhaps, it convinced the French that the Americans could win the war. The French then signed the **Treaty of Alliance** in 1778, which supplied the Americans with money, men, and ships. This treaty was in part negotiated by Benjamin Franklin. The French were not necessarily motivated by a spirit of goodwill towards the Americans; they hoped to gain back the territory they had lost in the French and Indian War. Moreover, the French believed that by aiding the Americans in the Revolutionary War they could position themselves to colonize parts of North America as yet unclaimed.

SOUTHERN CAMPAIGN IN THE REVOLUTIONARY WAR

The British military campaign in the **Southern colonies** was planned by Sir Henry Clinton and implemented by General Cornwallis in the years 1778 to 1781. Cornwallis quickly took **Savannah** and **Charleston** and then moved into the interior of South Carolina. Here and in North Carolina a series of bloody battles (many of them against the great American general Nathaniel Greene) weakened Cornwallis and forced him to make a supply run to **Yorktown** on the Virginia coast. There, the British suffered a naval defeat at the hands of the French, and then were routed by Washington-led troops. During their retreat, the British naval forces were further weakened by a violent storm, and Cornwallis was forced to **surrender** on October 17, 1781.

LEGACY OF THE REVOLUTIONARY WAR

After the conclusion of the Revolutionary War, neither the Proclamation of 1763 nor the Quebec Act applied, and thus colonists could **move west** across the Appalachians. A few British loyalists lost their land. After the war, many states moved to separate the church and state; in Virginia, for instance, Thomas Jefferson wrote the **Virginia Statute of Religious Freedom**, creating total separation in that state. States also revised the **Criminal Codes**, in an effort to make the punishment more closely fit the crime. Finally, whereas in 1750 most citizens did not question the institution of slavery, by 1780 many states began to examine this policy. Vermont was the first state to **abolish slavery**. Meanwhile, Southern states argued that the war would not have been won without slave labor.

> **Review Video: The Revolutionary War**
> Visit mometrix.com/academy and enter code: 935282

ARTICLES OF CONFEDERATION

The Articles of Confederation were largely ineffective because they gave too much power to the states and too little to a central government. Many historians now say that the best thing about the **Articles** were that they showed the authors of the Constitution what to avoid. Part of the Articles was the **Land Ordinance of 1785**, a plan created by Jefferson for dividing the Western land into organized townships. The sale of land in these territories helped generate money for the new government. The **Northwest Ordinance of 1787** divided the land above the Ohio River into five territories, which would soon become states. This ordinance would become the model for how all future states would be formed.

FOREIGN AFFAIRS

Both the Americans and the British violated the terms of the **Treaty of Paris**, which had ended the Revolutionary War in 1783. The British, for instance, never fully abandoned their lucrative fur trade in the Ohio Valley. Americans, on the other hand, never paid back their pre-war debts.

Meanwhile, the Spanish (who controlled Louisiana and Florida) openly challenged American borders in the South, at times encouraging Native Americans to make war on the fledgling nation. Americans sought the right of deposit on the Mississippi; that is, the right to load material from a boat to a dock. The Spanish were not quick to grant this right. Meanwhile, American ships were forced to pay tribute to the Barbary states in order to trade in the Mediterranean.

DEBT, PASSING LEGISLATION, LAW ENFORCEMENT, THE COURT SYSTEM, AND INFLATION AND DEPRECIATION

After the Revolutionary War, the United States found itself in a massive and troubling **debt**. Meanwhile, Congress was having great difficulty passing any **legislation** because in order to be made into law, a bill had to receive 9 of 13 votes, and there were often fewer than 10 representatives present. The government had no **chief executive**, and thus law enforcement was left to the states. Another major problem was that the lack of a **central court system** made it hard to resolve disputes between citizens from different states, or between the states themselves. Congress did not have the power to **tax** the people directly, and could only request funds. Furthermore, although Congress could issue **currency**, it had no authority to keep the states from issuing currency of their own, so wild inflation and depreciation were common.

COMPETING CURRENCIES AND LEGISLATIVE TROUBLES

Under the Articles of Confederation, Congress did not have the power to raise an **army** directly; it could only ask for troops from the states. The problems with this arrangement were amply demonstrated by **Shay's Rebellion** in Massachusetts in 1786 and 1787. This rebellion was in part a response to the economic uncertainty by competing currencies. Under the Articles, Congress did not have the power to regulate inter-state or foreign commerce. Each state in the confederation had different tariffs and trade regulations, and no foreign countries would enter into trade agreements with a nation so disorganized. In short, the **Articles of Confederation** left America unable to maintain order at home, unable to gain respect abroad, and unable to improve its economy.

PHILADELPHIA CONVENTION OF 1787

Although 55 delegates attended the **Philadelphia Convention of 1787**, only 39 signed the Constitution that emerged from this gathering. The attendees at the convention were exclusively rich men, but were all well-qualified to construct a new government. George Washington presided over the convention, and James Madison (the "father of the Constitution") served as secretary. The **representation** afforded to the people, as well as to states of different sizes, was a contentious issue throughout. Finally, in what is known as the **Great Compromise**, it was decided that the **lower house** (House of Representatives) would be chosen by the people, and the **upper house** (Senate) would be chosen by the state legislature. This convention also produced the **3/5 compromise**, whereby each slave was to be counted as 3/5 of a person. A 20-year moratorium was placed on the slave trade as well. Finally, it was decided at the convention that Congress should have control of commerce and tariffs.

CONSTITUTION

On September 17, 1787, the **Constitution** was presented to the people of the states. This document has three parts: a **preamble**; 7 **articles** outlining the powers and responsibilities of the 3 branches of government; and a section of **amendments**, the first ten of which are known as the **Bill of Rights**. The Constitution contains no bills of attainder, meaning that individuals cannot be denied life, liberty, and property without a trial. It does contain the concept of habeas corpus, meaning that arrested individuals must be charged with a crime within 72 hours. Federal judges are to be chosen for life, and there is an electoral college to select the president. In order to be in the House of

Representatives, individuals had to be land-owning white males. The Constitution is famous for its system of **checks and balances** whereby the president can veto Congress, but Congress can override the veto with a 2/3 vote, and the courts can call the acts of either body "unconstitutional."

RATIFICATION PROCESS, FEDERALISTS, AND ANTI-FEDERALISTS

In order for the Constitution to take effect, it had to be **ratified** by ¾ of the states. The **Federalists** were those in favor of the Constitution. They were primarily wealthy men who lived along the coast and wanted the commercial protection afforded by a strong federal government. **Anti-Federalists**, on the other hand, were mainly small farmers and artisans who felt that the Constitution was not truly democratic and would erode the power both of the states and of individuals. The Anti-Federalists wanted a Constitution that allowed for annual elections, a standing army, and a Federal fortress. They also disapproved of the atheism of the document. Unfortunately for the Anti-Federalists, the superior organization of the Federalists helped the Constitution become ratified, despite the fact that most Americans were opposed to it.

History of the United States: 1790 to 1898

BEGINNING OF THE FEDERALIST PERIOD AND THE JUDICIARY ACT OF 1789

After the ratification of the Constitution, **George Washington** was inaugurated as the first **president** in New York City. He immediately went outside the Constitution to form the first **Cabinet**: Thomas Jefferson, Secretary of State; Alexander Hamilton, Secretary of the Treasury; Henry Knox, Secretary of War; Edmund Randolph, Attorney General; and Samuel Osgood, Postmaster General. With the **Judiciary Act of 1789**, it was decided that there would be 6 justices and one chief justice on the Supreme Court. This act also established the federal court system and the policy of judicial review, whereby federal courts made sure that state courts and laws did not violate the Constitution. This policy was inspired by the case **Chisholm v. Georgia**, in which the Supreme Court ruled that a citizen of South Carolina could sue the state of Georgia, and that the case must be heard in a Georgia state court.

HAMILTON'S FUNDING AND ECONOMIC PLAN FOR THE FINANCIAL SYSTEM

The United States was born with $80 million in debt. **Alexander Hamilton**, however, was not terribly concerned by this; on the contrary, he encouraged **credit** as a means of financing the rapid capital improvements that would aid economic expansion. Hamilton introduced a **funding process**, whereby the government would buy back government bonds at full price in order to place money into the economy. Unfortunately, word of this plan leaked to some speculators, who bought the bonds at reduced rates and made huge profits. This led to accusations of a conspiracy. Another aspect of Hamilton's economic plan was for the federal government to **assume state debts**. This was done in part to tie state governments to the national government.

CUSTOM DUTIES, EXCISE TAXES, AND FEDERAL BANKS

In order to pay off the national debt, Hamilton promoted the **Revenue Act of 1789**, which was ostensibly a tax on imports, though it amounted to very little. Hamilton hoped to appease American industry with this measure without alienating foreign interests. The **Whiskey Tax**, instituted in 1791, was another attempt to generate revenue. This tax was wildly unpopular, however, and Washington was forced to call in several state militias to deal with various uprisings. At this time, Hamilton was also trying to establish a national bank, based upon the Bank of England. The **Bank of America** was established with $10 million in capital and aimed to repay foreign debts, provide a uniform national currency, aid in the collection of taxes, make loans, and act as a federal depository.

FOREIGN DIPLOMACY UNDER WASHINGTON

The United States stayed **neutral** during the wars of the French Revolution, even issuing a proclamation to that effect in 1793. Meanwhile, the British were constantly testing this neutrality: they did not leave their posts in the Northwest; they seized American ships and forced American sailors into service; and they frequently aided the Native Americans in their conflicts with the United States. This conflict eventually led to the **Jay Treaty** in 1794 which made the Spanish fear an Anglo-American alliance, causing them to become more willing to discuss American use of the Mississippi River. **Pinckney's Treaty**, also known as the **Treaty of San Lorenzo** (1795), gave the United States free use of both the Mississippi and the city of New Orleans.

> **Review Video: Pinckney's Treaty**
> Visit mometrix.com/academy and enter code: 866670

28

JAY TREATY

The Jay Treaty of 1794 aimed to calm the post-revolution conflicts between Britain and the United States. In it, the British promised to leave their forts in the northwest and to pay for all the recent damages to ships. The British also allowed the US to form a limited commercial treaty with the British West Indies. The **Jay Treaty** asserted that the rivers and lakes of North America could be used by both Britain and the United States. However, the treaty made no provisions for any future seizures of American ships, and made no mention of Native American attacks on the American frontier. The Southern states were annoyed that the treaty won no compensation for slaves freed during the Revolutionary War, and, moreover, stipulated that Southerners had to repay their pre-war debts. The controversy surrounding the Jay Treaty led to the formation of the first **political parties**.

RISE OF THE FIRST POLITICAL PARTIES

Unlike a faction, which exists in order to achieve a single goal, a **political party** endures beyond the accomplishment of a specific goal. The first two political parties in the United States were the **Federalists** and the **Democratic-Republicans. Hamilton** is the primary figure associated with the Federalists, who were wealthy northeasterners in support of a strong central government and a loose interpretation of the Constitution. The Federalists advocated a strong president, the economic policies implemented by Hamilton, and a strong relationship with the British. The Democratic-Republicans, on the other hand, were associated with the so-called "common man" of the South and West. Led by **Jefferson** and **Madison**, they advocated a strong central government, a strict interpretation of the Constitution, a close relationship with France, and closely-restricted government spending.

WASHINGTON'S FAREWELL ADDRESS AND PRESIDENTIAL ACCOMPLISHMENTS

In 1796, Washington decided he was too tired to continue as president. In his famous **Farewell Address**, he implored the United States to avoid three things: permanent alliances; political factions; and sectionalism. Washington felt that the nation could only be successful if people placed the nation ahead of their own region. For his own part, Washington made some significant improvements during his presidency. He avoided war at a time when the nation was vulnerable. He also avoided political alliances and promoted the national government without alienating great numbers of people. Washington oversaw Hamilton's creation of the economic system and guided expansion to the West (as well as the creation of three new states: Vermont, Kentucky, and Tennessee).

ELECTION OF ADAMS AND CONFLICT WITH THE FRENCH

John Adams became the second president of the United States in the election of 1796; his opponent, **Thomas Jefferson**, became vice president because he received the second-most electoral votes. Adams was immediately confronted by the French, who were angry about the **Jay Treaty** and the broken **Treaty of Alliance of 1778**. After the French began destroying American ships, Adams sent American diplomats to meet with the French ambassador **Talleyrand**, who demanded tribute and then snubbed the Americans. There followed an undeclared naval war between 1798 and 1800. During which, the American military grew rapidly, warships were built and the Department of the Navy was established. Finally, at the **Convention of 1800**, the Treaty of Alliance of 1778 was torn up and it was agreed in this new **Treaty of Mortefontaine** that the

Americans would pay for damages done to their ships by the French, among a host of other clauses including each country giving the other Most Favored Nation trade status.

> **Review Video: John Adams as President**
> Visit mometrix.com/academy and enter code: 156316

DOMESTIC EVENTS UNDER ADAMS

The Alien and Sedition Acts were established in 1798, in part because of xenophobia arising from conflict with the French. The **Alien Act** increased the number of years before one could obtain citizenship, gave the president the power to deport anyone and allowed the president to jail dangerous aliens during times of war. The **Sedition Act** made it a crime to libel or slander US officials or policies; many people believed this policy was a violation of First Amendment rights. The **Virginia and Kentucky Resolves**, promoted by Jefferson and Madison, stated that a contact exists between the state and national governments, but that the national government had exceeded its authority and broken the contract. This document advocated that states should have the power of nullification over national policies; only Virginia and Kentucky supported this policy, which had the potential to fatally undermine the Constitution.

> **Review Video: The Alien and Sedition Acts**
> Visit mometrix.com/academy and enter code: 633780

ELECTION OF 1800

In the election of 1800, the **Federalists** were represented by John Adams and C.C. Pinckney, and the **Democratic-Republicans** by Thomas Jefferson and Aaron Burr. The Federalists had been weakened both by the unpopularity of the Alien and Sedition Acts and the internal feud between Adams and Hamilton. They therefore focused their campaign on Jefferson, accusing him of being an atheist, of stealing money from the poor and of having an affair with a slave. In the election, Jefferson finished with the same number of electoral votes as his supposed running mate, Burr, who surprisingly refused to concede. This situation led to the **12th amendment**, which states that a candidate must stipulate his desired office. **Jefferson** finally won the tie-breaking vote in the House of Representatives, sweeping the Federalists out of office.

> **Review Video: The Election of 1800**
> Visit mometrix.com/academy and enter code: 992318

FEDERALIST PERIOD

The **Federalist period** had some remarkable successes and some bitter failures. It saw the establishment of the national bank and the Treasury system under Hamilton. The United States, amazingly, was able to pay off all of its debt during this period. The **Federalist administration** can also be credited with maintaining international neutrality, establishing the Pinckney Treaty, crushing the Whiskey Rebellion, and getting the British out of their northwest posts. On the other hand, over time the Federalists became known as an elitist party, and the Alien and Sedition Acts were very unpopular. The Jay Treaty was seen as a diplomatic failure by most Americans, and in general the Federalists were not able to maintain very cordial relations with Europe (especially France).

JEFFERSONIAN REPUBLICANS

After using his inauguration speech to try to pacify angry Federalists, Thomas Jefferson went on to introduce the "**spoils system**," replacing Federalist office-holders with **Republicans**. He also reversed many of the Federalist policies: the Alien Act was repealed, and the Sedition Act expired in

1801 (everyone arrested under its authority was pardoned, absolved, and had their fines repaid). Jefferson also sought to reform the judiciary. The **Judiciary Act of 1801**, otherwise known as the **Circuit Court Act**, was passed by the Federalists in order to cement some of their judges in place; Jefferson in turn forced through the **Judiciary Act of 1802**, which removed all 42 of these judges.

Review Video: Jefferson and the Spoils System
Visit mometrix.com/academy and enter code: 514178

MARBURY V. MADISON

William Marbury was one of the Federalist judges removed from office by the Judiciary Act of 1802. Marbury, having been promised a job, brought up the issue with **James Madison**, who pleaded ignorance. The issue became contentious and in 1803 came before the Supreme Court as **Marbury v. Madison**. Although Section XIII of the Judiciary Act of 1789 had a **Writ of Mandamus** which required Madison to honor the appointment, Chief Justice **John Marshall** declared this section unconstitutional. This was a historic act: although the power of the Supreme Court to declare state and local measures unconstitutional had been established, this had never before been done on the national level. Marshall thereby established an independent judiciary; he is quoted as saying, "The Constitution is the supreme Law of the Land, with the Supreme Court as the final interpreter."

Review Video: Marbury v. Madison
Visit mometrix.com/academy and enter code: 573964

YAZOO CLAIMS AND JOHN RANDOLPH

In 1795, the corrupt Georgia legislature sold some land known as the **Yazoo Claims** for almost nothing to a group of northeastern speculators in exchange for a bribe. When a new group of legislators came into office in 1797, they revoked the land sales, infuriating the speculators. In 1802, the land claims were ceded to the national government and Jefferson decided to grant the speculators a cash settlement. **John Randolph**, however, was the chairman of the House committee responsible for paying this settlement, and he refused to make the payment, stating that the deal was "bathed in corruption." Though the Supreme Court eventually granted the settlements in the case **Fletcher v. Peck** (1810), Randolph was permanently alienated from Jefferson and went on to form a group called the **Tertium Quids**. This group was the ultra-conservative pro-states' rights contingent of the Democratic-Republicans.

Review Video: Fletcher v Peck
Visit mometrix.com/academy and enter code: 652746

TREATY OF ILDEFONSO AND THE LOUISIANA PURCHASE

In an agreement between the French and Spanish known alternately as the **Treaty of Ildefonso** or the **Retrocession**, Napoleon Bonaparte acquired Louisiana. This, along with Spain's closing of New Orleans to American business, made Jefferson nervous, and he thus sent James Monroe to France in order to purchase New Orleans and West Florida. Bonaparte, himself made anxious by a rebellion in Haiti and a renewal of hostilities with the British, signed over 800,000 square miles to the US, making the **Louisiana Purchase** the largest land acquisition without bloodshed in human history. Napoleon hoped to curry favor with the United States, in order to forestall a possible Anglo-American alliance.

PERCEPTION OF THE LOUISIANA PURCHASE AND ACQUISITION OF EAST AND WEST FLORIDA

The Louisiana Purchase was probably the high point of Jefferson's presidency; it was seen at home as a diplomatic victory that also avoided drawing the United States into conflict with the European powers. It destroyed the Federalist party. After the **Louisiana Purchase** was completed, explorers set out to discover just what had been bought; among these explorers were **Meriwether Lewis** and **William Clark**. Meanwhile, the United States began to make inroads into Spanish-controlled **West Florida**. In 1810, rebels attacked Baton Rouge and James Madison claimed that West Florida was now part of the US. Of course, the Spanish protested, but they were unable to reestablish themselves. In 1818, Andrew Jackson would lead a group of soldiers into **East Florida** under the pretense of taming the Seminoles. In 1819, the Spanish would reluctantly sign the **Treaty of Onis**, in which the US formally acquired East Florida for $5 million, which the Spanish promptly returned to pay off some of their debt to the US.

AARON BURR

After losing his challenge for the presidency in 1800, **Aaron Burr** was left out of the 1804 election and became embittered. He then lost a bid for the governorship of New York, in part because of the mudslinging of **Alexander Hamilton**. At this point, Burr began to toy with the idea of forming a new country in the West. Hamilton, hearing of this plan, informed Jefferson. Burr promptly challenged Hamilton to a **duel**, and in 1806 killed him at Weehawken, NJ. Burr headed west, and planned to start a new country in Louisiana and the areas controlled by Spain. Jefferson formally charged Burr with treason, but, citing executive privilege, refused to attend the trial. Burr was eventually found not guilty, in part because he had only planned a new country, and in part because the US was unable to find any reliable witnesses.

> **Review Video: Aaron Burr**
> Visit mometrix.com/academy and enter code: 273358

FOREIGN POLICY UNDER THE JEFFERSONIAN REPUBLICANS

The most important event during the dominance of the Jeffersonian Republicans was the **War of 1812**, fought between France and Britain. In the United States, there was much speculation as to whether the young nation would side with the shark (Britain) or the tiger (France). In 1803, Jefferson had declared American ships neutral, an act which annoyed both sides. The British subsequently passed the **Orders-in-Council**, and the French the **Berlin and Milan Decrees**, all of which were designed to weaken American shipping in Europe. The US responded with the **Non-Importation Act of 1806**, though this was largely a failure. In 1807, an American ship called the **Chesapeake** was attacked by a British ship, leading Jefferson to issue the **Embargo Act of 1807**. This act forbade American ships from leaving for foreign ports; it was very unpopular, and was repealed in 1809.

> **Review Video: Opinions about the War of 1812**
> Visit mometrix.com/academy and enter code: 274558

MADISON AND "PEACEFUL COERCION," AND THE NON-INTERCOURSE ACT OF 1809

In the 1808 election, **James Madison** of the Democrat-Republicans easily defeated C.C. Pinckney. Madison continued Jefferson's policy of "**peaceful coercion**" with respect to France and Britain, but the lack of an organized American military made it difficult for him to get the attention of these major powers. In 1809, Madison convinced Congress to pass the **Non-Intercourse Act of 1809**, which forbade trade with Britain and France until they began treating American business fairly. When the British ambassador **David Erskine** vowed to improve the treatment of American

businesses, Madison agreed to trade with England. However, Erskine's superior quickly overruled him, making Madison look ridiculous and souring Anglo-American relations further.

MACON'S BILL NO. 2

Madison replaced the Non-Intercourse Act of 1809 with **Macon's Bill No. 2**, which declared that America would be open to trade with any country. The bill also stipulated that if either Britain or France agreed to neutral trading rights with the US, the US would immediately cease trade with the other. France jumped at this opportunity, and the US cut diplomatic ties with Britain. The British, weakened by the American embargoes and by a bitter winter, rescinded the **Orders-in-council**, although the US had already declared war upon them. After the British Prime Minister was assassinated, the new foreign secretary, **Castlereagh**, tried to mend relations, but the US went to war anyway. The **War of 1812** was very unpopular, especially among Federalists in the northeast. Many Americans felt that England could not be beaten, that engaging in a war would damage US business, and that Napoleon was not a very savory ally.

WAR OF 1812

CONTROVERSY

The conservative members of Madison's party, known as the **Tertium Quids**, opposed the **War of 1812** because they felt it would be too expensive, would result in the perpetuation of a standing army, would damage America economically, and would lead to the acquisition of Canada as a slave state. These critics were opposed in Congress by the **Warhawks**, so-called by the Federalists to imply that they were picking a fight. The Warhawks mainly represented the Southwest and the West, and included luminaries such as Henry Clay, John C. Calhoun, and Felix Grundy. They supported the war because they thought it would bolster foreign trade, would discourage the British from inciting Native Americans along the frontier, and could result in land gain. In selling the war to the American people, Madison stressed the British insult to American honor; he mentioned several stories about impressments of Americans into British military service.

EVENTS LEADING UP TO COMBAT

Despite a great deal of bloated rhetoric both for and against the war, the US fought against Britain for a few basic reasons, namely to gain more **land** and to destroy **alliances** between the British and Native Americans. Americans had become incensed when, following his defeat to the Americans at Tippecanoe Creek, **Chief Tecumseh** had fled north into British-controlled Canada. This provocation provided enough popular support to declare war. Unfortunately, the American military was both unprepared and overconfident. Most American military strategists thought it would be quite easy to take Canada, but the army had only 35,000 troops at the time. Moreover, the first Bank of the United States had just gone defunct, and so there were scarce economic resources to support a war.

MAJOR BATTLES

At the **Battle of Lake Erie** in September of 1813, the American Commander Perry secured Detroit for the US. At the **Battle of Lake Champlain**, the American General Thomas McDonough secured northern New York from British invasion. At the **Battle of the Thames**, the American General William Henry Harrison defeated a coalition of British and Native American forces; Tecumseh was killed. Andrew Jackson scored a decisive victory at the **Battle of Horseshoe Bend**. During this war, much of Washington, DC (including the White House) was torched. A crucial point of the war came when the US was able to successfully defend **Fort McHenry**, outside of Baltimore; this conflict inspired Francis Scott Key's composition of "The Star-spangled Banner." At the **Battle of New Orleans**, Andrew Jackson used a rag-tag collection of soldiers and pirates to defeat the British navy.

CONCLUSION OF THE WAR

Throughout the War of 1812, there was loud opposition from the **Federalists** in the northeast. At the **Hartford Convention**, they formally blamed Madison for the war, and proposed changes to the Constitution whereby a 2/3 vote would be needed for declaring war and for admitting new states to the union. The War of 1812 required several agreements to fully restore relations between the US and Britain. The **Treaty of Ghent** returned Anglo-American ties to their pre-war terms, and proposed that commissions be created to settle differences. The **Rush-Bagot Treaty of 1817** formally declared that there would be no naval race between the 2 countries. At the **Convention of 1818**, a line was drawn along the 49th parallel, dividing Canada from Louisiana, and it was declared that the 2 countries would jointly occupy Oregon. In the **Adams-Onis Treaty of 1819**, a western boundary for Louisiana was set, and the Spanish renounced their claims to Oregon.

> **Review Video: The Adams-Onís Treaty**
> Visit mometrix.com/academy and enter code: 802716

SIGNIFICANCE

The War of 1812 did not really accomplish its supposed goal of establishing neutral trading rights for American ships. The exodus of Napoleon during the war made this a moot point. Nevertheless, from Madison's perspective the war could only be seen as a major **success**. The United States lost no major territory, and scored enough victories to keep the British from making any extreme demands. More importantly, perhaps, Americans were overjoyed that the US was finally getting respect from the major European powers. **Nationalism** exploded in the US: people forgot the debacle of the failed national bank, and the economy boomed. Finally, the success of the War of 1812 effectively drove the final nail into the coffin of the **Federalist party**.

STRENGTHENING OF AMERICAN NATIONAL IDENTITY

The success of the War of 1812 and the prospering economy made Madison extremely popular. In the northeast, with the implementation of the British factory system, and in the southeast, with the invention of the cotton gin, manufacturing interests were booming. This sense of **national identity** was strengthened by the emergence of the United States' first generation of **post-colonial artists**. In literature, James Fenimore Cooper and Washington Irving (*The Legend of Sleepy Hollow*) were eminent. A uniquely American style of **architecture** developed, led by Jefferson, among others, emphasizing columns, symmetry, and classical proportions. The **Hudson River school** produced a group of painters influenced by the natural beauty of their region; among them John James Audubon.

TRIUMPH OF NEO-FEDERALISM

In 1816, Madison declared that that the government should increase the army, the national debt, and the banking interests, an agenda oddly reminiscent of Federalism. The **Second Bank of the United States** was shown to be necessary by the War of 1812, but it was poorly organized and came to be known as a "moneyed monster." The **Tariff of 1816** was established to protect fledgling industry; it was as popular in the northeast as it was unpopular in the south. Much of the tariff money went to developing infrastructure; the new method of **paving** invented by John MacAdam enabled the creation of long thoroughfares, mostly in the north. It was even proposed in the so-called "Bonus Bill" that all of the surplus money from the new bank should go to the roads; Madison vetoed this measure to avoid further alienating the south.

"THE ERA OF GOOD FEELINGS" FROM 1817 TO 1825

In the election of 1816, the Democrat-Republican **James Monroe** defeated the last Federalist candidate, Rufus King, by a landslide. The Federalist opposition to the War of 1812 doomed the party to extinction. Monroe's early term was not without its problems, however. A mild depression caused by over-speculation on western lands led to the **Panic of 1819**, and began a 20-year boom-bust cycle. These problems were exacerbated by the **Second Bank of the United States**; the Bank's pressure on the so-called "wildcat" banks to foreclose on properties, as well as the unwillingness of the Bank to loan money, made it very unpopular. The nationalism generated by the War of 1812 was damaged by these economic travails.

THE MARSHALL COURT (1801-1835)

The Supreme Court led by **John Marshall** is credited with increasing the power of the national government over that of the states. This court also gave the judicial branch more power and prestige, notably in the case of **Marbury v. Madison** (1803). Marshall was known as an arch-Federalist, and as a loose interpreter of the Constitution. In the case **McCullough v. Maryland** (1819), the court ruled that a national bank is allowed by the Constitution, and that states cannot tax a federal agency. In the case of **Gibbons v. Ogden** (1824), the right of Congress to regulate interstate commerce was reaffirmed, and indeed federal regulation of just about anything was made possible. In **Fletcher v. Peck** (1810), the sanctity of contracts was asserted; this case also established the right of the Supreme Court to declare state laws unconstitutional.

MONROE DOCTRINE

After a series of revolutions in Latin America, the United States was the first to recognize the **sovereignty** of the new countries. This was in part because the revolutionaries had used the United States as inspiration, in part because the US preferred to have weak, independent nations nearby, and in part because the US wanted to maintain and expand its lucrative trade with Latin America. The British attempted to persuade the US to sign an agreement preventing foreign intervention in Latin America, but Monroe decided to maintain American independence and issue his own document. This document, known as the **Monroe Doctrine**, had as its two main principles *non-intervention* and *non-colonization*. Many considered it a "paper tiger," because it was really only as effective as the American ability to enforce it. Still, it seemed to encourage foreign nations to come to the bargaining table rather than test the American military.

> **Review Video: <u>Monroe Doctrine</u>**
> Visit mometrix.com/academy and enter code: 953021

JACKSONIAN DEMOCRACY

The 1820s and 30s are known as the era of **Jacksonian democracy**, which was political rather than economic or social. Jackson was considered to be emblematic of the "common man." In the years after the conclusion of the War of 1812, it was generally considered that America was "safe for democracy," and thus **suffrage** was extended to poor people in many states. As more people became involved in politics, campaigning became more about image and perception than the issues. This change also ended the tradition known as "**King Caucus**," in which candidates were chosen by a small group of powerful men; now, candidates were to be selected by a series of primaries and nominating conventions. Furthermore, the members of the electoral college would be chosen by the voters rather than by the state legislature. The new system maintained the tradition of **patronage** (the spoils system), in which newly-elected officials would fill the government offices with their supporters.

ELECTION OF 1824 AND ADAMS' ADMINISTRATION

All the major candidates in the 1824 election were **Democrat-Republicans**. Although Andrew Jackson received more electoral votes than **John Quincy Adams**, he did not win a majority, and Adams (with the help of Henry Clay) won the run-off in the House of Representatives. Adams was a fierce **nationalist** at a time when many in the country were sectionalist. Although his initiatives for a national university and public funding for the arts were well-meaning, Adams was still believed to be out of touch with the common man. He further alienated the middle and lower classes with the **Tariff of 1828**, known in the South as the "Tariff of Abominations." The South was already on shaky economic ground and the tariff became a scapegoat for its troubles. **John C. Calhoun** was an especially ardent Southern voice; he futilely proposed that states should have the ability to nullify federal regulations.

> **Review Video: John Quincy Adams as President**
> Visit mometrix.com/academy and enter code: 797549

1828

The election of 1828 is considered the first **modern campaign** in American politics. **Andrew Jackson** had the first campaign manager, Amos Kendall, and produced buttons, posters, and slogans to support his candidacy. These men—Jackson, Kendall, John C. Calhoun, and Martin van Buren—formed the beginning of the **Democratic party**. Meanwhile, the incumbent John Quincy Adams ran a very formal campaign, with little of the "flesh-pressing" of Jackson. Adams tried to discredit Jackson as an adulterer and bigamist because Jackson's wife had not been officially divorced at the time of their marriage. When his wife died during the campaign, however, the popular sentiment returned to Jackson, and he won the election by a considerable margin. Jackson's inauguration was an over-crowded, chaotic affair; the president suffered three cracked ribs during the festivities.

> **Review Video: Martin Van Buren's Presidency**
> Visit mometrix.com/academy and enter code: 787203
>
> **Review Video: The Election of 1828**
> Visit mometrix.com/academy and enter code: 535830

JACKSONIAN DEMOCRACY

Andrew Jackson is often seen as a symbol of the rising power of the New West, or as an embodiment of the "rags to riches" fable. He spent much of his presidency trying to promote the idea of **nationalism** at a time when most of the country was ardently sectionalist. During his presidency, he dominated Congress, vetoing more legislation than all of the previous presidents combined. He was also famous for his so-called "**Kitchen Cabinet**," a group of close advisers without official positions. Many of these men later received formal appointments, including Secretary of State (Martin van Buren), Postmaster General (Amos Kendall), and Secretary of the Treasury (Roger B. Taney).

> **Review Video: Andrew Jackson as President**
> Visit mometrix.com/academy and enter code: 667792
>
> **Review Video: Nationalism**
> Visit mometrix.com/academy and enter code: 865693

MAJOR EVENTS OF THE JACKSON ERA

RAID INTO FLORIDA AND THE WEBSTER-HAYNE DEBATE

One of the least successful events in Jackson's presidency was a **raid into Florida** in 1828, made for the purpose of subduing the Seminoles. The raid did not go well, and even Jackson's Secretary of War, John C. Calhoun, referred to it as "idiotic." Another major event in Jackson's term was the **Webster-Hayne debate** of 1829-30, held to debate western expansion. The senators of the northeast were opposed to western migration, mainly because they felt it would weaken manufacturing and create a new political rival. Senator **Robert Hayne** of South Carolina blasted the war record of the Northeast, in the hopes of allying the West and the South. **Daniel Webster** (MA) retorted that the US is not a collection of states, but a union that happens to be divided into states; he asserted that if states could nullify federal measures, the only thing holding the union together was a "rope of sand."

MAYSVILLE ROAD VETO AND NATIVE AMERICAN REMOVAL

In 1830, Jackson set a precedent by **vetoing the funding of a road** that was to be entirely within one state (Kentucky). Many believed that Jackson vetoed this bill to spite Henry Clay, but the move had some positive political consequences as well: the Southerners appreciated the idea that states should tend to their own business and northerners liked it because the road would have given people easier access to the West. Jackson's attempts at **relocating Native Americans** were less successful. The passage of the **Indian Resettlement Act of 1830** was the first attempt by the national government to force migration. In the case of **Worcester v. Georgia** (1832), the Supreme Court ruled against those who sought to grab Native lands. John Marshall asserted that the **Cherokee nation** was sovereign, but a ward of the US. Despite Marshall's assertion of Native American rights, Jackson supported the slow and steady conquest of land in the South and West.

TARIFF OF 1832 AND THE FORCE ACT OF 1832

At a feast in celebration of Thomas Jefferson—a man noted for his nationalism—Andrew Jackson promoted the idea of the nation, saying, "Our Union, it must be preserved." John C. Calhoun responded with a speech in which he referred to "Our Union, next to our liberty most dear," indicating that the South was not going to back down. The milder **Tariff of 1832** was then offered by Jackson to appease the South and Calhoun; instead, Southern politicians declared it was not enough, and Calhoun resigned from Congress in order to organize the opposition to all tariffs. Henry Clay, who realized that Jackson could easily overpower South Carolina, was further disturbed by the **Force Act of 1832**, which stated that the president had the right to use military force to keep a state in the union. So, Clay proposed an even lower **Compromise Tariff of 1833**: the tariff would be lowered from 35% to 20-25% over the next ten years. Both sides agreed to this compromise.

BANK WAR OF 1836

It had already been arranged that the **renewal of the Second Bank of America** would be discussed in 1836. It was common knowledge that Jackson hated the Bank, and thus Henry Clay and others tried to renew it ahead of time, in 1832. Jackson was then forced to assert his position: he declared that the bank was anti-West, anti-American, unconstitutional and a "monopoly of money." The unpopularity of Clay's attempt to renew the Bank was a main reason that he was crushed by Jackson in the 1832 election. After making sure that the Bank would not be renewed, Jackson sought to mend fences with the Northeast by avidly promoting the Union. This was Jackson's genius as a politician; he always was careful to get what he wanted without fully alienating any faction.

ELECTION OF 1836 AND THE VAN BUREN PRESIDENCY

When Jackson decided not to pursue a third term as president, his vice president **Martin Van Buren** ran and won over a group of challengers including the Whig candidate William Henry Harrison. Van Buren's presidency was marked by frequent border disputes with Canada. Also, Van Buren suffered through the **Panic of 1837**; like in 1819, this was caused by over-speculation in the West. In the 1836 "Specie Circular," Jackson had declared that all land bought from the government must be paid for in gold coins. Because gold was hard to come by, many people lost their property. Further economic problems were created by over-spending on infrastructure in many states. One of the results of Van Buren's handling of the situation was that it became acceptable for the president to influence the amount of money in circulation. In 1840, a listless Van Buren was defeated by **Harrison**, who promptly died after a month as president. **John Tyler** became the next president.

TYLER PRESIDENCY

John Tyler, a Virginia aristocrat, was the first vice president to take over in mid-term. Oddly, even though he was the Whig candidate, he opposed almost all of the Whig agenda. Henry Clay hoped to dominate Tyler, but his attempts to create a third national bank and to improve infrastructure in the West were both vetoed by Tyler. Tyler's presidency was also fraught with conflict with the British; he endured the **Lumberjacks' War of 1842** and the **Hunters' Lodges skirmishes** in 1838, both of which were minor conflicts along the Canadian border. There was also the incident of the *Caroline*, an American ship sunk by the British for allegedly smuggling supplies to Canadian rebels. In the **Webster-Ashburton Treaty of 1842** fugitives were exchanged, the border of Maine was set at the St. John River and it was established that the British could no longer search American ships.

> **Review Video: John Tyler as President**
> Visit mometrix.com/academy and enter code: 791157

EXPANSION AND MANIFEST DESTINY

The phrase "**manifest destiny**," meaning the inevitability and righteousness of the American expansion westward, was coined by the editor **John O'Sullivan**. This idea was lent further credence by the work of Horace Greeley, the journalist responsible for the admonition, "Go West, young man!" Besides this mythology, however, there were some sound reasons why the United States expanded westward. For one thing, there was cheap and fertile land in the west, and the more that was claimed by the Americans, the less which could be claimed by the British. Americans also had an eye towards claiming the western ports to begin trading with Asia. Finally, many Americans felt that they would only be benefiting the world by spreading their ideals of liberty and democracy across as much land as possible.

> **Review Video: Manifest Destiny**
> Visit mometrix.com/academy and enter code: 957409

TEXAS' ROLE IN US EXPANSION

In 1821, **Mexico** received its independence from Spain. Mexico sold Texan lands to Americans, yet these people were still required to live under Mexican civil law (for one thing, people had to convert to Catholicism). In 1832, however, **Santa Anna** led a coup in Mexico and decided to crack down on the Texans. This led to the **Texas Revolution of 1836**, in which Texan General William Travis' men were massacred by the forces of Santa Anna at the **Alamo**, in which both Davy Crockett and Jim Bowie were killed. After suffering some other defeats, the Texans, led by Sam Houston, finally defeated Santa Anna at the **Battle of San Jacinto** in 1836 and he was forced below the Rio Grande.

Nevertheless, Texas was not made part of the US, mainly because the issue of slavery was so contentious at the time.

US EXPANSION INCLUDING SALT LAKE CITY, OREGON, AND CALIFORNIA

The territory of **Oregon** became more important to the US government as fur-trapping became a lucrative industry. Oregon was also known to contain rich farmland. As for **California**, its natural bounty had been described by whalers since the 1820s. In the 1840s, whole families (including the ill-fated Donner party) began to migrate there. Around this time the **Church of Jesus Christ of Latter-day Saints**, otherwise known as the Mormon Church, was founded by Joseph Smith. Among the beliefs espoused by the Mormons were polygamy, communalism and the abolition of slavery. After Smith's death, the Mormons were led by Brigham Young and settled in what is now **Salt Lake City**. Meanwhile, in 1848 gold was discovered in a California stream, generating still more excitement over the economic potential of the West.

PRESIDENCY OF JAMES K. POLK

The election of 1844 brought to the forefront a number of critical issues; the economy was still hurting from the Panic of 1837, there was growing support for abolitionism and the issue of manifest destiny was gaining steam. Somewhat surprisingly, the bland North Carolinian **James K. Polk** defeated Henry Clay and succeeded John Tyler as president. He instituted the **Walker Tariff**, which lowered the rate at which foreign goods were taxed from 35% to 25%. He also reinstated the **Independent Sub-Treasury system** in 1846. Mainly, however, Polk's presidency is associated with westward expansion; **Texas** was brought into the union as a slave state in December of 1845. Polk also spent considerable time trying to get possession of Oregon.

> **Review Video: James K. Polk as President**
> Visit mometrix.com/academy and enter code: 917254

MEXICAN WAR

CAUSES

The immediate causes of the **Mexican War** were the American annexation of Texas, disputes over the Southern border of Texas and the large amount of money owed to the United States by Mexico. Moreover, it was well known that the Mexicans held the US in contempt, considering them greedy land-grabbers. **Polk** sent an emissary to buy Texas, California, and some Mexican territory for $30 million; he was refused. **Zachary Taylor** then led an American expedition into a disputed area of Texas where some of them were killed. Polk was able to use these deaths as a rationale for war, despite considerable opposition in Congress. Overall, the Democrats supported the war, while the Whigs, led in part by Abraham Lincoln, were opposed.

MAJOR BATTLES AND CONCLUSION OF WAR

The United States scored major victories over Mexico at **Buena Vista**, where they were led by Zachary Taylor, and **Vera Cruz**, where they were led by Winfield Scott. The American effort in New Mexico was led by Stephen Kearney and in California by John C. Fremont. The **Treaty of Guadalupe-Hidalgo** was signed in 1848 after Polk sent an emissary with cash in an effort to persuade Santa Anna to stop the war. Under the terms of the treaty, the US got California, the rest of Texas, and all of the Mexican territory between Louisiana and California (including what would become Utah and Nevada). In exchange, the US erased a good deal of Mexico's debts. Controversy immediately erupted over whether the new territories would be allowed to have slaves; some abolitionists wanted to cancel the treaty while some Southern Democrats wanted to claim the entirety of Mexico.

ROAD TO CIVIL WAR

There was immense controversy surrounding the **slavery policy** in the new American territories after the war with Mexico: Polk wanted to simply extend the line of the **Missouri Compromise** out to the Pacific while abolitionists offered the **Wilmot Proviso**, which declared that none of the territories should have slaves. The Southern states felt slavery should be allowed, and a more moderate view was offered by Stephen Douglas, who declared that the people of the new states should decide whether they wanted slavery or not. In the election of 1848, the war-hero **Zachary Taylor** (Whig) defeated Lewis Cass (Democrat) and the former president Martin Van Buren (Free Soil party, a collection of abolitionist interests).

> **Review Video: Missouri Compromise**
> Visit mometrix.com/academy and enter code: 848091

GOLD RUSH AND THE COMPROMISE OF 1850

After **Zachary Taylor** won the election of 1848, he immediately had to deal with the issue of slavery in the new western territories. This issue was magnified by the California gold rush. Taylor declared that all of the lands would be free, enraging the Southerners. Soon after, however, Taylor died of food poisoning and was succeeded by Vice-president **Millard Fillmore**. In order to solve the problem of slavery in the west, Henry Clay proposed the so-called **Compromise of 1850**: California would be a free state, while New Mexico would be allowed to decide for itself; there would be no more slave trading in the District of Columbia; there would be tighter laws regarding fugitive slaves; and Texas would receive $10 million for its lost territories. Fillmore readily signed this agreement, but problems with it arose immediately. One of which was that the **Underground Railroad** of **Harriet Tubman** was already making it very difficult to catch fugitive slaves.

ELECTION OF 1852 AND THE GROWING CRISIS OF SLAVERY

In the election of 1852, Democrat **Franklin Pierce** easily defeated the Whig Winfield Scott who was hurt by his association with the abolitionist William H. Seward. At this time, despite the growing crisis of slavery, there were some positive changes in the US. One was that the introduction of **California** as a free state permanently upset the sectional balance. Immigration into the Northeastern cities was bringing a wealth of new ideas. The northern states resisted the fugitive slave laws by passing initiatives in support of personal liberties and by aiding the Underground Railroad. Harriet Beecher Stowe enraged the South with her novel Uncle Tom's Cabin (1852). In 1857, Hinton R. Helper published "The Impending Crisis of the South," an essay that suggested the South was becoming a slave to the North because of its reactionary view on slavery.

TRANS-CONTINENTAL RAILROAD, OSTEND MANIFESTO, AND KANSAS-NEBRASKA ACT

The construction of the **Trans-Continental Railroad** was begun in 1853 for the purpose of transporting easterners to California. With the **Gadsden Purchase**, the US had purchased some New Mexican lands so that the train could avoid the mountains. With the **Ostend Manifesto** in 1854, the US attempted to purchase Cuba from Spain for $120 million; Spain refused, and though the US threatened to take the island by force, they never did (in part because it was believed that the South wanted to make it a slave state). The **Kansas-Nebraska Act** (1854), authored by Stephen Douglas, divided the Nebraska territory into two parts (Kansas and Nebraska) and declared that slavery would be determined by popular sovereignty in those territories. This act drove northerners to the liberal side and caused the creation of the **Republican party**. The opposing factions engaged in violence to try and win the popular vote. Though Kansas worded its constitution in an attempt to have slaves, the document fell apart upon review by Congress, and Kansas entered as a free state.

SUMNER-BROOKS INCIDENT, ELECTION OF 1856, AND THE DRED SCOTT CASE

In 1856, Senator **Charles Sumner** (MA) gave an impassioned speech on the "Crime against Kansas," in which he blamed the south for the violence. One of the men whom he singled out for blame was the uncle of Senator **Preston Brooks** (SC); Brooks beat Sumner with his walking stick, and was glorified in the South. In the election of 1856, **James Buchanan** (Democrat) defeated several candidates, including Millard Fillmore (American party; some southern states had threatened to secede should Fillmore prevail). Next came the **Dred Scott** case. Scott was a slave taken to a free state by his owner, and then transported back to a slave state. Abolitionists said he should be a free man. The Supreme Court, however, ruled that slaves are property and can be transported across state lines without being changed. This decision effectively rendered the Kansas-Nebraska Act, the Missouri Compromise, and the whole idea of popular sovereignty unconstitutional.

> **Review Video: Dred Scott Act**
> Visit mometrix.com/academy and enter code: 364838

LINCOLN-DOUGLAS DEBATES AND JOHN BROWN'S RAID

During the campaign to become senator of Illinois in 1858, **Abraham Lincoln** and **Stephen Douglas** eloquently debated the issue of slavery. In the so-called **Freeport Doctrine**, Lincoln questioned whether the people of a territory could vote against slavery. The Supreme Court would say no, but Lincoln wondered whether the people should not have the final say. Douglas essentially agreed, stating that the people of the territory should decide. Douglas won the election, though his stance on slavery irritated Southerners. In 1859, the abolitionist **John Brown** led a raid on a federal arsenal at Harper's Ferry, Virginia. Brown's group was only able to take a fire station, and Brown himself was captured and executed by a battalion led by **Robert E. Lee**. Brown became a martyr to the North.

ELECTION OF 1860 AND SECESSION OF THE SOUTH

In the election of 1860, **Abraham Lincoln** defeated three other challengers. Lincoln's platform was anti-slavery, though he vowed to leave it intact where it already existed. He also promised full rights to immigrants, the completion of a Pacific Railroad, free homesteads, and a protective tariff. After the election, South Carolina **seceded**, followed by the rest of the Deep South (Mississippi, Alabama, Georgia, Louisiana, Florida and Texas). These states established the **Confederate States of America**, with its capital in Montgomery, Alabama. The president of the CSA was **Jefferson Davis**. Outgoing US President Buchanan claimed that he had no constitutional authority to stop the secession, but upon entering office Lincoln attempted to maintain control of all Southern forts. This led to the firing on **Ft. Sumter** (SC) by the Confederates. As Lincoln called for aid, the Upper South (Virginia, Arkansas, North Carolina and Tennessee) seceded as well, and the CSA made Richmond, Virginia its new capital.

> **Review Video: The Civil War: Abraham Lincoln and Secession**
> Visit mometrix.com/academy and enter code: 570281

COMPROMISES TO SAVE THE UNION

The US government made a number of compromises in an attempt to preserve the Union after Lincoln's election. The **Crittenden Compromise** extended the line of the Missouri Compromise and promised federal protection of slavery south of that line. The **House of Representatives Compromise** offered an extension of the Missouri Compromise and a Constitutional amendment to protect slavery. The **Virginia Peace Convention** produced an offer to extend the line of the Missouri Compromise and establish that slavery can never be outlawed except by the permission of

41

the owner. Finally, Congress offered $300 for each slave. The South said that this was not enough money and the North was appalled by the offer, regardless.

CIVIL WAR

The Civil War was fought for a number of reasons, but the most important of these was the controversy about **slavery**. The issue of slavery touched on moral, economic, and political themes. Also, the differing geography of the North and South had caused the latter to develop an **economy** that they felt could only survive through slavery. The Civil War also sprang from the ongoing debate over **states' rights**; many in the South felt that states should have the power to nullify federal regulations and believed that the North had too much representation in Congress; and, indeed, the North had received much more federal aid for infrastructure. Finally, there was a general difference in **culture** between the North and South; the North was more of a dynamic and democratic society, while the South was more of a static oligarchy.

ADVANTAGES OF THE NORTH

The **Northern side** in the Civil War contained 22 states with 22 million people. The North also contained most of the US' coal, iron, and copper, as well as 92% of the industry. The Union side had more than twice as much railroad track as the Confederacy and a vastly larger navy. Most importantly, perhaps, the Union had a huge advantage in **troops**. Most of the Northern troops were either volunteers or had been conscripted (starting in 1863). It was permissible to pay someone to take your space in the military. The North generally had between 2 and 3 times as many troops as the South during the war. The South was really only able to survive for so long because it fought a very defensive war.

ADVANTAGES AND DISADVANTAGES OF THE CONFEDERACY

The **Confederate States of America** was comprised of 11 states with only 9 million people. When the war began, the South had no organized army or navy. At first, the troops were strictly volunteers, but eventually the CSA established a draft to bolster the ranks. The Confederacy did have some advantages, however. One was that they were fighting on their own soil and thus they already had interior lines of defense as well as knowledge of the terrain. On the whole, the Confederate commanders were more experienced and talented. Finally, the Confederacy had a psychological advantage over the North: they were fighting for a **tangible reason** (namely, to preserve their lives and property, while the North had to motivate its troops with notions of "preserving the Union."

MILITARY STRATEGIES OF THE NORTH AND SOUTH

The North began the Civil War by trying to **blockade** the Southern coast and seal off the border states; they hoped to end the war quickly by preventing supplies from reaching the Confederacy. The North also wanted to divide the South into two parts by seizing control of the Mississippi River. This plan would later be adjusted, and **Sherman's March** would try to divide the South into a northern and southern half. The Confederacy, meanwhile, knew that its best chance for success was to fight **defensively** (the South did not want any Northern territory). They also knew that they would need help from European powers. The South hoped to outlast the North's will to fight, to capture Washington, DC, and to receive Maryland into the Confederacy.

MAJOR BATTLES

First Bull Run, Shiloh, and Second Bull Run: The **First Battle of Bull Run** was fought in Manassas, VA in July of 1861. The North believed that an easy victory here would allow them to quickly take Richmond. Washingtonians even picnicked around the battlefield, anticipating a pleasant spectacle. It was not to be, however: led by Stonewall Jackson (who actually earned that nickname at this battle), the South won a shocking victory. As a result, the South became somewhat overconfident, and the North realized it was in for a long war. At the **Battle of Shiloh** (TN) in April of 1862, Ulysses S. Grant led the Union to its first major victory. At the **Second Battle of Bull Run** in August of 1862, Stonewall Jackson again defeated a Northern army, this time with the help of Robert E. Lee.

> **Review Video: Robert E. Lee**
> Visit mometrix.com/academy and enter code: 637719

Antietam: At the **Battle of Antietam** (MD) in September of 1862, the Confederate General Robert E. Lee went on the offensive, hoping to bring Maryland into the Confederacy, sever the channels between Washington, DC and the North, and attract the recognition of the European powers. This was the bloodiest battle of the Civil War and ended in a draw. It was after this battle that Lincoln issued his famous **Emancipation Proclamation**. This document freed the slaves in any area that was taken by the Union, or in areas from which slaves could enter the Union. It did not, however, free slaves in the Border States, because Lincoln wanted to maintain loyalty to the Union in these areas. The aims of the Emancipation Proclamation were three: to keep the British from assisting the South, to motivate the Northern troops and to effect a positive moral change.

> **Review Video: Emancipation Proclamation**
> Visit mometrix.com/academy and enter code: 181778

Fredericksburg, Chancellorsville, and Gettysburg: At the **Battle of Fredericksburg** (VA) in December of 1862, Robert E. Lee successfully repelled the attacks of the Union General Burnside. At the **Battle of Chancellorsville** (VA) in May of 1863, Lee scored his greatest victory of the war; it was during this battle, however, that the Confederate General Stonewall Jackson was mortally wounded by his own troops. At the **Battle of Gettysburg** (PA) in July of 1863, the Confederacy troops led by Lee suffered a damaging defeat. Lee had hoped to take some pressure off the South with a successful surge into the North, but instead got caught in an unfavorable tactical position and endured massive casualties. Most historians believe the Union victory at Gettysburg was the turning point in the war.

Vicksburg, Atlanta, and Sherman's March: The Union General mounted a siege against the crucial Confederate city of **Vicksburg** (MS) in July of 1863. When the Confederates had finally been starved into surrender, the Union had total control of the Mississippi River. Then, between July and October of 1864, the major Southern rail hub of **Atlanta** was conquered and burned by Union troops under General William Sherman. This victory guaranteed that Lincoln would be reelected in the election of 1864. It also marked the beginning of **Sherman's March to the Sea**, a campaign of devastation mounted by the Union in late 1864 and early 1865. Sherman's troops melted Southern rails and destroyed Southern crops and factories, creating a swath of chaos that stretched from Atlanta to Savannah.

> **Review Video: Civil War**
> Visit mometrix.com/academy and enter code: 239557

ELECTION OF 1876 AND COMPROMISE OF 1877

In 1876, **Rutherford B. Hayes** (Republican) defeated Samuel Tilden (Democrat) after an electoral commission composed mostly of Republicans ruled that certain votes by carpet-bag governments should have gone to him. As part of the ensuing **Compromise of 1877**, the South was given federal money for improvements to infrastructure, a Southerner was placed in Hayes' Cabinet, and the Union troops propping up the carpetbag governments were removed. This election established the tradition of the "**Solid South**": it was assumed that every year the majority of Southerners would vote for the Democratic candidate.

NEW SOUTH IN THE 1880S

In the 1880s, the old Southern plantations began to break up, in part because the high taxes imposed by the new governments made them unprofitable. The land was mainly worked by tenant farmers and sharecroppers: **tenant farmers** worked and paid rent on someone else's land, while **sharecroppers** worked the whole plantation and got a share of the crop. Tenant farmers were mostly poor whites, while sharecroppers were mostly freed blacks. There was considerable diversification in agriculture around this time, brought on not only by innovation (cotton picker, tractor), but by the **Morrill Land Grant Act**, which gave grants for the creation of agricultural colleges. Clarence Birdseye's development of the refrigerated railroad car spurred farming as well. Also, as the road and rail infrastructure improved in the South, so did Southern industry.

REDEEMERS

The Redeemers sought to prevent blacks from voting and to return power to the "natural leaders." In response, the **Populist party** was formed; it was an uneasy alliance of blacks and poor whites. Southern Democrats tried to exploit the tension within the Populist party. In order to keep blacks from voting, Democrats subjected voters to literacy tests, property tests, criminal background checks, residency requirements and the so-called **Grandfather Clause**, which stated that individuals could not vote unless their ancestors had voted before January 1, 1867. These restrictions, known collectively as the **Mississippi Plan**, were actually upheld by the Supreme Court, which ruled in **Williams v. Mississippi** (1898) that they were legal because they never explicitly stated that blacks could not vote.

BLACK SOUTHERNERS AND SEGREGATION

Most Southern Democrats supported **segregation**, or the separation of the races. Although the **Civil Rights Act of 1875** had outlawed segregated restaurants and hotels, among other things, the Supreme Court ruled in 1883 that this act violated the 14th amendment because only states, and not individuals, could be forbidden from segregation. The **Jim Crow laws** were those rules that segregated blacks and whites. Although de facto (by custom) segregation had existed in the North for years, the South began to implement segregation de jure (by law). In **Plessy v. Ferguson** (1896), the Supreme Court ruled that accommodations should be "separate but equal." In **Cummings v. Board of Education** (1898), the Supreme Court allowed public schools to be segregated.

BOOKER T. WASHINGTON AND W.E.B. DUBOIS

Booker T. Washington was an ex-slave who founded the Tuskegee Institute; he felt that blacks should establish economic independence before worrying about political rights. In his **Atlanta Exposition speech**, he declared that blacks needed to humble themselves to whites. Professor **W.E.B. DuBois** attacked Washington's speech as a compromise; DuBois believed blacks should take everything they were due. In 1914, both Washington and DuBois met with Marcus Garvey, who believed that blacks should return to Africa and establish a separate country (interestingly, most of Garvey's financial support came from the KKK). At around this time, Paul Laurence Dunbar was achieving renown as the "poet laureate of the Negro race," and Charles Waddell Chestnut was admired as a popular black novelist.

SUBORDINATION OF WESTERN NATIVE AMERICANS UNTIL 1874

The Native Americans who roamed the Great Plains were known as fierce hunters and there were a few bloody encounters between settlers heading west and the natives. In 1851, the US established the **Concentration policy**, which encouraged Native Americans to live close to one another. This strategy was untenable, however, and the period from 1860-90 was marked by frequent conflict. In the **Sioux Wars** of 1865-7, the Sioux were led by **Red Cloud**; they fought and lost to American troops after their sacred hunting ground was mined. For a while, the US tried to group tribes on reservations in Oklahoma and the Black Hills; from 1869-74, Generals Sherman and Sheridan engaged in a **War of Extermination** to kill those who refused to move.

SUBORDINATION OF THE WESTERN NATIVE AMERICANS FROM 1875-1887

According to **Grant's Peace Program**, each Native American tribe would be put under the control of different religious groups. In 1875, miners were allowed back into the Black Hills, prompting the **Sioux War** of 1875-6, during which Sitting Bull defeated Custer at the **Battle of Little Big Horn**. Around this time, Chief Joseph attempted to lead his Nez Perce tribe to Canada; this mission failed and the Nez Perce were sent to Oklahoma. The Apache leader Geronimo was defeated in Arizona in 1887. At the **Battle of Wounded Knee**, the US army massacred 300, mostly women and children. Native Americans were doomed by their inferior weapons; by the destruction by whites of their food supply, the buffalo; and by railroads which made it easier for whites to encroach on their hunting grounds.

SOLUTIONS TO THE "INDIAN PROBLEM"

The US government constructed several policies in an attempt to solve the so-called "**Indian Problem.**" The **Dawes (Severalty) Act of 1887** asserted that Natives needed to be assimilated into American society; tribes were moved onto "allotments of severalty" (reservations), which they supposedly owned, although they had no control of the land. The **Indian Reorganization (Howard-Wheeler) Act of 1934** encouraged a return to tribal life, and offered Natives money for college. In 1953, with the so-called "**termination policy**," Natives became the responsibility of the states rather than the federal government. In 1970, the new strategy was "self-determination without termination": Natives were allowed to move where they choose, and were promised money (which they did not receive).

ERA OF BONANZAS

Between the years 1848 and 1858, the miners known as the "**forty-niners**" dug about $555 million out of the Western soil. In particular, the **Comstock Lode** of Virginia City, Nevada was famous for producing vast amounts of gold and silver. After buffalo were largely eradicated from the Great Plains, there was a "cattleman's bonanza," aided by the invention of barbed wire. The **Cattleman's Association** was a union of cattle dealers joined together to preserve the integrity of the industry, to stop cross-breeding, and to stop cattle thievery. This era marked the end of the open range, mainly because of horrible droughts and bad winters, range wars between the cowboys and sheep farmers, the railroads and barbed wire.

HOMESTEAD ACT OF 1862 AND THE TRANSCONTINENTAL RAILROAD

The US government tried many different ways to improve conditions for farmers in the West. Under the **Homestead Act of 1862**, farmers were sold 160 acres for $10, with the proviso that they had to improve the land within 5 years. Between the years 1865 and 1900, only one in six farms began this way. The **Timber Culture Act of 1873** gave more land to farmers, with the proviso that they had to plant some trees on that land.

One thing that helped to populate the West was the completion of the **Transcontinental Railroad** in 1869. The Union Pacific met the Central Pacific railway at Promontory Point, Utah. In 1889, the US government opened Oklahoma for settlement, and by 1893 it was completely settled.

SECOND INDUSTRIAL REVOLUTION

The Second Industrial Revolution was possible in the United States because of the abundance of raw materials and the laissez-faire economic policies of the government. In the space between the years 1860 and 1914, industry grew to about twelve times its original size. This rapid progress was made possible by the rapid growth of the **American railway system**. The railroads were subsidized by the federal government. Around this time, Samuel Morse developed his **telegraph code**, enabling almost instantaneous communication across vast distances. Jay Gould and James J. Hill were among those who made immense fortunes as railroad managers. Cornelius Vanderbilt and his son William were both railroad magnates with a reputation for ignoring the plight of their workers.

> **Review Video: Second Industrial Revolution**
> Visit mometrix.com/academy and enter code: 608455
>
> **Review Video: Second Industrial Revolution: Standard Oil Company**
> Visit mometrix.com/academy and enter code: 616068
>
> **Review Video: Second Industrial Revolution: The American Railroad System**
> Visit mometrix.com/academy and enter code: 843913

INDUSTRIAL ERA SCANDALS AND INNOVATIONS

The infamous **Credit Mobilier scandal** occurred during Grant's presidency in 1972 and involved the Union Pacific Railroad. A more egregious crime was perpetrated on the stockholders of the Erie Railroad; the owners were trying to avoid being bought out by Vanderbilt, and thus they printed up a huge amount of new stock, making it impossible for Vanderbilt to get a majority interest but also vastly diminishing the value of each share. During this era, the following **innovations** and inventors accelerated industry: sleeper cars (George Pullman); air brakes for trains (George Westinghouse); time zones; double tracking (so that two trains could run on the same line); and the standardization of the distance from one rail to another.

COMPETITION AND DISORDER IN THE INDUSTRIAL ERA

The late eighteenth century was marked by intense **competition** between the railroads. Railroads offered secret illegal refunds to big customers and in areas where they had no competition, they charged exorbitant prices. After the 1870s, various states tried to tame the railroads; one such instance of this kind of regulation was the **Granger Laws**. Farmers often felt that they were charged more than others. In **Munn v. Illinois** (1877), the Supreme Court asserted that the state governments had the right to regulate the railroads. In Wabash, St. Louis, and **Pacific Railroad Co. v. Illinois** (1886), the Supreme Court reversed its former opinion and declared that only the federal government could regulate the railroads. Finally, with the **Interstate Commerce Act of 1887**, the federal government forbade discriminatory practices like refunds and price fixing; unfortunately, these laws were rarely enforced.

J.P. Morgan and Banker Control

The **Panic of 1893** was brought on by the collapse of the **Philadelphia and Reading Railroads**; soon after, 192 railroads failed. In a panic, railroad magnates turned to bankers, especially the "Railroad Doctor," **J.P. Morgan**. Morgan insisted that all of the business' records be opened to him. His usual strategy was to encourage old investors to reinvest, to sell more, "watered-down" stock, and to place either himself or one of his associates on the Board of Directors. In this way, Morgan was able to create a set of "interlocking directories," conglomerations of businesses in which he had an interest. He created many large companies this way, among them General Electric, Western Union, and Equitable.

Andrew Carnegie and Steel

The potential for making money in **steel** was made possible by the development of the **Bessemer process**, whereby iron ore was converted into wrought iron and then has its impurities removed with cold air. **Andrew Carnegie**, an immigrant from Scotland who rose to the top of the Pennsylvania Railroad, was one of the first to make his fortune in steel. He was not especially knowledgeable about steel, but he was the first manager to make a point of **vertical integration**: that is, control of every step of the production process. Carnegie bought out most of his competitors, until he was eventually bought out by J.P. Morgan. Carnegie and his fellows believed in a sort of "gospel of wealth," the idea that they had risen to the top through a process like natural selection. They also believed in using their money for the community.

> **Review Video: <u>Andrew Carnegie and the Steel Industry</u>**
> Visit mometrix.com/academy and enter code: 696753

John D. Rockefeller and the Trust

John D. Rockefeller came from a working-class background, but gradually rose to become the owner of the wildly profitable **Standard Oil company**. Rockefeller was known for spying on his competitors and intimidating his employees. In 1870, Standard allied itself with 40 other companies; when this alliance began, the group controlled 10% of the market, but by 1881 they controlled almost 95%. In 1882, Standard Oil created a **trust**: alliance members gave their stock to Standard in exchange for trust certificates. The federal government began to get suspicious of these powerful trusts, and in 1890 the **Sherman Anti-trust Act** was passed. This act forbade trusts, but it was worded so vaguely that it was ineffective. In the case of **US v. E.C. Knight Co.** (1895), the Supreme Court ruled that the Knight sugar refinery was not a monopoly because it didn't hurt interstate trade; businesses saw this ruling as a call to monopolize.

Laissez-Faire Conservatism and the Gospel of Wealth

The so-called "**Gilded Age**" of American history, which ran roughly from 1880 to 1900, only looked prosperous from a distance. Many at this time believed that wealth justified itself, and that God showed his favor in people by making them rich. Many business leaders did not trust politicians because they did not feel that they had had to fight their way to the top. Businessmen believed that the role of the government was to protect property and trade through tariffs. **William Graham Sumner** wrote the essay "What the Social Classes Owe Each Other," in which he declared that corporations shouldn't demand high tariff rates, but the government shouldn't respond to requests to clean up the slums. There was a general sense that the poor were responsible for their plight.

Around this time, the popular imagination was inspired by the rags-to-riches fables of **Horatio Alger**.

SOCIAL CRITICS AND DISSENTERS IN THE GILDED AGE

In his book *Dynamic Sociology*, **Lester Frank Ward** railed against the Social Darwinism espoused by the upper class; he declared that humans were more than mere animals. In *Progress and Poverty*, **Henry George** asserted that poverty was the result of poor legislation rather than any inherent weakness in the poor. **Edward Bellamy** promoted socialism in his novel *Looking Back* (1888); in it, a man of the year 2000 describes how America was turned into a utopian society through the abolition of corporations. Also, at this time, **Thorstein Veblen** exposed the phenomenon of "conspicuous consumption" in his *Theory of the Leisure Class*. All of these critics were disgusted by the hypocrisy of the **robber barons**; these magnates claimed to support laissez-faire government, yet they wanted high tariffs to protect their businesses.

AMERICAN LABOR IN THE GILDED AGE

As the US emerged from the Civil War, one of the main economic problems was that most workers were **unskilled**. In general, working conditions were horrendous and wages were low. There was little homogeneity in the labor force, either, making it difficult for workers to switch jobs. **Immigrants** were usually willing to take more dangerous jobs than natives; during the 1880s, more than 5 million immigrants entered the US. In 1882, the **Chinese Exclusion Act** put a 10-year moratorium on Chinese immigration. In 1885, the **Foran Act** prohibited American business men from traveling to China to recruit workers. Both of these acts were open violations of the **Burlingame Treaty of 1868**, which had provided for open Chinese immigration.

LABOR ORGANIZATIONS AFTER THE CIVIL WAR

NATIONAL LABOR UNION AND NOBLE AND HOLY ORDERS OF THE KNIGHTS OF LABOR

At the end of the Civil War, only about 2% of all US workers were **unionized**; many believed joining a union was an admission that one would never move up. Over time, though, people began to realize that the consolidation of business interests (trusts) had to be met by a consolidation of labor. In 1866, the **National Labor Union** was founded by William H. Sylvis; this idealistic organization advocated an 8-hour work day but disbanded after backing the loser in the 1872 election. In 1869, Uriah Stephens founded the **Noble and Holy Orders of the Knights of Labor**; this group excluded doctors, lawyers, and bankers and supported the end of sexism; the 8-hour workday; paper money; income tax; and the prohibition of alcohol.

HAYMARKET SQUARE AND AMERICAN FEDERATION OF LABOR

In 1886, the **Knights of Labor** gathered in **Haymarket Square** in Chicago to protest an attack against another union. During the protest, a bomb was thrown and several people were killed; 7

members of the union were arrested, and some were executed. This incident linked labor unions with violence in the popular imagination. At the same time, less idealistic labor unions like the American Railway Union (led by Eugene V. Debs), the United Mineworkers, and the Molly McGuires were making great inroads in working communities. The **American Federation of Labor** was an alliance of many unions formed in 1881. This group sought a shorter workday, better working conditions, and workman's compensation: they were also not afraid to strike. The AFL frequently engaged in collective bargaining, in which a strike was threatened in order to bring management to the negotiation table.

GREAT STRIKE OF 1877, THE HOMESTEAD STRIKE, AND THE PULLMAN STRIKE

The Great Strike of 1877 occurred in West Virginia when state police and militiamen were sent to break up a railway strike and joined it instead. President Hayes sent in the army and at least 100 people were killed breaking up the strike. This debacle set a bad precedent for future strikes. In the **Homestead (PA) Strike** of July 1892, a group of soldiers called by Henry Clay Frick (temporarily in charge of one of Carnegie's steel mills) brutally broke up a strike. In 1894, a group of **Pullman railcar employees** began a strike, supported by the American Railway Union of Eugene V. Debs. All rail workers then went on strike out of sympathy for the Pullman workers. The rail owners got an injunction, claiming that the rail workers were interfering with interstate trade and therefore violating the **Sherman Anti-trust Act**. This did not end the strike, and thus President Grover Cleveland had to send in the army under the false premise that the strike was holding up the US mail.

OPPOSITION TO ORGANIZED LABOR

The general public **opposed** labor unions because they disliked the idea of closed shops (those places in which one had to be a union member to work) and because they had a reputation for violence. Unions were also fiercely competitive with one another, and there was some animosity between the unions for skilled and unskilled workers. Unions were always at a disadvantage in their dealings with management, in part because management could hire lobbyists (to promote anti-union legislation in Washington) and lawyers, and could bribe politicians. Owners often had blacklists of union trouble-makers who would not be hired, and plenty of "yellow-dog" workers who had signed contracts pledging never to join a union. Owners often hired spies to obtain information among workers, and, in the event of strike, they could always hire "scabs" to cross the picket lines. It was not unheard of for managers to hire thugs to cause trouble among strikers and perpetuate the rowdy reputation of the unions.

GILDED AGE

CHARACTERISTICS

The period in American history between Reconstruction and the Progressive Era is commonly known as the **Gilded Age**. During this period, the US seemed to be simultaneously abandoning the ideals of the past and failing to anticipate the future; this was in large part due to the confusion of a horrendous Civil War and massive immigration, industrialization, and urbanization. During this period, many Americans sought refuge in **community organizations** like the Moose Lodge, the Elks Club, and the Masonic Lodge. The politicians of the Gilded Age tended to avoid the major issues of **social injustice and inequality**, instead focusing on minor issues like public v. parochial schools, and the blue laws (laws restricting commercial activity on Sunday).

> **Review Video: The Progressive Era**
> Visit mometrix.com/academy and enter code: 722394

49

POLITICS

Although the **Republicans** dominated the executive branch during the Gilded Age, Congress was evenly divided. The Republican party was composed mainly of people from the Northeast and Midwest. Blacks typically were Republicans (that is, when they were allowed into the political process). In general, the Republicans supported high tariffs and sound money. One of the main internal disputes in the Republican party was between the **stalwarts**, who supported the spoils system, and the **half-breeds**, who did not. As for the **Democrats**, they were largely based in the South or in the big cities of the North. The Democrats and Republicans butted heads over ethnic, religious, and cultural issues, but they tended to avoid larger economic and social issues. Extremely talented individuals were more likely to go into business than politics during this era. Another trend of the Gilded Age was the domination of the president by Congress.

HAYES PRESIDENCY

HIGHLIGHTS

Foolishly, **Rutherford B. Hayes** made himself a lame-duck president by announcing soon after taking office that he would not seek a second term. Hayes' wife was nicknamed "Lemonade Lucy," because she would not allow any alcohol in the White House. Hayes tried to restore the power of the presidency after the debacle of Grant, but he was weakened by intense struggles over his Cabinet confirmations. One thing Hayes can be credited with is making a gallant attempt to destroy the **spoils system**. He replaced the Collector of the Customs House after discovering the corruption of that body, and he appointed Carl Schurz Secretary of the Interior on the basis of merit. In turn, Schurz established a merit system in his department, creating an entrance exam for potential employees.

LOW-POINTS

One of the failures of the Hayes administration was its handling of the **Great Rail Strike of 1877**. When over two-thirds of the rail lines were shut down by strikes, Hayes sent in federal troops, and there was considerable bloodshed. This set a bad precedent for how strikes would be handled in the future. Hayes vetoed an attempt by western labor unions to restrict Chinese immigration, saying that this would be a violation of the **Burlingame Treaty**. One of the main issues in the Hayes years was monetary policy. Farmers, who were often in debt, wanted a soft currency not backed by anything; they were willing to settle for a silver standard. In **Hepburn v. Griswold** (1869), the Supreme Court had ruled that there could not be paper money without a gold standard; in the **Legal Tender cases of 1871**, however, the Court reversed itself. The bickering over these conflicting rulings plagued the Hayes administration.

HAYES VS. GREENBACKERS AND THE SILVERITES

After the **Specie Resumption Act of 1875**, Hayes worked to minimize the effects of the oncoming "day of redemption," in which paper money could be exchanged for gold coins. He began a policy of contraction, wherein the government gradually took in paper money and issued gold, and he funded attempts to mine more gold. The **Greenbackers** were those who wanted Hayes to postpone the day of redemption; he did not, and it ultimately proved anticlimactic, as people assumed their paper money was "good as gold" and didn't bother to redeem it. Hayes also had to deal with the **Silverites**. In 1873, the government had enraged silver prospectors by announcing that it would no longer make coins out of silver. In answer to their fury, Hayes pushed through the **Bland-Allison Act**, which established that a minimum of $2 million of silver had to be purchased and coined by the government every month.

ELECTION OF 1880

In the election of 1880, the **Republican party** was beset by internal squabbling between the stalwarts and half-breeds over the issue of patronage. This led to a chaotic nominating convention in which a campaign manager, **James A. Garfield**, became the candidate. Garfield won a narrow victory over the Democrat Winfield Scott Hancock, a war hero with no political experience. Garfield was a charismatic figure whose administration began with a successful compromise among Republicans; unfortunately, he was shot and killed in 1881. Garfield was succeeded by his vice-president, **Chester A. Arthur**. The major event of his presidency was the **Civil Service Act of 1883**, which established a commission to create competitive examinations for potential government employees. Arthur also helped create the modern US navy.

ELECTION OF 1884

In 1884, the incumbent Arthur was passed over by his party in favor of Secretary of State James G. Blaine. This proved to be a bad move, as the **Democratic** candidate, **Grover Cleveland**, was able to win the support of conservative Republicans (Mugwumps) and claim a narrow victory. The highlights of the Cleveland administration include the further reform of civil service and the government's successful stand against ex-Union soldiers who were protesting for large pensions. Cleveland reluctantly signed the **Interstate Commerce Act**, and he was correct in predicting that it would not be enforced. Cleveland also spent a great deal of time on tariffs: he attempted to reduce the overall duty with the **Mongrel Tariff** and the **Mills Bill of 1888**, neither of which were very successful.

ELECTION OF 1888

In 1888, the Republican **Benjamin Harrison** narrowly upset the incumbent Cleveland, despite having less of the popular vote. Harrison did not accomplish much civil service reform, and spent a great deal of time managing insubordination in Congress. Harrison's Republican agenda promoted the **Federal Election Bill**, which was a response to the Mississippi Plan designed to protect the voting rights of freedmen. The **Silver Purchase Bill** was favored by the west, but lacked the votes to get through. In the **Compromise of 1890**, the Western Republicans got the silver purchase (Sherman Silver Purchase Act), Southern Democrats got the defeat of the Federal Election Bill, and the Northern Republicans got a higher tariff (McKinley Tariff of 1890). Harrison's administration became known for giving money away for virtually any reason: pensions were excessive; the silver purchase cost federal money; and all of the income tax taken during the Civil War was given back to the people.

AGRICULTURAL PROBLEMS DURING POPULISM

In the years following the Civil War, the US heartland suffered from an **overabundance** of wheat and rice; these surpluses, coupled with the advances in transportation and communication, drove prices down. Farmers were forced into high debt which they could never repay, leading to **deflation** and a scarcity of currency. Since many farmers didn't own the land that they worked, the banks often had to **foreclose** when farmers were unable to pay their debts. Farmers blamed their problems on a number of different factors. They blamed the railroads, which usually gave discount rates to bigger shippers. They blamed the banks, which loaned money to the rich but were unforgiving of farmers' economic plight. They also blamed the tax system, claiming that it was easy for businesses to hide their assets and impossible for farmers to do so. Additionally, they blamed the tariff, which discouraged other countries from buying US goods.

EARLY FARM ORGANIZATION DURING POPULISM

The **Patron of Husbandry (Grange)** was founded in 1867 by Oliver Kelley to establish cooperatives, in which individuals bought goods directly from the whole-sale distributor. His group was also responsible for the **Granger Laws**, which attacked railroad and grain elevator interests. The Grange had basically disappeared by 1875. The **National Farmer's Alliance and Industrial Union** pursued a number of different initiatives: more national banks; cooperatives; a federal storage system for non-perishable items; more currency; free coinage of silver; reduction of tariffs; direct election of senators; an 8-hour workday; government control of railroads and telegraphs; and one term for the president. This group's success led to the formation of the **Populist Party** in 1890. This party aimed to speak for the farmers and included all of the farmers' unions as well as some labor unions, the Greenbackers, and the Prohibitionists. The party suffered from internal divisions from its inception.

ELECTION OF 1892 AND THE PANIC OF 1893

Grover Cleveland (Dem) defeated Benjamin Harrison (Rep) in the election of 1892 primarily because of his financial conservatism, his promise to change the tariff and because the epidemic of strikes in 1892 had weakened Harrison. Then came the **Panic of 1893**, caused by labor troubles, over-speculation in the railroads, and an agricultural depression. First the Philadelphia and Reading Railroads collapsed, then the stock markets collapsed, then the banks folded, draining the gold reserves, then the other railroads folded, and finally the factories were forced to close. Cleveland believed that the cause of this Panic was the **Sherman Silver Purchase Act**, so he repealed it. This plan did absolutely nothing financially, and it split the Democratic party politically.

PANIC OF 1893 AND DOMESTIC AFFAIRS UNDER CLEVELAND

After the Panic of 1893, a group known as the **Silverite school** declared that the economic problems could be solved if the US would begin coining silver again. Cleveland, however, ignored this advice, and elected to buy gold with the profits from the sale of government bonds. This strategy was somewhat successful. It was during the **Panic of 1893** that the suggestion to battle economic depression by employing people on public works was first made. One of Cleveland's major policy moves in his second term was the **Wilson-Gorman Tariff of 1894**. This lowered the tariff rate and established trade with Latin America. It also established a small income tax on wealthy individuals, though this income tax would be repealed in the **Supreme Court case Pollock v. Farmer's Loan and Trust** (1895). Cleveland's last term was diminished by ineffective enforcement of the **Sherman Anti-trust Act** and the **Interstate Commerce Act**.

REPUBLICAN ASCENDANCY IN THE ELECTION OF 1896

The Republicans had been successful in the Congressional elections of 1894, and they nominated **William McKinley** for president in 1896. McKinley was in favor of high tariffs and the gold standard. He was opposed by William Jennings Bryan of the Democrats. McKinley had a wealth of political experience and money, and the Democrats were blamed by many for the economic depression under Cleveland: McKinley won fairly easily. This election marked a 36-year period of domination by the **Republicans**. It also spelled the end of the Populist party. Around this time, gold was found in the Yukon, lending credence to the Republican belief in the gold standard.

IMPERIALISM
DURING THE PERIOD OF WITHDRAWAL (CIVIL WAR TO 1880S)

In the period after the Civil War, the US for the most part withdrew from **foreign affairs**. The Secretaries of State in this period, however, were very aggressive: **Seward** interfered in Korean politics, tried to assert influence in the Caribbean, and famously purchased Alaska from Russia in

1867 for $7.2 million. **Hamilton Fish** tried and failed to annex Santo Domingo. Aside from these instances, though, the US kept its distance. For the most part, this was because it was preoccupied with its own problems. There was also a common belief that invading and colonizing other countries would be a violation of our own **Declaration of Independence**. Many were remembering Washington's farewell address, in which he advised the US to avoid military entanglements, and others were wary of violating the **Monroe Doctrine**.

DURING THE NEW MANIFEST DESTINY (1880S TO 1920S)

In the 1880s, the US began to take a stronger interest in **foreign affairs**. This was in part due to humanitarian concern: the US felt it could improve the standard of living around the world. There was also, of course, an economic motive; manufacturers wanted to find a new source of raw materials, as well as a new market for their products. Missionaries began to travel abroad in this period, trying to convert foreigners to Christianity. There were also military reasons for the increased activity abroad; the US decided it would be a good idea to acquire naval bases in the Pacific and a group known as the **Jingoists** openly looked for a military conflict. Theodore Roosevelt and Henry Cabot Lodge were both Jingoists.

BERING SEA, PAN-AMERICAN UNION, AND SAMOAN ISLANDS CONFLICT

The "**Seal Battle**" was fought in the Bering Sea between British Canada and the US mainly over boundary lines. In 1893, the two sides met and established mutual boundaries between Alaska and Canada. In 1889, the first meeting of the **Pan-American Union** was held in Washington, DC. In 1878, the US had established a naval base at Pago Pago. Both the British and Germans demanded access to the base. In 1889, the US allowed both the British and Germans to jointly occupy the base. In 1899, the **Samoan islands** were divided up among the US and the European powers.

CONFLICT WITH ITALY, BALTIMORE INCIDENT, BOUNDARY DISPUTES IN SOUTH AMERICA, AND HAWAII

Between the years 1889 and 1891, the US came into conflict with **Italy** after members of the **Sicilian Black Hand**, a terrorist group, were lynched without just cause in New Orleans. The US also sparred with Chile after 2 sailors from the *USS Baltimore* died during a bar fight in Valparaiso, Chile. At around this time, a boundary dispute erupted between **British Guiana** and **Venezuela** after gold was discovered in the vaguely-defined border region. Britain was ready to send troops into South America but the US dissuaded them from doing so, citing the Monroe Doctrine. Meanwhile, all throughout the nineteenth century the US had been closing in on a conquest of **Hawaii**. After New England missionaries stumbled upon the islands, the US had gotten the natives to sign trade treaties with various US companies. In the 1890s the US army, led by pineapple magnate Sanford Dole, ousted the native leadership. Hawaii was annexed by the US in 1898.

> **Review Video: Anti-Colonial Struggles: Central and South America**
> Visit mometrix.com/academy and enter code: 158300

SPANISH-AMERICAN WAR

CAUSES

The **Spanish-American War** centered around **Cuba**. There had already been several revolts against the Spanish leadership on that island, and the **Wilson-Gorman Tariff** had damaged the Cuban economy. In 1896, the Spanish sent General Valeriano Weyler to establish a reconcentration camp, where the dissenting Cubans could be weeded out. Many in the United States pushed the government to intervene in Cuba; businessmen were worried about their crops, Christians and humanitarians were worried about the Cuban people, and imperialists saw a good chance to seize the island. The two final causes of the war were the **DeLome letter**, in which the Spanish minister to the US insulted President McKinley, and the explosion of the *USS Maine* in Havana Harbor. Although the Spanish still claim to not have caused this explosion, the US nevertheless declared war on April 25, 1898.

OVERVIEW

The Spanish-American War only lasted between six and eight weeks before the US claimed victory. The first phase of it was fought in the Philippines, and the second in Cuba. In Cuba, the United States scored a crucial victory when a rag-tag group of soldiers known as the **Roughriders** (Theodore Roosevelt among them) took Kettle Hill and secured Santiago. Although the **Teller Amendment of 1898** had promised independence to Cuba after the war, the **Platt Amendment**, which was inserted into the Cuban Constitution in 1901, made Cuba a protectorate of the US. The US control of **Guantanamo Bay** dates back to this amendment. In 1934, Cuba received its independence. The Spanish-American War formally ended with the signing of the **Treaty of Paris** in 1898. The US received Guam, the Philippines, Puerto Rico, Cuba, and Wake Island. The US also paid the Spanish $20 million because Manila had supposedly surrendered after the end of the war, making it an invalid wartime concession.

DEBATE OVER THE PHILIPPINES AND THE FILIPINO WAR

In the years 1898 and 1899, the question of what to do about the **Philippines** was hotly debated in the US. **Imperialists** (including Henry Cabot Lodge and Theodore Roosevelt), wanted to make the group of islands into a state, argued against **Anti-imperialists** (e.g., Andrew Carnegie, Mark Twain) who felt that the US would be drawn into Asian conflicts. Some politicians, like William Jennings Bryan, voted for the Treaty of Paris and the acquisition of the Philippines because they felt it would be a disaster that would discourage further imperialism. In 1899, the Filipino leader **Aguinaldo** led the people against US forces. This uprising was only crushed after much cruelty. Later, the **Tydings-McDuffie Act of 1934** promised independence to the Philippines within 10 years but they did not receive it until 1946. Some relevant Supreme Court rulings from this period were in the **Insular Cases of 1901**: the Court asserted that citizens of US territories do not have the same rights as citizens of the continental US.

HAMPTON ROADS PEACE CONFERENCE, LAST BATTLES OF CIVIL WAR, AND ASSASSINATION OF LINCOLN

At the Hampton Roads Peace Conference in February of 1865, **Lincoln** and Secretary of State **Seward** met with the vice president of the CSA, **Alexander Stephens**. Lincoln made a stern offer: reunion of the states, emancipation of the slaves, and immediate disbanding of the Confederate army. The Confederates, however, were not yet ready to return to the Union. The Northern General U.S. Grant then led troops toward the CSA capital at Richmond. Finally, at **Appomattox** (VA) in April of 1865, Lee surrendered to Grant. Soon after, the Confederate President **Jefferson Davis** would be caught and jailed. Finally, on April 14, 1865, Lincoln was fatally wounded by two shots from the gun of **John Wilkes Booth** in Ford's Theater in Washington.

LINCOLN'S RECONSTRUCTION PLAN

According to Lincoln, the relation between the North and the South after the completion of the Civil War would include "malice for none, charity for all." He imagined that the President would lead the **Reconstruction** effort, and, in 1863, he vowed that once 10% of the 1860 voters in a Southern state pledged loyalty to the Union, they could draft a new state constitution and receive "executive recognition." Lincoln was unsure whether blacks should be gradually emancipated or relocated, but he knew they should be free. As for his own **Republican party**, Lincoln asserted that it should

54

Copyright © Mometrix Media. You have been licensed one copy of this document for personal use only. Any other reproduction or redistribution is strictly prohibited. All rights reserved.

become a national party, and that it should include freed blacks, who would receive the right to vote.

CONGRESS' RECONSTRUCTION PLAN

With the **Wade-Davis Bill of 1864**, Congress outlined their plan for the rehabilitation of the South after the Civil War. Unlike Lincoln, who had only asked for a 10% (of 1860 voters) loyalty nucleus, Congress wanted a majority before admitting Southern states back into the **Union**. Participants in the state constitutional conventions would be required to sign an "ironclad oath" pledging eternal loyalty to the Union. Ex-Confederate officials would not be allowed to vote or hold office. Slavery, of course, would be **abolished**. Finally, the Confederate debt would be repudiated, and those who loaned money to the Confederacy would be unable to get it back. Lincoln **vetoed** this bill, mainly because he wanted the abolition of slavery to be an amendment rather than a law.

PRESIDENTIAL RECONSTRUCTION PLAN UNDER ANDREW JOHNSON

Andrew Johnson, a Jacksonian Democrat from Tennessee, became president after the assassination of Lincoln. Though a Southerner, he believed the yeoman farmers of the South had been tricked into war by "cotton snobs." Johnson's plan for reconstruction called for **amnesty** to be granted to all ex-Confederates except for high-ranking officials and wealthy cotton planters, who would be allowed to apply for special pardons. Johnson also called for a **provisional Unionist governor** to be appointed in each Southern state; this leader would hold a constitutional convention at which it would be necessary to disavow secession; repudiate the CSA debt; and accept the 13th amendment. This plan was largely a failure, however, because it infringed on the powers of Congress, was seen as too lenient on the South, threatened the Republicans by giving too much power to Southern Democrats, and ignored freed blacks, who were repressed in the South by the so-called **Black Codes**.

RADICAL REPUBLICAN RECONSTRUCTION PLAN

By 1867, Johnson's Reconstruction plan had largely failed. His unwillingness to change drove many moderate congressmen to become radicals. Radical Republicans came up with their own Reconstruction plan. First, a "Joint Committee of 15" went South to explore the damage done by the war; while there, they discovered the "Black Codes" repressing freed slaves. With the **Civil Rights Act of 1866**, they provided basic rights for ex-slaves (not including the right to vote). The **14th amendment** then gave blacks citizenship, and said that state governments could not deny anyone life, liberty and property without due process. This amendment disqualified ex-Confederates from holding public office, and declared that states could lose representation if they infringed on the rights of blacks. With the **Congressional Reconstruction Act** (Military Reconstruction Act) of 1867, the South was divided into 5 districts and placed under martial law; Congress forced this bill through, and eventually all of the Southern states capitulated.

> **Review Video: Reconstruction Era**
> Visit mometrix.com/academy and enter code: 790561

TENURE OF OFFICE ACT AND THE SUPREME COURT'S ACTIVITY

The Tenure of Office Act of 1867 established that in order to fire any Cabinet member, the president had to get the approval of the Senate. Though basically unconstitutional, this act almost ended the presidency of Johnson when he tried to dismiss **Edwin Stanton**, his Secretary of War. Johnson was charged with a crime, **impeached** by the House of Representatives, and missed being impeached by the Senate by one vote. The Supreme Court, though generally quiet during this period, made a couple of significant rulings. In **ex parte Milligan** (1866), the Supreme Court asserted that it is unconstitutional for military rule to continue after regular courts have been reinstated. In **ex parte**

McCardle (1868), a similar case, the Supreme Court was actually too afraid of Congressional radicals to make a ruling.

RADICAL REPUBLICAN RECONSTRUCTION GOVERNMENTS IN THE SOUTH

Carpetbaggers were those Northerners who, under the guise of reinvesting in the Southern economy, took advantage of the situation by acquiring positions in local governments and raising taxes. **Scalawags** were those white Republican Southerners who took similar economic advantage. During the rule of the Reconstruction governments, blacks were allowed to hold some public offices, though not if they were freed slaves; the black Senator **Hiram Revels** (MS) served in Jefferson Davis' old seat. Blacks had very few economic rights and had no land. **Thaddeus Stevens** declared that blacks should receive "40 acres and a mule," but nobody was willing to take this land from its present owners. **Sharecropping** became basically another form of slavery. In short, the Reconstruction governments were corrupt, spent too much and levied too many taxes, and took advantage of newly-freed slaves. Still, these governments established state constitutions, built roads and schools, and made education compulsory.

KU KLUX KLAN AND AMNESTY ACT OF 1872

In the 1870s, Southern whites, as members of the Conservatives or Redeemers, began to regain control of the local governments; they sought to do away with "Negro rule." The **Ku Klux Klan** was founded in 1867 by former Confederate General Nathan Bedford Forrest and other ex-Confederates. Though founded as a social club, this group quickly got out of hand, causing the passage of the **Ku Klux Klan and Force Acts** (1870-1), unsuccessful attempts to subdue the Klan by allowing for black militias. The **Amnesty Act of 1872** extended the right to vote to many more ex-Confederates. Gradually, the North began to lose interest in the South for the following reasons: they were disgusted by the corrupt governments; they were frustrated by the persistent racism; and they had agreed to remain distant in exchange for a higher tariff.

ELECTION OF 1868 AND THE GRANT ADMINISTRATION

After the Civil War, the US was consumed by **materialism**. The election of 1868 pitted **Ulysses S. Grant** (Republican) against Horatio Seymour (Democrat). Grant was a war hero, and Seymour spent much of the campaign defending himself from allegations that he aided the Confederacy. The Democrats proposed that states should decide for themselves the question of black suffrage, and they wanted to give amnesty to former Confederates. Republicans had much more success with their campaign, blaming the Democrats for the war (a strategy known as "waving the bloody shirt"), and Grant won handily. Grant's presidency would not be as easy as his campaign, however. He had no political experience and was unused to compromise. He frequently fought with his Cabinet, though Secretary of State Hamilton Fish was able to convince him to sign the **Treaty of Washington** (1871), in which Britain compensated the US for aiding the Confederate navy.

GRAFT AND CORRUPTION UNDER GRANT
CREDIT MOBILIER SCANDAL, SCHUYLAR COLFAX, AND FISK-GOULD SCANDAL

The Grant administration was so corrupt that the president himself had to apologize. One of the most famous fiascos of the era was the **Credit Mobilier scandal**: the Union Pacific gave a contract to the Credit Mobilier after the federal government secretly loaned Credit Mobilier money for their bid. Then, Vice-president **Schuyler Colfax** was caught accepting a bribe in return for ceasing the investigation. In the **Fisk-Gould scandal**, Jim Fisk and Jay Gould convinced Grant to keep government gold out of the New York Stock Exchange, because they hoped to corner the market. Grant became angry with the men and dumped $4 million worth of gold onto the market. September 24, 1869 is known as **Black Friday** on Wall Street; this was the day that Grant's gold

flood caused the price of gold to drop so rapidly that the entire market crashed. Gould was able to survive this catastrophe; Fisk was not.

TAMMANY HALL, CONGRESSIONAL SALARY GRAB, AND WHISKEY RING SCANDAL

William Marcy "Boss" Tweed was the political boss of New York City. He ran the **Tammany Hall** political machine, a group that fixed elections by recruiting voters with food and jobs. Another instance of corruption under Grant was the **Congressional salary grab**: Congress voted to give themselves a 50% raise, set retroactively by two years. The public was outraged by this avarice, and so, though they kept the pay raise, Congress gave up the back pay. In the **Whiskey ring scandal**, some tax agents who were supposed to be taxing barrels of whiskey were found to have been accepting bribes; this scandal went up as high as Secretary of the Treasury Benjamin Bristow. When historians look at this period and try to figure out why there was so much corruption, they generally decide that it was a carryover from the brutality of the war, combined with the naiveté of the president.

OPPOSITION TO GRAFT AND CORRUPTION UNDER GRANT

Thomas Nast was one of the first famous political cartoonists; he made his name satirizing corrupt politicians like Boss Tweed. Grant established the **Civil Service Commission** in 1871, an organization whose mission was to study corruption and make recommendations to the president. Grant paid little attention to this group, however, and it died a quiet death in 1875. During Grant's first term, a group of upper-class Republicans, calling themselves the **Mugwumps**, began to call for a civil service based only on merit. At the same time, the **Liberal Republicans**, another splinter group of the Republican party, spoke out against the graft in civil service, the use of paper money and the Republican Reconstruction policy. This group supported a lower tariff and better treatment for farmers.

ELECTION OF 1872 AND FINAL COLLAPSE OF GRANT

In the election of 1872, **Grant** won a second term (over Liberal Republican Horace Greeley) because of his enduring status as a war-hero, and because the worst scandals of his administration had yet to be exposed. Quickly, though, Grant's administration fell apart. Five Cabinet members would be found guilty of **corruption**. Then came the **Panic of 1873**. This was the result of three factors: the withdrawal of European investment (Europeans were funneling their money into the Franco-Prussian War); the stock market crash caused by the Fisk-Gould scandal; and the inflexibility of the banks caused by heavy investment in non-liquid assets. As a result of these factors, **Jay Cooke and Co.**, one of the largest banks in the US, collapsed, taking several other banks with it. 89 railroads soon went under, and then the iron and steel mills had no business. By 1875, half a million Americans were unemployed, and farmers were beginning to lose their land to foreclosure.

SOLUTIONS TO THE PANIC OF 1873

By 1873, **currency deflation** was a major problem in the US. There were a number of supporters of cheap money, and they encouraged the US government to issue $26 million in greenbacks to stimulate the economy; this plan failed. There was another group of hard-money advocates who suggested using a gold standard, so the government made a compromise called the **Specie Resumption Act of 1875**. This act increased the number of national banks in the South and West; allowed national banks to issue as many notes as they wanted (up to a $300 million limit); and named a "day of redemption," on which all greenbacks could be exchanged for gold coins. The day of redemption never came to pass, however, which seemed to be a victory for the cheap money supporters. Instead, it became evident that the promise of gold exchange caused the public to treat greenbacks as if they were "good as gold." By 1879, the economy was back on track and the Republicans had acquired the reputation as the party in favor of business.

ELECTION OF 1876 AND NATIONAL SELF-EVALUATION

The election of 1876, won by **Rutherford B. Hayes** (Republican) over Samuel J. Tilden (Democrat), coincided with the **US centennial**, and so people were compelled to consider the history of the country thus far. When Americans of 1876 looked back, they had some reason to be pleased: they had survived a Civil War intact and had witnessed the end of slavery. They also had developed a strong national government. On the other hand, many Americans were disillusioned at this time by the scandals of the Grant administration. There had also been violent and disheartening struggles between black militiamen and the Ku Klux Klan in the South. Finally, many in the country were still reeling from Custer's bloody defeat at the Battle of Little Big Horn.

GEOGRAPHY OF THE CONTINENT OF NORTH AMERICA

North America is the third largest continent in the world. It includes all the mainland of the northern landmass in the western hemisphere, as well as all the related offshore islands that lie north of the Isthmus of Panama. People often will call Canada and the United States "**Anglo-America**," and Mexico, Central America, and the Caribbean "**Middle America**." North America is bounded on the north by the Arctic Ocean, on the west by the Pacific Ocean and the Bering Sea, and on the east by the Atlantic Ocean and the Gulf of Mexico. The Gulf of Mexico is the largest body of water to indent the coast, the second-largest being the Hudson Bay. The Gulf of St. Lawrence and the Gulf of California also indent the coast of North America severely.

COASTAL ISLANDS, HIGHEST POINT, LONGEST RIVER, AND OTHER MAJOR RIVERS

There are a number of large **islands** off the coast of North America: Greenland, the Arctic Archipelago, the Greater and Lesser Antilles, the Alexander Archipelago, and the Aleutian Islands. The highest point in North America is **Mt. McKinley**, Alaska, and the lowest point is in **Death Valley**. The **Missouri-Mississippi River System** is the longest in North America; it is also the world's largest inland waterway system. Ships are able to enter the heart of the North America by means of the Saint Lawrence Seaway. Other major rivers of the North American continent are the Colorado, Mackenzie, Nelson, Rio Grande, St. Lawrence, Susquehanna, Columbia, and Yukon.

CLIMATE OF NORTH AMERICA

The continent of North America contains every climatic zone, ranging from the tropical rain forests and savannas in the lowlands of Central America to the permanent ice caps in the middle of Greenland. In northern Canada, the climate is mostly subarctic and tundra. These are also found in northern Alaska. The two major mountain ranges of the continent affect the climate greatly. In the interior regions close to the Appalachian and Rocky Mountains, the climate and terrain is mostly semiarid and desert. These areas are largely prevented from receiving westerly winds and storms. Most of North America, however, has a temperate climate and is hospitable to settlement and agriculture.

PHYSIOGRAPHY OF NORTH AMERICA

North America can be divided into five regions. The **Canadian Shield** is an area of stable, ancient rock that occupies the northeast corner of the continent, including Greenland. The **Appalachian Mountains** are an old and worn-down mountain system extending from the Gaspe Peninsula to Alabama. The **Atlantic-Gulf Coastal Plain** is a stretch of lowlands running from New England to Mexico. The **Interior Lowlands** extend from central Canada to the Gulf Coast. The **North American Cordillera** is a mountain system that includes both the Pacific Margin and the Rocky Mountains. Another lesser formation, the **Transverse Volcanic Range**, extends below Mexico City.

NATIVE AMERICANS

NATIVE AMERICANS OF THE NORTHWEST COAST AREA

The main Native American tribes in the Northwest Coast are the **Kwakiutl**, **Haida**, and **Nootka**. These people lived in a densely forested area, with a temperate climate and heavy rainfall, and they survived mainly on salmon. The Native Americans in this region built their houses out of wood, and made canoes from cedar. These tribes built totem poles in their permanent winter villages which were elaborately carved with the faces of the tribal animal gods. They had a strict social hierarchy, with chiefs, nobles, commoners, and slaves. The Native Americans of the Pacific Northwest would be largely untouched by Europeans until the 18th century, when **fur trappers** began to encroach upon their territory.

NATIVE AMERICANS OF THE PLAINS AREA

The Plains area extends from barely north of the Canadian border to Texas. Before the arrival of Columbus, the tribes in this region were either nomadic or sedentary. The **sedentary** tribes settled in the great river valleys and grew corn, squash, and beans. The **nomads**, meanwhile, moved their goods around on sleds pulled by dogs. They hunted buffalo by driving them into enclosures or by herding them with fires. There was also a fair amount of trade with the sedentary tribes. Many Native American tribes migrated into the Plains region; among them were the **Sioux**, **Comanche**, **Kiowa**, **Navajo**, and **Apache**. The tribes were typically governed by a chief, who would eventually be supplanted in a violent coup.

NATIVE AMERICANS OF THE PLATEAU AREA

The Plateau area runs from just above the Canadian border into the American southwest. Some of the larger tribes in the region were the **Spokane**, **Nez Perce**, and **Shoshone**. The area where these tribes dwelled was not especially hospitable, so they spent much of their time trying to eke out a living. The tribes in the south gathered fruits and nuts, and hunted small animals. The tribes in the north fished for salmon and gathered roots and berries. Later on, these tribes would begin to hunt buffalo. Many of the northern tribes had permanent winter villages, most of which were along waterways. They borrowed the architecture of the tepee from the Plains Indians, though some tribes had long houses covered with bark.

NATIVE AMERICANS OF THE EASTERN WOODLANDS

The Eastern Woodlands extend from the Mississippi River east to the Atlantic Ocean. The tribes of this region included the **Natchez**, **Choctaw**, **Cherokee**, and **Creek**. The people of the northeast region mostly farmed and hunted deer. They used canoes made of birch bark. The people in the Iroquois family of tribes lived either in dome-shaped wigwams or in long houses, and would typically wear clothing made from the skin of deer, often painting their faces. In the southern part of the Eastern Woodlands, there were semi-nomadic tribes who survived by hunting, fishing, and gathering. These people hunted with a bow and arrow or with a blowgun. They developed highly detailed pottery and surrounded their villages with elaborate defenses.

NATIVE AMERICANS WHO INHABITED THE REGION NOW KNOWN AS CANADA

The Native Americans that inhabited the region now known as Canada included the **Chippewa**. This region was not especially hospitable to life and therefore there was little farming. Instead, the tribes hunted, gathered, fished, and trapped in order to survive. There were many groups of nomadic hunters who moved around from season to season. Caribou was the most popular game, and people would make all kinds of products out of parts of the animal, including caribou shoes, caribou nets, and caribou bags. These people relied on snowshoes to allow them to move quickly

and without falling into icy lakes. Many of the tribes in this region had a shaman, a mystic who provided spiritual guidance to the members of the tribe.

NATIVE AMERICANS OF THE SOUTHWEST AREA

The Southwest area extends across Arizona, New Mexico, Colorado, and Utah. A seminomadic people known as the **Basket Makers** hunted with the atlatl, a device that made it possible to throw a spear accurately over a great distance. The tribes in this area lived in pit dwellings which were partly underground. Later, ancestors of the Pueblo Indians would develop community houses set into the side of cliffs and canyons. These **cliff dwellings** often had a ceremonial fire pit, or kiva. These people grew corn, beans, squash, cotton, and tobacco, they killed rabbits with a wooden stick, and they traded their textiles to nomadic tribes for buffalo meat. The tribes of the Southwest also had a complex mythology and religious system.

History of the United States: 1899 to the Present

JOHN HAY'S DEFENSE OF CHINA

From 1898 to 1905, **John Hay** was the Secretary of State. One of his great achievements was establishing the **Open Door Policy** with respect to China. China had just been defeated by Japan and was in the process of being carved up by the European powers into various spheres of economic influence. Hay asserted that each nation should allow equal access for all nations and should respect the rights of the Chinese. Somewhat surprisingly, Europe agreed to this policy of goodwill. The Open Door Policy did not, however, keep China from being exploited by foreign traders. In the **Boxer Rebellion of 1900**, the Chinese rose up against foreigners and were promptly routed by an international coalition (including the US).

> **Review Video: Anti-Colonial Struggles: The Boxer Rebellion**
> Visit mometrix.com/academy and enter code: 352161

ELECTION OF 1900 AND THEODORE ROOSEVELT

In the election of 1900 **McKinley** and Theodore Roosevelt of the Republicans defeated William Jennings Bryan of the Democrats. McKinley was then assassinated on September 6, 1901, and **Roosevelt** took over. Roosevelt is known as a follower of the African proverb, "Speak softly and carry a big stick." He was known for having very little respect for the system of checks and balances: if the Constitution were too rigid on an issue for his tastes, he ignored it; if Congress acted up, he would subdue them with a mixture of compromise and coercion. Roosevelt displayed his blunt skill in diplomacy in the **Alaska Panhandle dispute of 1903** (in which he decided which islands the US would get, and which would belong to the British) and in the **Morocco Dispute of 1905**, in which he (along with Britain and France) dissuaded Germany from trying to take the North African country.

PANAMA CANAL

BEGINNINGS UNDER ROOSEVELT

The Spanish-American War had demonstrated that the US needed a **Latin American canal** in order to become a major naval power. At that time, however, their hands were tied by the **Clayton-Bulwer Treaty of 1850**, which had stated that neither the US nor Britain would build a canal in Latin America without the other. Fortunately for the US, the British were distracted by the Boer War in South Africa and thus were willing to sign the **Hay-Pauncefote Treaty** in 1901, allowing the US to go it alone. Many in the US, including Roosevelt, wanted to build the canal in Nicaragua because it has a number of lakes that could be connected, and because it is mostly flat. Others lobbied for Panama, pointing out that a French contractor had already started work on a canal there and that Panama was narrower than Nicaragua.

ORGANIZATION REQUIRED TO BUILD

In 1902, the United States struck a deal with a Panamanian builder for the control of the canal project. The US then needed to acquire the land. Panama at this time was owned by Colombia; the Colombians rejected the first offer made by the US, leading Roosevelt to call them "blackmailers." Then, in 1903, a rebellion broke out in Panama; Roosevelt recognized the new, independent country after less than a day of fighting. 15 days later, the US purchased the **Panama Canal Zone** from the new foreign minister for $10 million initially and $250,000 per year. Many observers were embarrassed by the deal the United States had won from a fledgling country. Nevertheless, Roosevelt then hired engineer John Stephens to finish the job.

BUILDING AND OPENING

Once Roosevelt finally secured the building supplies and the land to construct the Panama Canal, the brutal and dangerous work began. In order to prevent malaria, the US paved streets, drained swamps, and built houses so that the workers would not have to sleep in tents. Nevertheless, the workdays were long and the pay was low. In the end, the canal cost about $400 million; it was finished in 1913, but did not open until the next year. Roosevelt's visit to Panama made him the first president to leave the US during his term. In 1920, a guilty Democratic Congress gave Colombia $25 million. At present, about 12,000 ships go through the canal every year and it takes about 8 hours to get from one end to the other.

ROOSEVELT AND THE 2ND VENEZUELAN CRISIS

In 1902, many Latin American countries were deep in debt to Europe and were not making any moves to repay their debts. Enraged, European countries began to use military force. At first, Roosevelt supported this policy, but he gradually changed his mind, in part because the American public was opposed to it. When Germany, therefore, sent ships to Santo Domingo in 1904, Roosevelt announced the **Roosevelt Corollary** to the Monroe Doctrine: this document stated that nations may not use force to collect debts. Roosevelt asserted that the US would peaceably arbitrate these disputes before Europe could get violent; he felt these interventions would help Latin America and prevent European recolonization. The US developed a reputation as "the policeman of the Caribbean."

SECOND HAGUE DISARMAMENT CONFERENCE, TREATY OF PORTSMOUTH, JAPANESE LABORERS, AND GREAT WHITE FLEET

At the Second Hague Disarmament Conference in 1907, a number of nations gathered to reaffirm the **Hague Conference rules** of humane warfare and agreed upon how the collection of debts should be pursued. After the **Russo-Japanese War**, Roosevelt rather reluctantly agreed to mediate between the two countries. The result was the **Treaty of Portsmouth**, in which the Japanese lost some land (though not as much as the Russians felt was appropriate). For this, Roosevelt received the 1906 **Nobel Peace Prize**. After the Russo-Japanese War, many **Japanese workers** came to the US; Roosevelt had to intervene and prevent them from being discriminated against. Finally, Roosevelt promoted the **US Navy** by painting a number of ships white and parading them past the Asian coast.

PROGRESSIVE MOVEMENT
DEMOGRAPHIC TRENDS AND WORKING CLASS

The **Progressive Movement** was marked by advances in rights for workers, women and minorities. As the twentieth century began, it seemed as if the rich were getting richer and the poor were becoming more numerous. Per capita income and population had both increased dramatically, but wealth seemed to be concentrated in a smaller and smaller group. Between one-third and one-half of all factory workers lived in poverty and management showed no concern for these workers in the form of unemployment or worker's compensation. Many of the wealthy magnates felt the poor were that way because of their sinfulness and thus had no desire to provide aid. At the same time, many in the middle class feared that the lower class would revolt, although they didn't want to cause trouble themselves.

LABOR UNIONS, IMMIGRANTS, AND BLACKS

By 1914 the **American Federation of Labor** had 2 million members, although most Americans still did not trust labor unions. Meanwhile, immigrants had withstood several challenges to their legitimacy. The **Immigration Restriction League** had tried many times to require immigrants to pass a literacy test. For their part, immigrants were annoyed that they had to go to school, they hated Prohibition, and they hated the settlement houses into which they were often forced by the government. Blacks were one group that would not receive much help during the Progressive era. In 1905 W.E.B. DuBois had spearheaded the Niagara Movement, which led to the formation of the **National Association for the Advancement of Colored People**. In 1911 the **National Urban League** was formed to help blacks move into the cities.

EFFECTS ON WOMEN AND FARMERS

During the early part of the twentieth century, women aggressively pursued more rights. **Sarah Platt Decker** led the **General Federation of Women's Clubs**, a group that worked hard to improve working conditions for women and children. The **International Ladies' Garment Workers Union** was also popular; it received a great deal of publicity after 146 women died in a fire at the Triangle Shirt factory. **Jane Addams** supported Prohibition, as did the Women's Christian Temperance Union and the Anti-Saloon League. **Carrie A. Nation** became famous for attacking saloons with an axe. For their part, farmers were doing much better in the early years of the twentieth century than in years past; those who were still struggling joined with the Progressives.

SOCIAL CRITICS AND STATE REFORMS

Eugene V. Debs was a prominent Socialist leader during the Progressive era. The **Industrial Workers of the World**, established in 1905 by "Big Bill" Haywood and known as the "Wobblies," was a radical and militant labor union that appealed to unskilled workers. There were some interesting state and local experiments in this period. In Galveston, Texas, the city switched to a commission system in which the heads of various departments were elected. In Staunton, Virginia, the office of the mayor was done away with in favor of a managing council. **Robert LaFollette's** many reforms in Wisconsin led Roosevelt to refer to this state as the "laboratory of democracy." LaFollette tied the university system, the railroads, and the banks to the state government. Governor Woodrow Wilson of New Jersey planned to use corporate taxes to pay for public education.

NATIONAL REFORMS

The **16th amendment** (1913) allowed for an income tax. The **17th amendment** (1913) provided for the direct election of US senators. The **18th amendment** (1919) prohibited alcohol. The **19th amendment** (1920) gave women the right to vote. In the case of **Muller v. Oregon** (1908), the Supreme Court upheld Oregon's 10-hour workday for women. In **Hammer v. Dagenhart** (1918), the Supreme Court declared the Keating-Owen Act of 1916 was unconstitutional. This act had prohibited interstate shipping of goods made in factories that employed children. The Court declared that the regulation of factories was the concern of the states. In response to this decision, many states passed acts banning child labor. The first **minimum wage** (25c) was established in Massachusetts in 1912. New York established the first lasting workman's compensation rules in 1910. In 1896, Utah had become the first state to limit the workday, to ten hours.

SUMMARY

It is important to note that Progressivism is not synonymous with Socialism; **Progressives** wanted to change the system, while **Socialists** wanted to destroy it altogether. Progressives believed that the government should regulate all business. Moreover, the Progressives wanted to take government out of the hands of the rich and put it into the hands of the common people. Often,

Progressives had difficulty getting organized. This problem had been the death knell of the Populists; the Progressives were able to succeed in spite of their turmoil because they had great leaders: Roosevelt, Taft, and Wilson. The Progressive philosophy was started by a small minority of liberal intellectuals, including William James and Henry Adams. Among the authors who wrote on Progressive themes were Jacob Riis (*How the Other Half Lives*), Frank Norris (*The Octopus*, on railroad corruption), and Upton Sinclair (*The Jungle*, on corruption in the meatpacking industry).

ROOSEVELT REPUBLICANS AND ROOSEVELT AS A "TRUSTBUSTER"

For Roosevelt Republicans, the principles of good **domestic policy** could be summed up as the "3 Cs": control of the corporations; consumer protection; and the conservation of natural resources. Roosevelt had made his name as a member of the **Roughriders** in the Spanish-American War. Interestingly, his presidency was a result of his unpopularity in his own party: his fellow Republicans had nominated him as vice-president because this was felt to be a weak position. They were of course quite displeased when McKinley was assassinated and Roosevelt became president. Roosevelt quickly became famous for his attacks on the trusts. He went after the **Northern Securities Company**, run by, among others, J.P. Morgan and John D. Rockefeller. Morgan attempted to bribe Attorney General Philip Knox to halt the investigation; Knox promptly reported this to Roosevelt. In all, 44 **anti-trust cases** were heard during Roosevelt's presidency.

ROOSEVELT'S SQUARE DEAL

Roosevelt's Square Deal was a domestic agenda designed to help the working class and diminish the power of the corporations. The **Elkins Act** made railroad rebates illegal, making it difficult for preferential treatment to be given to corporations. Roosevelt formed the **Department of Commerce and Labor** to help workers. One telling episode was the **Anthracite Coal Strike** in 1902. When the owner of the mines asked Roosevelt for an injunction forcing the employees back to work, Roosevelt instead sent troops in to mine the coal for the government! The owner and the labor leader then met at the White House to settle their differences. This was the first time both sides in a strike had accepted an executive commission, and the first time the president had threatened to seize property. It was also the first time a president had sided with a labor union.

ELECTION OF 1904

In the election of 1904, Roosevelt used the **Square Deal** as his platform, and was able to defeat the Democrat Judge Alton B. Parker. As part of the Square Deal, Roosevelt mandated an **open shop policy**; workers would be free to join a union without being obliged to do so. A case in which Roosevelt's government did not benefit workers was the **Danbury Hatters' Strike**. During this dispute, the workers organized a general boycott of Danbury Hats. The management argued that this boycott violated the **Sherman Anti-trust Act** and the **Interstate Commerce Act**, and the Supreme Court agreed. Many workers blamed Roosevelt for this decision.

ROOSEVELT'S REFORMS

The **Hepburn Act of 1906** gave the ICC the authority to set shipping prices in the event that a shipper complained about the rates. This act also allowed the government to regulate pipelines and express and sleeping car companies. The **Pure Food and Drug Act of 1906** established the Food and Drug Administration to regulate what had become a very corrupt industry. The **Meat Inspection Act of 1906** was inspired by Upton Sinclair's novel *The Jungle*, which exposed the corruption of the meatpacking industry. It established tougher regulation of meat handlers. Not all of Roosevelt's legislation passed, however. He was unable to pass laws against child labor, establish a national worker's compensation, or restrict the power of the **National Association of Manufacturers** to gain injunctions against strikers.

ROOSEVELT'S NEW PROGRAMS AND THE OLD GUARD REPUBLICANS

Many Old Guard Republicans disagreed with Theodore Roosevelt on the issue of resource conservation. The **Newlands Reclamation Act of 1902** tried to reclaim the wilderness through the construction of dams. Roosevelt believed that the United States only had about a quarter of its original trees; this act set aside land in the Grand Canyon, Yosemite and Yellowstone for the preservation of forests. Roosevelt also had to endure the **Panic of 1907** caused by too much supply, a decrease in demand, and a short money supply resulting from a lack of gold. The **Aldrich-Vreeland Act of 1908** authorized national banks to issue emergency currency. Over time, it seemed that Roosevelt had become more radical. The **Employers Liability Act of 1906**, for instance, had provided for workman's compensation but was struck down by the courts. Roosevelt promptly went after the courts.

THEODORE ROOSEVELT'S LEGACY AND THE ELECTION OF 1908

Theodore Roosevelt, like Andrew Jackson, was truly a public servant. Most of his domestic policies really seemed aimed at improving the lot of the common American. During his administration, Roosevelt greatly enlarged the powers of the president. He created the national parks system and gave the Progressive Movement some respectability. In the 1908 election, Roosevelt chose **William Howard Taft** to become his successor. Roosevelt felt confident that Taft would carry on the mission of the Progressives. Taft ran against William Jennings Bryan of the Democrats, a veteran leader who favored a lower tariff and limited injunctions against strikers. Taft won the election, primarily because of his association with Roosevelt.

TAFT PRESIDENCY
FOREIGN POLICY OF TAFT (1909-13)

Roosevelt was succeeded in the White House by **William Howard Taft**, who became known for "**dollar diplomacy**"; the United States would loan money to Latin American countries so that these countries could pay off their European debts. The US would also dabble a bit in Latin American politics, trying to influence the governments for the benefit of American business. The Taft administration also wanted to encourage trade with China and therefore helped prop up some American banking interests there. Taft is also known for his association with the creation of the **World Court**. The US, Britain, and France tried to establish an international judiciary. This idea enraged former president Roosevelt; he preferred settling differences on the battlefield.

TARIFFS AND THE PAYNE-ALDRICH ACT

Taft was a very cautious president. His administration saw the deepening of the gradual split between Progressive and Old Guard Republicans. Though Roosevelt had promoted him as a Progressive, Taft slowly began to act more like a member of the **Old Guard**. These tensions came to a head over the tariff in 1909. The Old Guard wanted to keep the tariff as it was, while Progressives fought for reductions. After the House and Senate came up with conflicting tariff bills, Taft was able to engineer a compromise; the **Payne-Aldrich Act of 1909** brought the tariff down to 40.8%. This act also contained a corporate tax and the promise of an income tax in the future.

SPLIT BETWEEN TAFT AND ROOSEVELT

In the Congressional elections of 1910, the radical Progressives (known as the **insurgents**) were able, with the help of the Democrats, to diminish the power of the Old Guard republicans in the House. Meanwhile, President Taft drifted closer and closer to the side of the Old Guard. In 1909, Secretary of the Interior **Richard Bollinger** leased national land to corporations, incurring the wrath of forester Gifford Pinchot, who asked for a Senate investigation. Bollinger was forced to resign to take the heat off of Taft. In the Congressional election of 1910, former President Roosevelt

announced a mixture of Progressive and Liberal ideas called the **New Nationalism program** and was labeled a Marxist. Then, finally, Taft destroyed a merger between US Steel and Tennessee Coal and Iron that Roosevelt had supported, infuriating the former president.

1912 ELECTION AND THE LEGACY OF TAFT

At the Republican convention before the election of 1912, the incumbent **Taft** was nominated even though **Theodore Roosevelt** had won most of the primaries. Enraged, Roosevelt left the Republicans and formed the **Progressive (Bull-Moose) party**. Roosevelt ran on his platform of **New Nationalism**: voting rights for women and a ban on child labor were among the initiatives. On October 14, 1912, Roosevelt was shot in the torso during a speech; he finished the speech. The election came down to a contest between Roosevelt and **Woodrow Wilson** of the Democrats. These two candidates had similar views on a number of issues, but while Roosevelt was willing to allow some trusts, Wilson wanted to eliminate trusts across the board. Wilson ended up winning a rather comfortable victory. As the Taft presidency came to a close, most observers saw his greatest accomplishments as the "rule of reason," in which the judiciary was allowed to pick which trusts to bust; the **Mann-Elkins Act**, which brought the telephone and telegraph industries under control of the federal government; and the creation of the **Department of Labor**.

WILSON PRESIDENCY

TARIFF REFORM AND THE FEDERAL RESERVE ACT

Woodrow Wilson appointed **William Jennings Bryant** as his Secretary of State; Bryant became known for his policy of "cooling off," wherein volatile situations would be ignored until all parties had a chance to reconsider their positions. One of Wilson's first major acts as president was to push through the **Underwood-Simmons Tariff of 1913**. This reduces the duty rate to 27% and drastically reduced the tariff on a thousand other items. It also included a slightly greater income tax. Another important economic move was the **Federal Reserve Act of 1913**: this set up a national banking system to be overseen by a Federal Reserve Board. The Federal Reserve system would become the first effective national banking system since the Second Bank of the United States, and would be one of the great legacies of Wilson's term. It gave the government a ready means to adjust the amount of currency in circulation.

EFFECTS ON TRUSTS

When Wilson entered office, he declared that there was no such thing as a good trust. With the **Federal Trade Commission Act of 1914**, a bi-partisan committee of 5 was created to investigate trusts and issue reports to the government and to the public. The creation of the FTC slowed the growth of monopolies. Peeved by the ineffectiveness of the Sherman Anti-trust Act, Wilson supported the passage of the **Clayton Anti-trust Act of 1914**. This prohibited business from selling at reduced prices to favored customers if this price discrimination helped create a monopoly. It also prevented so-called "tying contracts," which forbade a purchaser from buying or selling the products of a competitor. The act also outlawed large interlocking directories; formally allowed the existence of labor unions and farm organizations, as well as strikes and boycotts; and declared that no injunctions could be issued unless property was at stake.

ACCOMPLISHMENTS OF WILSON'S NEW FREEDOM AGENDA

The **Smith-Lever Act of 1914** brought public education into rural areas. The **Smith-Hughes Act of 1917** allocated money for vocational training and home economics courses. The **Federal Farm Loan Act of 1916** divided the US into 12 agricultural districts, and established federal farm loan banks with low interest rates. The **Adamson Act of 1916** asserted that railway workers should be paid for a 10-hour day, though they should only be required to work 8 hours. During Wilson's presidency, **Lewis Brandeis** became the first Jewish member of the Supreme Court. In general,

then, Wilson believed in regulating business and improving social welfare. He did not, however, see anything wrong with segregation.

WILSON'S MORAL DIPLOMACY

Along with his Secretary of State William Jennings Bryant, Woodrow Wilson promoted the view that nations should treat one another ethically. For instance, the **Panama Canal Tolls Act of 1912** had made it so that the US did not have to pay tolls to use the canal, unlike every other nation; Wilson did away with this measure. Wilson's actions in the **Dominican Republic** were more dubious. The Dominican Republic had been in deep debt early in the twentieth century, and the Roosevelt administration had been glad to help in exchange for keeping some troops in the country. When in 1916 the Dominican Republic asked the US to leave, Wilson refused and sent in the Marines. It was only in 1940 that the Dominican Republic was no longer considered a US protectorate. A similar scenario occurred in **Haiti**: the US offered to help the tiny nation, but was unwilling to leave when asked (mainly because of economic interest).

US AND MEXICAN REVOLUTION

Mexicans traditionally resented the US for its seizure of Texas and the Southwest. When the US-friendly leader **Porfirio Diaz** was overthrown in 1910, and eventually replaced by the murderous dictator **Victorian Huerto**, the US sent weapons to his opponents. Then, in April 1914, two American soldiers of the *USS Tampico* were jailed in Mexico and the US did not receive an apology upon their release. This angered the US, and they in turn seized a German ship that was believed to be unloading war materials to Mexico. The only thing that kept the US out of a more serious conflict was the **ABC Mediation**: Argentina, Brazil, and Chile met and convinced Huerto to retire. Still, **Pancho Villa**, a challenger for control of Mexico, continued to antagonize the US; he killed several Americans and was unsuccessfully pursued by American forces.

WORLD WAR I

AMERICA'S ROLE IN THE BUILD-UP TO WAR

There had been relative peace in Europe since the end of the Napoleonic Wars in 1815. Many even felt that the age of great wars was over. In 1910, the US had become involved in the **Pan-American Union**, which was organized to settle differences with diplomacy rather than violence. At the **First Hague Conference** in 1899, 26 nations agreed on the principles of mediation, the humane rules of war, and on the creation of a permanent court of arbitration. At the **Second Hague Conference** in 1907, 44 nations reaffirmed the old agreements and declared that the payment of debts could not be forced through war. Unfortunately, there would be no Third Hague Conference; it was cancelled due to World War I.

CAUSES

The rise in **nationalism** at the beginning of the twentieth century helped contribute to the possibility of war. There was also some conflict between the **imperialist** (France, Britain, and the US) and the **non-imperialist** (Germany, Italy) nations. Many large nations were seeking economic expansion outside of their own borders, and the competition for foreign markets was intense. There was also a complex system of entangling alliances; many countries were involved in several different alliances at the same time. The spark for World War I, though, was the assassination of **Archduke Franz Ferdinand**, heir to the throne of Austria-Hungary, in April of 1914 by a Serbian nationalist. When Emperor Franz Joseph declared war on Serbia, it set off a chain reaction that involved virtually every nation in Europe.

US Attempts at Neutrality

For a while, the US tried to remain **impartial** in World War I, not least because it was making a great deal of money producing supplies for both sides. Among the general public, there was general support for Britain and France, but many German and Irish immigrants supported the Central powers. There were a small group of American citizens who flew missions for the French, known as the Lafayette Escadrille. Gradually, the US government became angry with both sides, even as it tried to maintain trade with both sides. The British blockade of neutral Scandinavia annoyed the US, as did the German's flouting of the rules of war with their aggressive U-boats. In 1915, the British ship *Lusitania* was sunk off the coast of Ireland, killing 128 Americans. This convinced many Americans that neutrality could not be maintained.

Increasing American Involvement

During the early years of WWI, the tide of **nationalism** was rising in the US. Many people felt it would be impossible for America to remain neutral; even Theodore Roosevelt decried conscientious objectors. Nevertheless, many **pacifists** objected to any involvement. William Jennings Bryant resigned as Secretary of State after the sinking of the *Lusitania*, advising the US to stay off of British ships; to stop selling weapons to both sides; and to not side so unthinkingly with the British. At around this time, Roosevelt began recruiting and training men as part of the **Plattsburg Experiment**. Finally, Wilson increased the number of troops in both the Army and the Navy with the **National Defense Act of 1916**. Wilson also set into motion a campaign to build more ships.

Election of 1916 and Entrance into WWI

In the election of 1916, **Wilson** narrowly defeated the Republican Charles Evans Hughes. Wilson ran on a **peace platform**. Soon after, however, diplomatic relations were broken off with the Central powers, and submarine warfare began. The American entrance to WWI was accelerated by the "**Zimmermann Note**," in which the German minister to Mexico encouraged that country to attack the United States. In 1917, merchant vessels were ordered by Wilson to arm themselves. Among the reasons the US sided with the Allies was the fact that American business was more deeply connected with these countries than with the Central powers. Also, the US had traditionally had stronger ties with Britain and France.

Wilson's War Agenda

On April 2, 1917, Wilson addressed the nation on the subject of World War I. He declared that the conduct of the German U-boats was "a war against humanity itself," and that, if managed successfully, WWI would be "a war to make the world safe for democracy." Four days later, a **declaration of wa**r was passed. The **Selective Service Act of 1917** registered and drafted millions of American men for military service; about 4.7 million Americans served in the war. The American war effort was mainly paid for with borrowed money, though an increased income tax and the sale of war bonds contributed. Wilson also mobilized American industry; the **War Industries Board**, headed by Bernard Baruch, strove to cut waste and create new industries to aid the war effort. The **National War Labor Board**, headed by ex-President Taft, tried to streamline the labor force to aid the war effort.

Contributions of the American Public and Public Opinion of the War

The **18th amendment** to the Constitution, otherwise known as the **Volstead Act**, outlawed alcohol in 1920. This amendment was purported to conserve food, though it was really an attempt to influence public morality. Through the **Food Administration**, Wilson encouraged people to plant "victory gardens," and to skip meat one day a week. The war was also supported through the **Espionage and Sedition Acts of 1917-8**, which made it illegal to say negative things about the war

68

or to interfere with the sale of war bonds. In **Schenck v. US** (1919), the arrest of the Socialist leader Charles Schenck for criticizing the war was upheld by the Supreme Court which asserted that First Amendment rights were only exercisable when they did not present a clear and present danger to the nation. In **Abrams v. US** (1919), a Russian immigrant critical of the US actions in Russian was also declared to be a clear and present danger.

PERCEPTION OF AMERICANS SOLDIERS

The situation for the Allies was desperate after Russia left the war under the **Brest-Litovsk Treaty of 1917**. The US began to convoy British and French ships in an attempt to prevent U-boat attacks. The American soldiers in Europe were referred to as Doughboys, Yanks, and Devil Dogs. Some of the American heroes in the war were **Alvin York** ("Sergeant York"), who reportedly killed 20 and captured 132; **J.J. Pershing**, who led the American Expeditionary Force; and **Eddie Rickenbacker**, a pilot credited with 22 kills. Americans were praised for their efforts at Cantigny, Reims, and in the Argonne Forest campaign, where there were over 128,000 American casualties.

WILSON'S FOURTEEN POINT PROGRAM

Wilson issued his Fourteen Point program supposedly to try to create a quick and lasting peace. Also, however, Wilson hoped to draw the Russians back into the war, to inspire the war-weary Allies, and to demoralize the enemy nations by appealing to the dissenting contingents. Some of the changes called for in the **Fourteen Points** were open diplomacy, freedom of the seas, no tariffs, reduced land artilleries, right of self-determination for all people, a temporary international control of colonies (not imperialism) and the creation of the **League of Nations**. Wilson's proposal encouraged the Slavic peoples in Germany and Austria-Hungary to resist the war. Its success in defusing the German war effort allowed Wilson to insist that he would only negotiate with a ruler of the people's choice; **Kaiser Wilhelm** was forced to abdicate the throne.

ARMISTICE OF WWI AND THE TREATY OF VERSAILLES

On November 11, 1918, the Germans agreed to an **armistice** provided that Wilson's Fourteen Points be used as a treaty. Overall, between 9 and 10 million people died in the war, including 320,000 Americans. In the **Treaty of Versailles** (1919), the **League of Nations** was created to handle international disputes. A number of new countries such as Poland and Czechoslovakia, were created by this treaty; also, Germany was disarmed and forced to pay war reparations. Later, the Treaty of Versailles would come to be seen as an uneasy mixture of vengeance and conciliation. It also relied too much on the good faith of the signers. Wilson recognized many problems with the treaty, but he felt the League of Nations would be able to correct them in the future.

US AND THE LEAGUE OF NATIONS

The League of Nations had five permanent members: Japan, Britain, Italy, France, and the US. Germany and Russia were not included. The League would have a **General Assembly** and a **Court of International Justice**. It would try to use economic sanctions and, if necessary, force to guarantee the territorial integrity and political independence of every nation. The problems the League developed in practice were many: it was almost impossible to set into motion, because a unanimous vote was required for action; it created a number of artificial and unsuccessful countries

69

(Sudetenland, for example); it had no power to regulate economics; it excluded two major nations (Russia and Germany); and it had no power to force a nation to disarm.

Review Video: WWI Overview
Visit mometrix.com/academy and enter code: 659767

Review Video: World War I: European Alliances
Visit mometrix.com/academy and enter code: 257458

Review Video: World War I: Outcomes
Visit mometrix.com/academy and enter code: 278666

US RESPONSE TO THE TREATY OF VERSAILLES AND THE LEAGUE OF NATIONS

The US Senate rejected both the Treaty of Versailles and the League of Nations. Republicans, including Henry Cabot Lodge, created the "**Round Robin Manifesto**" guaranteeing that the Treaty would not be approved; some felt that the Republicans were hurt that none of their members had been invited to the table in Versailles. Other politicians were simply angry that the Kaiser had not been killed. Wilson attempted to take the matter of the treaty directly to the American people but he suffered a stroke in 1919 and both the Treaty and the League were rejected by Congress. Lodge issued the **Lodge Reservations**, a rebuttal to Wilson's Fourteen Points, in which he declared that it was an infringement on Congress' power for Wilson to assert that the US military would be used to protect other nations. In the national climate of isolationism and disillusionment that followed the war, it was perhaps inevitable that the US would never sign the Treaty or join the League.

1920s

ELECTION OF 1920 AND THE BACKGROUND TO THE 1920S

The election of 1920 was known as the "solemn referendum." In it, Republican **Warren G. Harding** (who had voted against the League of Nations) defeated Democrat James Cox (who had Franklin Roosevelt as his running mate). Harding's election was in part due to his opposition to the League, but also it was due to his being a radical departure from Wilson. As the 1920s began, Americans felt disillusioned: few people felt that WWI would be the end of war, and massive immigration had left the US scrambling for an identity. There was also hostility lingering from the war: anti-radical, anti-immigration, anti-black, and anti-urban groups had broad followings. The general negativity at the beginning of the decade was not helped by the post-war **recession** and a massive outbreak of **influenza** that killed half a million people.

IMMIGRATION AND LABOR ISSUES AT THE BEGINNING OF THE 1920S

The radical **International Workers of the World** was defunct by 1920, but many people still feared the influx of new ideas (including communism) and immigrants to the US. Indeed, immigrants became the scapegoat for many of the nation's problems. With the **Immigration Restriction Act of 1921**, only a certain quota of immigrants would be allowed into the country. The **National Origins Act of 1924** restricted immigration even further, and stipulated that no Japanese would be allowed into the US. Basically, Americans only wanted Nordics to be able to enter the country. Anti-communist sentiment flared up for the first time during this period; **A. Mitchell Palmer**, the attorney general under Wilson, encouraged citizens to "rouse the Reds."

RACE RELATIONS IN THE EARLY 1920S

In July 1919, there were violent **race riots** because of competition for jobs; in Chicago, a black swimmer crossed into the wrong area of Lake Michigan, sparking another riot. At around this time, the **KKK** increased in popularity in part because of D.W. Griffith's movie "Birth of a Nation," which

depicted the Old South as a paradise led by the Klan. The KKK was led by Hiram Evans and had between 4 and 5 million members; it was anti-black, anti-immigration, anti-Jewish, anti-Catholic, and anti-alcohol. Membership in the Klan declined slightly in the wake of some lynchings and as the economy improved. Nevertheless, many blacks sought refuge in the big cities, as part of the **Great Black Migration**. Also, at this time, the **Harlem Renaissance** was reinvigorating black culture: this movement included Langston Hughes, Countee Cullen, Duke Ellington, Paul Robeson, and Louis Armstrong. Many blacks subscribed to the beliefs of Marcus Garvey, who thought blacks should return to Africa.

PROVINCIALISM V. MODERNITY

At the beginning of the 1920s, the American population was evenly divided between city-dwellers and country-dwellers. While the cities were booming in the post-war period, **farmers** found themselves in economic trouble because of their surpluses. At around this time many writers including Ernest Hemingway, F. Scott Fitzgerald and the members of the **Ashcan School** sharply criticized the growing materialism of the **urbanites**. In 1920, the "noble experiment" of **Prohibition** began; it was constantly undermined by corrupt government and organized crime, and the government lost the money it had made on the taxation of alcohol. Another incident which brought the differences between Americans into sharp relief was the **Scopes Monkey Trial** in Dayton, Tennessee (1925). In this trial, Clarence Darrow successfully defended a science teacher who had taught the students Darwin's theory of natural selection.

> **Review Video: 1920's**
> Visit mometrix.com/academy and enter code: 124996

HARDING PRESIDENCY

When Warren G. Harding came into office, he promised a "return to normalcy." He almost immediately passed the **Esch-Cummins Act of 1920** which allowed for virtual trusts in the railroad industry. Harding raised tariffs and was known for having a strong Cabinet, which included **Herbert Hoover** as Secretary of Commerce. Harding's administration was also known for a large number of scandals. It was discovered at one point that Attorney General Harry Daugherty was selling pardons, parole, and liquor; his successor, Jesse Smith, was later found to be doing exactly the same thing. In the **Forbes Scandal**, the head of the Veterans Bureau was found to have embezzled $250 million from the organization. In the **Teapot Dome Scandal**, the Secretary of the Interior was discovered to have sold government oil reserves to private interests. Near the end of his term, Harding had a stroke and was succeeded by **Calvin Coolidge**.

COOLIDGE PRESIDENCY AND THE ELECTION OF 1924

Calvin Coolidge succeeded Harding after the latter succumbed to a stroke; Coolidge then won the election of 1924 by distancing himself from the scandals of the Harding administration. He is famous for saying, "The business of America is business," and his administration embodied that credo. He allowed the return of **trusts** (now known as "mergers") and he made major efforts to protect American business abroad. When struggling farmers looked to the government for help, Coolidge responded by vetoing the **McNary-Haugan Bill**, which would have established a minimum price for agricultural products. The **Clayton Anti-Trust Act** was totally ignored during the Coolidge presidency.

ELECTION OF 1928 AND HOOVER'S AGRICULTURAL PROGRAM

The election of 1928 pitted **Herbert Hoover** of the Republicans against **Alfred E. Smith** of the Democrats. Hoover, who had served as Secretary of Commerce under Harding, was associated with rural voters, Prohibition, and Protestantism and earned a solid victory over Smith after a dirty

71

campaign. Hoover immediately put into action his "self-help" program for agriculture. With the **Agricultural Marketing Act,** he established cooperatives. He also established the **Federal Farm Board** to loan money to farmers and the Grain and Cotton Stabilization Corporation to buy surpluses. Hoover passed the **Hawley-Smoot Tariff of 1930**, which allowed the president to adjust the tariff at his own discretion; Hoover set it at the highest peacetime rate in American history.

CAUSES OF THE GREAT DEPRESSION

The Great Depression was the result of a number of converging factors. For one thing, there was an agricultural depression in the 1920s brought on by tremendous post-war surpluses. The automobile and housing industries both experienced diminished demand in the 20s. One major problem was that wealth was so unevenly distributed: one-third of the nation's wealth was controlled by 5% of the population. There was not much in the way of international trade, in part because of Hoover's high tariff. Overproduction on assembly lines led to factory surpluses and unemployment. Finally, there was persistent unsound speculation in the stock markets. By 1929, many stocks were considered to be overvalued and thus no one was buying them. This caused the catastrophic market crashes of **Black Thursday** and **Black Tuesday** (October 24 and 29, 1929), in which 40% of the market value (about $30 billion) was lost.

HOOVER AND THE GREAT DEPRESSION

Hoover's first strategy for combating the Great Depression was to balance the budget, reduce federal spending, keep the US on the gold standard, and just wait it out. Later, he developed some **work-relief programs**, employing people on public work projects. The **Hoover Dam** was one of those projects. Hoover also created the **Reconstruction Finance Group**, which loaned money directly to state and local governments as well as to railroads and banks. Hoover's aid projects were unprecedented; still, he resisted giving direct aid to the people in the form of welfare. World War I veterans descended on Washington in 1932 when they were told that their pensions would not be paid until 1945. These so-called "**Bonus Marchers**" eventually had to be dispersed with force, leading many citizens to believe that the country was descending into anarchy. The **20th amendment**, known as the anti-Hoover amendment, actually brought the date of the next inauguration forward.

> **Review Video: The Great Depression**
> Visit mometrix.com/academy and enter code: 635912

FRANKLIN DELANO ROOSEVELT AND THE NEW DEAL

Franklin D. Roosevelt was elected president in the election of 1932. He was determined to preserve the US government and tried to calm the general public with his folksy "**Fireside Chats**." As the governor of New York, Roosevelt had been able to experiment with social welfare programs. He was a pragmatist and a follower of the **Keynesian school of economics** which insisted that the government had to spend money in order to get out of the Depression. Unlike Hoover, then, Roosevelt supported massive government spending and little volunteerism; he wanted the government to regulate agriculture and industry and also for it to take an interest in the daily economic decisions of the people.

In the early days of his term, FDR promoted the **3 Rs**: relief, recovery, and reform. He announced a bank holiday for five days to stop the drain on the cash flow. The **Emergency Banking Act** authorized the **Reconstruction Finance Group** to buy bank stocks in order to finance repair. The **Glass-Steagall Act** made it illegal for banks to loan money to people for the purpose of playing the market and established the **Federal Deposit Insurance Corporation** to protect banks. The

Economy Act cut $400 million from veterans' payments and $100 million from government salaries. Roosevelt had the gold standard and prohibition repealed. The **Federal Emergency Relief Administration** was established to provide $3 billion in direct relief to people.

The **Civil Works Administration**, headed by Harry Hopkins, was established to give people work. The **Civilian Conservation Corps** was a civilian army that built things such as the Blue Ridge Parkway. Other organizations created to **employ** people were the Public Works Administration, the Works Progress Administration, the Tennessee Valley Authority (responsible for the construction of 21 dams), the National Youth Administration (gave work to high school students) and the Rural Electrification Administration. The **National Industrial Recovery Act** tried to encourage fair competition and create scarcity to drive prices up. It established a minimum wage, a maximum number of weekly hours, and the right of labor to organize. In **Schechter Poultry v. US** (1935), the Supreme Court would rule that the NIRA should have been made up of laws instead of codes, because there were too many loopholes.

As part of his **New Deal program** to help the US recover from the Great Depression, FDR established the **First Agricultural Adjustment Administration**. This agency provided farmers with loans to help them with mortgage payments and paid them not to plant or sell agricultural products. The formation of the **AAA** was economically successful, but was one of the least popular measures in the New Deal; it would later be declared unconstitutional in Butler v. US (1936). The **Federal Securities Act** stated that the securities dealers must disclose the prices of stocks and bonds. The **Wagner Act of 1935** made it illegal for employers to have blacklists of unionized workers. The **Federal Housing Administration** was established to provide lower interest rates for people willing to repair or purchase a house. The **US Housing Authority** was created to loan money to state and local governments for the construction of low-cost housing.

RESISTANCE TO FDR'S NEW DEAL

Father Coughlin was a priest who became famous for his radio broadcasts; he blamed the banks and an "international Jewish conspiracy" for the Depression. **Dr. Francis E. Townsend** was a famous advocate for senior citizens who advocated a national sales tax. **Alf Landon** ran against FDR in the 1936 presidential election, and was defeated soundly because of his ties to big business. In the **"Court Packing" controversy** of 1937, FDR tried to overcome Supreme Court resistance to the New Deal by increasing the number of justices on the Court from 9 to 15. This attempt was unsuccessful, but Roosevelt was able to fill Court vacancies with New Deal supporters. A final bit of resistance to the New Deal occurred during the so-called "**Roosevelt Recession**" of 1937-8, in which the economy seemed to be making much less progress than before. Many historians attribute this recession to the fact that New Deal programs were getting much less use in this era.

LIFE OF BLACK AMERICANS AND THE GREAT DEPRESSION

In the **Scottsboro (AL) case of 1932**, 9 young black men were accused of raping 2 white women. Although the evidence was scant, all 9 of the men were convicted. In **Powell v. Alabama**, the Supreme Court would rule that the men had not been given a fair trial because they had not had adequate representation. At around this time, the white **Harold Ickes** was the head of the NAACP. He worked hard to get New Deal jobs for blacks, Thurgood Marshall among them. **Eleanor Roosevelt** also was an advocate for blacks in this period. She came into open conflict with the Daughters of the American Revolution after this group denied Marian Anderson, a black opera singer, the right to sing at Constitution Hall. In general, the New Deal helped many blacks obtain leadership positions that otherwise would have been closed to them. The Roosevelt administration was the first to show any real concern for blacks, so most blacks became life-long Democrats.

LATIN AMERICAN FOREIGN POLICY FROM 1920 TO 1945

The US had tremendous financial investments in **Latin America** and most of the government's policy there was aimed at securing these investments. In 1921, the US paid $21 million to **Colombia**, in part for stealing the land for the Panama Canal and in part to keep them from seizing US oil investments. At this time, the US also had bad relations with **Mexico** until the election there of President Calles, a pro-American politician. During the Hoover administration, the US tried to promote "good neighborism" with respect to Mexico and the rest of Latin America. In 1934, the **Platt Amendment** gave Cuba full independence. When Batista came to power, however, the US backed him completely and refused to acknowledge any other elected leaders.

AMERICA'S INTRODUCTION TO WWII

After the First World War, the US became obsessed with isolating itself from foreign conflicts. The **Nye Committee** studied the war, and determined that it had been fought for financial reasons, and could have been avoided. Isolationist parties achieved some popularity during this period, including the **America First Committee**, led by Charles Lindbergh, and **SOS** (Stop Organized Slaughter). The **Neutrality Laws** of 1935-7 declared that the US could not sell weapons to another country in a time of war, and that US citizens could not travel on the ships of a nation at war. In 1937, FDR delivered the **Quarantine Speech**, in which he asserted that the Nazi "disease" must be contained. Finally, after conflict in Europe had escalated considerably, FDR declared that the US needed to help Britain, and be an "arsenal of democracy in the world." The **Neutrality Act of 1940** made it legal for the US to sell weapons on a cash and carry basis. In August of 1941, FDR and Churchill drew up the **Atlantic Charter**, which vowed to destroy Nazism, protect the right of self-determination, and create a World Peace Organization.

BUILDUP TO THE ATTACK ON PEARL HARBOR

A number of events had created a stormy relationship between the US and Japan long before the invasion of Pearl Harbor. The US influence over the **Treaty of Portsmouth**, which ended the Russo-Japanese War, created a great deal of tension between the two countries. The Japanese were also antagonized by Theodore Roosevelt's parade of the **Great White Fleet**, and by the **National Origins Act of 1924** and the **Segregation Laws**, which kept Japanese from entering and assimilating into the US. America also had a cordial relationship at this time with Japan's longtime rival, China. As the Japanese became more belligerent, the US froze all Japanese assets in America and denied Japan the purchase of any more oil or scrap metal. The Japanese then launched surprise attacks both on the American naval base at **Pearl Harbor** and on the **Philippines**, where they hoped to secure some oil.

US INVOLVEMENT IN WWII CONCERNING EUROPE AND AFRICA

After the Japanese attack on Pearl Harbor in 1941, the US declared **war** on Japan, after which Germany declared war on the US. Before going after Japan, however, the US first attacked Germany; this was done because the US underestimated Japan industrially and militarily, and because the US feared Britain was on the verge of defeat. **Operation Overlord**, the Allied invasion of the European continent at Normandy, was led in part by General **Dwight D. Eisenhower**. The American generals Omar Bradley and George Patton took part in the **Allied Operation Torch**, aimed at taking back North Africa. At the **Battle of the Bulge**, in Belgium, the Germans tried to break the Allied lines, but were unsuccessful, in part because of the heroism of American soldiers.

US INVOLVEMENT IN WWII CONCERNING ASIA AND THE PACIFIC

The US strategy for controlling the Pacific was known as "island hopping." In the **Coral Sea Battle of 1942**, Americans stopped the Japanese from taking Australia and New Guinea. In the same year,

the **Doolittle raids** of Japanese naval bases boosted American morale. In the **Battle of Midway** (1942), the US sunk four Japanese aircraft carriers. In the **Battle of Leyte Gulf**, General Douglas MacArthur took back the Philippines, and also took control of Iwo Jima and Okinawa. During this period, a team of American scientists led by Robert Oppenheimer were developing the **atomic bomb** in Los Alamos, New Mexico. Japan was warned several times by President Truman that the bomb would be used if they did not surrender. Surely enough, Americans dropped atomic bombs on **Hiroshima** on August 6, 1945, and on **Nagasaki** three days later. Japanese leaders surrendered aboard the USS Missouri on August 15, 1945.

ELECTION OF 1940 AND AMERICAN HOME FRONT DURING WWII

In 1940, **FDR** easily defeated the Republican Wendell Willkie. After his election, Roosevelt pledged that every resource would be devoted to winning the war. FDR created a number of war-time bureaucracies including the **War Production Board** (which was devoted to manufacturing goods for war), the **War Manpower Commission** (which organized the draft and created jobs for women) and the **Office of Price Administration**, which set prices and rations. In total, the US war effort cost between $330 and $360 billion. Most of this cost was covered through taxation and the sale of government bonds. The US frequently denied civil liberties to Japanese-Americans during this period, forcing many to live in internment camps. In **Korematsu v. US** (1944), the Supreme Court ruled that the internment camps were legal, but in **ex parte Endo** (1944), the Court adjusted its decision to state that the US could only intern those whose disloyalty could be proven.

YALTA CONFERENCE

The Yalta Conference was held on an island in the Crimean Sea in February of 1945. It was attended by FDR, Churchill, and Stalin. At the Conference, FDR tried to make sure that Germany would not be split into smaller nations (this would happen later). Stalin "liberated" the countries along the border of Nazi Germany, and in exchange FDR allowed the Red Army to remain in those countries. This Conference established boundaries and a provisional government for Poland (this provisional government was led by the Soviets, and would last until 1989). One of the more important moves of this Conference was that the US and Britain allowed a Communist government under **Mao Zedong** to remain in Mongolia; this group of Communists would eventually take over China in 1949.

TRUMAN AND THE FAIR DEAL

When Truman came into office after the death of Franklin Roosevelt in 1945, he was already fighting an uphill battle. Many people felt that the Democrats had controlled the executive branch for too long, and many expected **Truman** to have the personal charisma of FDR. Truman gamely attempted to continue the reforms of the New Deal, which he renamed the **Fair Deal**. Nevertheless, he was frequently thwarted by the Republican Congress. Truman surprisingly won a narrow victory over Dewey in the election of 1948, and continued to pursue reforms in education, health care, and civil rights. He gradually became worn down by his conflicts with Congress, however, and he declined to run in 1952.

KOREAN WAR

The Korean War took place during the Truman presidency. Korea had been divided after WWII into a **northern half** (under Soviet control) and a **southern half** (under American control). When foreign troops finally withdrew from the peninsula, North Korea attacked South Korea in an attempt to unify. The United Nations Security Council declared that North Korea was an aggressor, and sent troops led by the American General **Douglas MacArthur** to the region. MacArthur had some early victories, but progress slowed when China began to send men and supplies to the North

Koreans. Gradually, combat gave way to armistice talks, yet those these too seemed to drag on endlessly.

ELECTION OF 1952, EISENHOWER, AND THE SUEZ CANAL

General **Dwight Eisenhower**, a Republican, defeated the Democrat Adlai Stevenson in the election of 1952. One of the first crises of the Eisenhower administration concerned the **Suez Canal** in Egypt. The conflict began after Israel attacked Egypt in response to attacks on the new Jewish nation that were launched at Egyptian bases; at the same time, England and France withdrew plans to build a dam on the Suez Canal because of Egypt's recognition of Communist China. Angered by these events, the Egyptian President **Nasser** seized the assets of the European company that administered traffic on the canal. The United States was eventually able to defuse the situation; this marked the introduction of the so-called **Eisenhower Doctrine**, in which American troops and money would be used to undermine Communism in various regions around the world.

ANTI-COMMUNISM IN THE UNITED STATES

As the US was becoming more embroiled in the Cold War, Americans became increasingly paranoid about the spread of **Communism**. There were numerous investigations aimed at weeding Communist spies out of the government, and two people, Julius and Ethel Rosenberg, were executed for spying. The leader of much of this was Senator **Joseph McCarthy**, who was famous for promoting and prolonging the "**Red Scare**" as the often-termed witch-hunt for communists in the government was known (Soviet communications released after the fall of the Soviet Union confirmed the vast majority of his accusations). The tide of anti-communism extended into a general disapproval of organized labor. The **Taft-Hartley Act** restricted the ability of labor unions markedly. In order to survive, the nation's two largest labor unions combined, forming the **AFL-CIO**.

CIVIL RIGHTS UNDER EISENHOWER

For a long time, the problems of blacks had been considered a Southern issue; however, massive black migration into the Northern cities made civil rights a national question. In **Brown v. Board of Education** (1954), the Supreme Court ruled that segregation in public schools is unconstitutional. After some southern states defied this decision, Eisenhower was forced to send in federal troops. At the same time, blacks were staging nonviolent protests across the south. **Rosa Parks** famously refused to give up her bus seat in Montgomery, Alabama, and four black men staged a sit-in at a whites-only lunch counter in Greensboro, North Carolina. With the **Civil Rights Acts** of 1957 and 1960, blacks were given the right to vote; these acts were not enforced.

US FOREIGN POLICY UNDER EISENHOWER

The Secretary of State under Eisenhower was **John Foster Dulles**, who wanted to pursue an aggressive foreign policy to "roll back Communism." This was also the period in which the national defense budget skyrocketed, as both the US and USSR believed that peace could be maintained by threatening the other side with total annihilation. It was in this climate that the US first became involved in **Vietnam**. The French had been kicked out of this Southeast Asian nation for good in 1954, and the country had been divided into a northern and southern half in the **Geneva Truce** of the same year. The US then tried to bolster the standing of the non-communist leader **Ngo Dinh Diem** in the south, as he batted the communist **Viet Cong**. Increasingly, Eisenhower was funneling money to the anti-communist forces in South Vietnam, believing that if this country became communist, others would follow (the "Domino effect").

ELECTION OF 1960, KENNEDY AND THE SPACE PROGRAM, AND ASSASSINATION OF JFK

In the election of 1960, the Democrat **John F. Kennedy** defeated Richard Nixon; this was the first election in which television was a major factor. One of the most important issues of the Kennedy presidency would be the **space race** with the Soviet Union. It was under Kennedy that the **National Aeronautics and Space Administration** was established. Alan Shepard became the first American in space in 1961, and in 1969 Neil Armstrong would become the first human to walk on the moon. Kennedy, unfortunately, would not witness this event: he was shot and killed by **Lee Harvey Oswald** in Dallas in November of 1963. Though some still claim that Oswald was a part of a broader conspiracy, an investigation led by Chief Justice Earl Warren declared that he had acted alone.

CIVIL RIGHTS DURING THE KENNEDY YEARS

The black struggle for **civil rights** intensified during the Kennedy administration. After integration at Southern universities was mandated, National Guardsmen were deployed to keep the peace. The situation was especially tense in Alabama, where Governor George Wallace declared that segregation would stand in his state forever. In July of 1963, **Martin Luther King, Jr.** led the famous **March on Washington**, during which he made his "I Have a Dream" speech. King would receive the **Nobel Peace Prize** in 1964. The **23rd and 24th amendments** to the Constitution were aimed at redressing the issue of black suffrage; they gave electoral votes to Washington, DC, and eliminated the poll tax.

LBJ AND ELECTION OF 1964

Lyndon Baines Johnson took over as president after the assassination of Kennedy. He was able to use the "ghost" of the assassinated president to pass the **Civil Rights Act of 1964**. Johnson also declared a "war on poverty," a system of programs aimed at helping the poor. In the election of 1964, the escalating conflict in Vietnam was much in the public's mind, and the Republican candidate, Barry Goldwater, was viewed as a war-monger. The election of Johnson, however, did not keep the US out of Vietnam. After being elected, Johnson promoted legislation under the banner of the "Great Society." He created Medicare and Medicaid with the **Social Security Act of 1965** and established the agency of **Housing and Urban Development**.

CIVIL RIGHTS MOVEMENT DURING THE JOHNSON YEARS

The summer of 1964 saw more violence in the South as three civil rights workers were murdered while trying to register voters. After the passage of the **Voting Rights Act of 1965**, Johnson would have to deploy Federal Marshals to escort blacks to the polls. Frustrated by the slow advance to equality, many blacks became more militant. During the summer of 1967, there were riots in 150 cities, most of which were sparked by economic concerns, as blacks felt they were being mistreated in the marketplace. Advocates of **Black Power** joined groups like the Black Panthers and the Mau Mau, and even formerly moderate groups like the SNCC would begin to endorse violence. Many white Americans who sympathized with the black struggle were alienated by this militancy. There were more riots in 1968 after the assassination of Martin Luther King, Jr. in Memphis. The **Civil Rights Act of 1968** gave full rights to blacks, but contained restrictions aimed at reducing racial violence.

FOREIGN POLICY UNDER JOHNSON

After an American ship came under fire from **North Vietnam** in the Gulf of Tonkin, Johnson received a blank check for American involvement in the region. **General Westmoreland** oversaw troops during this period of escalation. Soon, 184,000 American soldiers were in Vietnam, and the government was spending a million dollars every day. Coupled with inflation, this expense bled

Johnson's domestic program dry. The **peace movement** in the US took off during this period. Many people protested what they saw as inequities in the draft system (for instance, blacks seemed to be unfairly overrepresented). The US problems in Vietnam were exposed to the world during the **Tet Offensive** of January 1968; during this period, the Viet Cong damaged American forces in virtually every city in the region.

ELECTION OF 1968 AND DOMESTIC POLICY OF NIXON

In the election of 1968, the Republican **Richard M. Nixon**, who had narrowly lost to Kennedy in 1960, defeated the Democrat Hubert Humphrey. The **Democratic National Convention** had endured violent protests over the Vietnam War. Though much of Nixon's administration would be concerned with the war (and later with the Watergate investigation), he did institute a somewhat successful policy of sharing revenue with states. The economy was languishing in a state of stagflation (high inflation and high unemployment) during this period and thus Nixon tried to jolt it with a ninety-day wage and price freeze. This move, known as the **New Economic Policy** (or Nixonomics) was a total failure.

NIXON AND VIETNAM

Nixon had won the election on a platform of "Peace with Honor," and upon entering office he began slowly withdrawing troops from Vietnam. The **Nixon Doctrine** asserted that the US would honor its commitment to South Vietnam with material rather than men. Nixon did, however, order an invasion of purportedly neutral **Cambodia**, where the Viet Cong were stockpiling weapons. It was also during Nixon's presidency that four students at Kent State University were killed by the National Guard during a protest. In the election of 1972, Nixon crushed George McGovern after Foreign Advisor Henry Kissinger claimed that peace was "at hand." After the election, Kissinger and Le Duc Tho would negotiate the **Paris Peace Accords of 1973**.

WATERGATE SCANDAL

On June 17, 1972, a break-in was thwarted at the **Democratic National Committee office** at the Watergate Hotel in Washington, DC. It was eventually discovered that the burglars had ties to the Nixon administration. This began the unraveling of an enormous conspiracy of corruption in the Nixon administration. Many of Nixon's advisers would be forced to resign, though Nixon still refused to cooperate with the investigation. Eventually, though, evidence would mount against him, and Nixon would be forced to release tapes of his Oval Office conversations. Nixon **resigned** on August 8, 1974, although he never admitted any guilt. The **Watergate scandal** left a permanent stain on the presidency.

GERALD FORD INTERLUDE

Gerald Ford, a congressman from Michigan, had been appointed vice president under Nixon after the resignation of Spiro Agnew, and after the resignation of Nixon he became president. His was a mostly uneventful term, as the nation recovered from the shocks of Vietnam and Watergate. Ford talked a great deal about battling inflation, but never did very much to back up his rhetoric. It was during the Ford administration that **South Vietnam** fell once and for all to the North Vietnamese. Ford's most famous act may have been his full **pardon** of Nixon. Though Ford at the time declared that "our long national nightmare is over," this unpopular move may have cost him the election in 1976.

ELECTION OF 1976 AND THE CARTER ADMINISTRATION

The Democratic governor of Georgia, **Jimmy Carter**, defeated the incumbent Gerald Ford in the election of 1976. Carter was popular with black voters, and was generally believed to be outside the cesspool of Washington politics. Carter immediately made an $18 billion tax cut, and inflation soared. Carter also made the controversial move of pardoning all those who evaded the draft during the Vietnam War. As for foreign policy, Carter became known for his humanitarian efforts: working for peace between Israel and Egypt at Camp David earned him the **Nobel Peace Prize**. Carter signed a bill to give the **Panama Canal** back to the Panamanians, and endured a severe oil shortage. This, along with the failed rescue of fifty American hostages in Iran, led to Carter's defeat in 1980.

ELECTION OF 1980 AND FOREIGN POLICY UNDER REAGAN

In the election of 1980, known as the **Conservative Revolution**, **Ronald Reagan** easily defeated Jimmy Carter. Reagan presided over the last few years of the Cold War. In 1983, Reagan authorized the invasion of Grenada, where there was an airstrip that was supposedly being used by the Cubans and the Soviet Union. Later in 1983, a Marine barrack in Lebanon was blown up by terrorists, killing hundreds of American soldiers. Reagan introduced the **"Star Wars" program**, a strategic defense initiative in which incoming missiles would be destroyed from outer space by laser-armed satellites. Reagan promoted the "**Peace through strength**" method of foreign policy, whereby the economic might of the United States would furnish such an intimidating military that the Soviet Union would be unable to compete financially and thus fail. This eventually played a major role in the **fall of the Soviet Union** in 1989. Reagan nevertheless improved relations with the Soviet Union diplomatically, even signing a treaty with Soviet Premier **Mikhail Gorbachev** to ban a certain class of Nuclear Weapon.

DOMESTIC AFFAIRS UNDER REAGAN

Upon entering office, Reagan implemented **tax cuts** in the hopes of stimulating the economy. While this had a very positive effect on the economy by the end of his first term, the American trade deficit continued to grow wider. Reagan's presidency was tarnished by the **Iran-Contra affair**, in which it was determined that the US had sold weapons to a hostile nation. In 1984, due to an impressive economic recovery and unprecedented growth, Reagan defeated Walter Mondale (whose running mate was Geraldine Ferraro, the first female vice-presidential candidate) in a landslide, winning 49 states electorally. In the case **Wallace v. Jaffree** (1985), the Supreme Court ruled that schools could provide for a moment of silence, but could not endorse any particular religion. In **US v. Eichman** (1990), the Court ruled that burning the American flag qualified as expressive conduct, and was therefore permitted under the First Amendment.

OVERVIEW OF GEORGE BUSH'S FOREIGN AND DOMESTIC POLICIES

In the election of 1988, the Republican Vice President **George H.W. Bush** defeated Michael Dukakis easily. Under Bush, the **federal deficit** continued to rise, and the US role in the Iran-Contra affair continued to cast a shadow over the executive branch. One of the major crises during the Bush administration was the wreck of the **Exxon Valdez**, which created the largest oil spill ever along the Alaskan coast. Meanwhile, Bush led the US military into the **Persian Gulf War** in 1990-1 after Iraq invaded neighboring Kuwait. American troops routed the Iraqis. It was also during Bush's administration that the **Berlin Wall** fell and the Communist regime in the Soviet Union finally crumbled.

ELECTION OF 1992 AND DOMESTIC POLICY UNDER CLINTON

The Democratic governor of Arkansas, **Bill Clinton**, defeated the incumbent George H. W. Bush and H. Ross Perot (Independent) in the election of 1992. Clinton tried to reduce the federal deficit. He also pushed for gays to be allowed into the military. Clinton appointed Janet Reno as the first female Attorney General and also reversed most of the restrictions on abortions that had been established by the Reagan and Bush administrations. Clinton's presidency would be plagued by scandals throughout; he and his wife were accused of making illegal land deals in the **Whitewater**

scandal and Clinton would later be **impeached** for lying under oath and obstructing justice in regard to an extramarital affair. A Democrat majority in the Senate elected not to remove him from office.

ELECTION OF 1996 AND FOREIGN POLICY UNDER CLINTON

In the election of 1996, the incumbent **Bill Clinton** narrowly defeated Kansas Senator Bob Dole. During Clinton's two terms, the United States trade deficit would continue. In the aftermath of the collapse of the Soviet regime, the US gave substantial aid to Russia and many of the new republics. The United States would also supply troops for a **NATO peacekeeping effort** during the Civil War in the former Yugoslavia between the years 1992 and 2000. American troops also participated in peacekeeping missions in Somalia, Bosnia, and Haiti. Finally, Clinton ordered air strikes against Iraq after it was determined that Iraqi leader **Saddam Hussein** had been part of a conspiracy to assassinate President Bush.

ELECTION OF 2000 AND GEORGE W. BUSH

In the election of 2000, **George W. Bush**, the son of ex-President Bush, defeated Vice-President Al Gore, despite losing to Gore in the popular vote. Bush immediately instituted a major tax cut; critics claimed that this tax cut only benefited the very rich. On September 11, 2001, the US suffered the worst **terrorist attack** in its history, as four planes were hijacked and two of them destroyed the **World Trade Center** towers in New York. The attacks were planned and funded by **al-Qaeda**; an Islamic fundamentalist group led by Osama bin Laden. The United States almost immediately launched **Operation Enduring Freedom**, an attack on the Taliban government of Afghanistan that had harbored bin Laden.

SAT Practice Test

U.S. History Practice Test #1

1. Which of the following is true regarding the Treaty of Tordesillas?

    a. It was executed during the 1500s.
    b. It set up a "Line of Demarcation."
    c. It moved a line of demarcation east.
    d. It was initiated by the Pope.
    e. It was between Spain and Portugal.

2. Which of the following conquistadores unwittingly gave smallpox to the Indians and destroyed the Aztec empire in Mexico?

    a. Balboa
    b. Ponce de Leon
    c. Cortes
    d. De Vaca
    e. De Soto

3. Which conquistador discovered the Mississippi River?

    a. Coronado
    b. De Soto
    c. Cortes
    d. De Leon
    e. De Narvaez

4. Which of the following statements is true regarding New Spain in the 1500s?

    a. New Spain had not yet developed any kind of class system.
    b. The Spanish originally imported Africans to use as slaves for labor.
    c. The *hacienda* system eventually gave way to the *encomienda* system.
    d. Conquistadores experienced shortages of labor in the New World.
    e. About 300,000 Spanish came to America to escape overpopulation.

5. Which of the following explorers was *not* involved in the search for a Northwest Passage?

    a. Verrazzano
    b. John Cabot
    c. Jacques Cartier
    d. Magellan
    e. All of the above explorers were involved in the search for a Northwest Passage.

6. Which of the following statements is *not* true regarding English expansionism in the 16th century?

a. England's defeat of the Spanish Armada in 1588 brought a decisive end to their war with Spain.
b. King Henry VIII's desire to divorce Catherine of Aragon strengthened English expansionism.
c. Queen Elizabeth's support for the Protestant Reformation strengthened English expansionism.
d. Sir Francis Drake and other English sea captains plundered the Spaniards' plunders of Indians.
e. Sir Francis Drake's voyages to and conquests of new territories were supported by Elizabeth.

7. Which of the following is incorrect regarding the Virginia Companies?

a. One of these companies, the Virginia Company of Plymouth, made its base in North America.
b. One of these companies, the Virginia Company of London, made its base in Massachusetts.
c. One company had a charter to colonize America between the Hudson and Cape Fear rivers.
d. One company had a charter to colonize America from the Potomac River to north Maine.
e. The Virginia Companies were both joint-stock companies that raised funds by selling stock.

8. Which of the following statements is *not* true regarding the colony of Jamestown?

a. The colony of Jamestown was established by the Virginia Company of London in 1607.
b. The colony of Jamestown became the first permanent English colony in North America.
c. The majority of settlers in early Jamestown died of starvation, disease, or Indian attacks.
d. Many settlers were English gentry who would not farm or explorers looking for treasure.
e. John Smith's governance helped Jamestown more than John Rolfe's tobacco discovery.

9. Which of the following is *not* a correct statement regarding the Pilgrims?

a. The Pilgrims left England in 1620 on the ship known as the *Mayflower* and landed at Cape Cod.
b. The Pilgrims were led by William Bradford with a charter from the London Company.
c. The Pilgrims were a group of Puritans who left England to escape religious persecution.
d. The Pilgrims were a group of separatists who migrated to leave the Church of England.
e. The Pilgrims wrote and signed the Mayflower Compact on the ship before going ashore.

10. Which of the following is *not* true regarding the early colonization of New York?

a. Dutch fur traders first created the New Amsterdam settlement on Manhattan Island in 1624.
b. King Charles II of England entitled his brother James to conquer New Amsterdam in 1664.
c. James, Duke of York, prohibited assemblies in New York as he was against representation.
d. Colonel Richard Nicols granted very few civil or political rights to the New York colonials.
e. New York colonial citizens, especially Puritans on Long Island, demanded self-government.

11. Which of the following did *not* contribute to differences in the lives of New England colonists vs. the lives of Chesapeake colonists during the 17th century?

a. In Virginia and Maryland, female settlers greatly outnumbered male settlers.
b. New England colonists had significantly longer life expectancies than did Chesapeake colonists.
c. New England colonists had a better organized, more stable society than did Chesapeake colonists.
d. New England colonists had educational advantages over Chesapeake colonists.
e. New England could not support large farms, which resulted in a richer economy.

12. Which of the following is *not* true regarding British mercantilism and the American colonies?

a. English mercantilists held the belief that the government should regulate all economic enterprise.

b. The many crops produced on American colony farms contributed to English mercantilism.

c. The Navigation Acts were passed by Parliament between 1650 and 1700 to further mercantilism.

d. British mercantilism fueled wars with Holland, but did not contribute to American prosperity.

e. Mercantilism raised prices of British goods for Americans and lowered prices of colonial goods.

13. Which of the following statements is *not* true about the Quakers?

a. The colonies of Pennsylvania and Delaware were originally established to provide Quakers with religious freedom.

b. The Quakers, though pacifists regarding war, were also aggressively subversive of social institutions and classes.

c. The Quakers, while religious, did not assign much significance to the Bible or most human institutions.

d. The Quakers were one of several radical religious groups formed in England around the time of the English Civil War.

e. William Penn, a Quaker, established Pennsylvania to provide religious freedom, but there was initially no representative assembly.

14. Which of the following wars included no major army battles on American soil and no major changes in territories?

a. Queen Anne's War

b. King William's War

c. King George's War

d. The French and Indian War

e. None of the above

15. Which of the following statements is *incorrect* regarding the inception of the Georgia colony?

a. Georgia was originally founded to create a buffer zone between South Carolina and Florida.

b. British philanthropist General James Oglethorpe and his followers founded Georgia.

c. The charter to establish a British colony in what is now Georgia was granted in 1765.

d. Due to the founders' extensive rules, few settlers came, and those few were unhappy.

e. Georgia's original settlers were British subjects who were economically unsuccessful.

16. Which of the following is true about the Enlightenment?

a. The Enlightenment was a philosophical movement that began in America and spread to Europe.
b. One of the most central premises of the Enlightenment was the importance of God in the world.
c. John Locke believed that governments should not be deposed for violating social or political rights.
d. In Enlightenment philosophy, traditional values, practices, and institutions were always upheld.
e. Of those who embraced the Enlightenment in America, the best known was Benjamin Franklin.

17. Which of these Americans was *not* particularly associated with the Great Awakening?

a. William Tennent
b. Gilbert Tennent
c. Theodore Frelinghuysen
d. Benjamin Franklin
e. Jonathan Edwards

18. Which of the following is a correct statement concerning the French and Indian War?

a. Then-Major George Washington, dispatched to Pennsylvania to oust the French, succeeded.
b. In 1756, this war extended over to Europe, where it became known as the Seven Years' War.
c. Colonial delegates included Thomas Jefferson, who proposed an intercolonial government.
d. English Major General Edward Braddock defeated an ambush on the way to Fort Duquesne.
e. The Treaty of Paris gave Britain all France's territories in Canada, but not in all of North America.

19. Which of these factors was *not* a direct contributor to the beginning of the American Revolution?

a. The attitudes of American colonists toward Great Britain following the French and Indian War
b. The attitudes of leaders in Great Britain toward the American colonies and imperialism
c. James Otis's court argument against Great Britain's Writs of Assistance as breaking natural law
d. Lord Grenville's Proclamation of 1763, Sugar Act, Currency Act, and especially Stamp Act
e. James Otis, Samuel Adams, Patrick Henry, the Sons of Liberty, and the Stamp Act Congress

20. Which of the following statements is *not* true regarding the Tea Act of 1773?

a. The British East India Company was suffering financially because Americans were buying tea smuggled from Holland.
b. Parliament granted concessions to the British East India Company to ship tea straight to America, bypassing England.
c. Colonists found that even with added taxes, tea directly shipped by the British East India Company cost less, and they bought it.
d. American colonists refused to buy less expensive tea from the British East India Company on the principle of taxation.
e. Many colonists felt the Boston Tea Party was wrong, but changed their minds upon the passage of the Intolerable Acts.

21. Which of the following was/were *not* dispatch rider(s) notifying Americans of British troop movements reported by American surveillance in 1775?

a. Paul Revere
b. William Dawes
c. John Parker
d. (a) and (b)
e. (a), (b), and (c) were all dispatch riders.

22. Which of the following was/were British generals who came to Boston in May of 1775 to push General Thomas Gage to become more aggressive toward the American colonists?

a. William Howe
b. Henry Clinton
c. John Burgoyne
d. (a) and (c) only
e. (a), (b), and (c)

23. When Americans captured Fort Ticonderoga on Lake Champlain, who was/were leading them?

a. Ethan Allen
b. Benedict Arnold
c. Richard Montgomery
d. (a), (b), and (c)
e. (a) and (b) only

24. Which of the following events happened earliest on the eve of the American Revolution?

a. The Declaration of Independence, drafted mainly by Thomas Jefferson, was officially taken up by America's Second Continental Congress.
b. Thomas Paine published his famous pamphlet, *Common Sense,* influencing even more moderate Americans to agree upon independence.
c. The Second Continental Congress issued the "Olive Branch Petition," begging King George III to ask Parliament to make peace with them.
d. King George III of England approved the Prohibitory Act, an official declaration that the colonists were in rebellion and no longer protected.
e. Virginia's Richard Henry Lee submitted several resolutions to Congress proposing American independence and a formal government.

25. Which of the following battles was/were won by George Washington against the British?

a. Long Island and Washington Heights, New York
b. Trenton and Princeton, New Jersey
c. Both (a) and (b)
d. Neither (a) nor (b); they were all losses.
e. Neither (a) not (b); Washington led no battles at these places.

26. Which of the following battles persuaded France to enter America's war against Britain?

a. The Battle of Saratoga
b. The Battle of Brandywine Creek
c. The Battle of Oriskany
d. The Battle of Bennington
e. None of the above

27. Which of the following statements is accurate concerning the Battle of Yorktown?

    a. General Cornwallis won a victory in Yorktown, Virginia, overlooking Chesapeake Bay.
    b. Washington's army defeated Cornwallis's troops single handedly in Yorktown, Virginia.
    c. Cornwallis's and Washington's troops fought for three weeks to an indecisive conclusion.
    d. Washington defeated Cornwallis with the help of a French naval fleet and a French land army.
    e. None of the above

28. The 1783 Treaty of Paris included which of the following agreements?

    a. Boundaries were established for the United States, including the southern tip of Florida as the southernmost boundary.
    b. Britain was allowed to keep both Canada and Florida as imperial British territories under the terms of the Treaty of Paris.
    c. The treaty stipulated that all private creditors in Britain were prohibited from making future debt collections from Americans.
    d. Property of loyalists that was confiscated by American states was allowed by Congress to be kept by the states in this treaty.
    e. Britain and the other most powerful countries of Europe recognized the United States' independence as a nation.

29. Which of the following is true concerning the formation of new state governments in the new United States of America following freedom from British rule?

    a. By the end of 1777, new constitutions had been created for twelve of the American states.
    b. The states of Connecticut and Massachusetts retained their colonial charters, minus the British parts.
    c. The state of Massachusetts required a special convention for its constitution, setting a good example.
    d. The state of Massachusetts did not formally begin to use its new constitution until 1778.
    e. Pennsylvania, Maryland, and Virginia all started with viable constitutions with checks and balances.

30. Which of these statements is *incorrect* regarding the Northwest Ordinance?

    a. Congress officially passed this ordinance in 1785.
    b. This ordinance provided a bill of rights for settlers.
    c. This law stopped slavery north of the Ohio River.
    d. This law allowed some territories to become states.
    e. All of the above statements are correct.

31. Which of the following is *not* true with respect to the Constitutional Convention of 1787?

    a. The delegates to the Convention had a common opinion that people are inherently selfish.
    b. Convention delegate Benjamin Franklin was quite instrumental in the Great Compromise.
    c. Edmund Randolph designed the "Virginia Plan," which was introduced by James Madison.
    d. Paterson's New Jersey Plan favoring smaller states was an alternative to the Virginia Plan.
    e. The Three-Fifths Compromise resolved differences between the North and South over slavery.

32. In what year was George Washington inaugurated as the first President of the United States?

    a. 1786
    b. 1787
    c. 1788
    d. 1789
    e. 1791

33. Which of the following amendments is included in the Bill of Rights?

    a. The amendment stating states could not be sued by individuals
    b. The amendment stating that slavery was abolished in America
    c. The amendment stating that senators were to be elected directly
    d. The amendment stating that income taxes would be made legal
    e. The amendment stating non-federal powers were kept by states

34. Which of the following is a power held only by the federal government?

    a. The power to levy taxes, borrow money, and spend money
    b. The power to award copyrights and patents to people or groups
    c. The power to establish the criteria that qualify a person to vote
    d. The power to ratify proposed amendments to the Constitution
    e. The power to keep police control of public health and safety

35. Of the following actions, which one requires a three-fourths majority?

    a. State approval of a proposed amendment to the Constitution
    b. Submitting a proposal for an amendment to the Constitution
    c. Ratification for appointments to the Presidency in the Senate
    d. The introduction of charges for an impeachment in the House
    e. The overriding of any veto that the President has declared

36. Which of the following was *not* a provision of the Judiciary Act of 1789?

    a. The initial establishment of the Supreme Court of the United States
    b. Constitutional validity of state laws to be judged by the Supreme Court
    c. The appointment of nine justices as members of the Supreme Court
    d. The establishment of a district court system for original jurisdiction
    e. The establishment of three courts of appeal, as well as district courts

37. Which of the following is correct regarding the emergence of political parties in the new United States of America?

    a. The Federalists were followers of Thomas Jefferson and their opponents followed Alexander Hamilton.
    b. The Anti-Federalists, as they were originally called by the Federalists, eventually developed into Democrats.
    c. The Federalists believed in a close, literal interpretation of the Constitution, while their opponents did not.
    d. Those who opposed the views of Alexander Hamilton and sided with Thomas Jefferson became Republicans.
    e. James Madison primarily supported Treasury Secretary Alexander Hamilton's philosophies and policies.

38. Which of these is true concerning the French Revolution, America, and Europe?

a. When France's revolution spread and they went to war with other European countries, George Washington allied with the French.

b. During the time period around 1792, American merchants were conducting trading with countries on both sides of the war.

c. American traders conducted business with various countries, profiting the most from the British West Indies.

d. The Spanish navy retaliated against America for trading with the French by capturing American trading ships.

e. When Citizen Genêt encouraged American people to support the French government, Washington agreed with him.

39. Which statement is *not* true about American Indians and American settlers in the 1790s?

a. Indian tribes were fighting back against American settlers encroaching on their territory along the Northwestern border of the country.

b. Indian tribes were fighting back against American settlers encroaching on their territory along the Southwestern border of the country.

c. In Canada, British officials were actually encouraging Indian tribes to continue to wage attacks on American frontier settlements.

d. General Anthony Wayne's defeat of the Indians and the Treaty of Greenville removed all Indian tribes from the Ohio territory.

e. The 1794 Treaty of Greenville following the Battle of Fallen Timbers effectively restored peace between the settlers and the Indians.

40. Which of the following is *not* true regarding the Whiskey Rebellion?

a. Washington's dispatching federal troops did not resolve the revolt, a setback for the government.

b. An excise tax levied on whiskey was central to Treasury Secretary Hamilton's revenue program.

c. Farmers in Pennsylvania objected to the excise tax on whiskey, and were refusing to pay the tax.

d. Farmers in Pennsylvania committed acts of terrorism against tax collectors over the whiskey tax.

e. President Washington sent a federal militia of 15,000 troops to address the Whiskey Rebellion.

41. Which of the following is correct about the Presidential election of 1796?

a. John Adams ran for President as the Republican Party's candidate.

b. Thomas Jefferson ran for President as the Federalist Party's candidate.

c. John Adams and Thomas Jefferson ran for opposing political parties.

d. John Adams ran for President with running mate Thomas Jefferson.

e. Thomas Jefferson ran for President with running mate John Adams.

42. What is *not* true concerning the election and "Revolution" of 1800 in America?

a. Thomas Jefferson and Aaron Burr ran as Republicans during this election.

b. John Adams and Charles Pinckney ran as Federalists during this election.

c. The Republican candidates received an equal number of electoral votes.

d. The Federalist candidates received an equal number of electoral votes.

e. Alexander Hamilton eventually shifted his support to Thomas Jefferson.

43. Which of these is *not* a correct description of the 1803 Supreme Court case Marbury v. Madison?

a. William Marbury sued Secretary of State Madison, demanding Madison appoint him Justice of the Peace.

b. Supreme Court Justice John Marshall stated Marbury's claim was unconstitutional, a first in U.S. history.

c. This case established the precedent of judicial review, which states that courts may cancel other branches' actions.

d. The Supreme Court's decision in this case was instrumental in defining the American system of checks and balances.

e. John Marshall continued to act as Secretary of State after being appointed Chief Supreme Court Justice.

44. Which of the following is *not* a true statement regarding the Louisiana Purchase?

a. Jefferson sent a delegation to Paris to endeavor to purchase only the city of New Orleans from Napoleon.

b. Napoleon, anticipating U.S. intrusions into Louisiana, offered to sell the U.S. the entire Louisiana territory.

c. The American delegation accepted Napoleon's offer, though they were only authorized to buy New Orleans.

d. Jefferson wanted Congress's approval of this purchase, which they gave based on his power to make treaties.

e. The Louisiana Purchase, once it was completed, increased the territory of the U.S. by 50% overnight.

45. Which of these was *not* a factor that contributed to the duel in which Aaron Burr killed Alexander Hamilton?

a. Some Federalists who opposed U.S. Western expansion were attempting to organize a movement to secede from the Union.

b. Alexander Hamilton challenged Aaron Burr to a duel because he objected to U.S. expansion into the West, which Burr supported.

c. Secessionist Federalists tried to enlist Aaron Burr's support for their cause by backing him in his run for Governor of New York.

d. Alexander Hamilton was the leader of the group that opposed Aaron Burr's campaign to run for New York Governor.

e. When Aaron Burr lost the election for Governor of New York, he challenged Hamilton to a duel and killed him.

46. Which of these events was the *least* important contributing factor leading to the War of 1812?

a. Macon's Bill No. 2 empowered the President to ban trade with any country that violated U.S. neutrality.

b. British officials running Canada were egging Indian tribes on in their border attacks of U.S. settlements.

c. The Spanish, who were allied with the British, were in favor of the Indian tribes' attacks on U.S. settlements.

d. The Non-Intercourse Act put an embargo on trade with Britain and France, but opened trade to other countries.

e. Henry Clay and John C. Calhoun, both members of Congress, led the War Hawks in agitating Britain to push them to go to war.

47. Which of the following did *not* occur during the War of 1812?

a. Early in the war, the U.S. executed a three-pronged invasion of Canada and succeeded on two of three fronts.

b. Early in the war, Americans won naval battles against the British, but were soon beaten back by the British.

c. Admiral Oliver Hazard Perry's fleet defeated the British navy on Lake Erie in September, 1813.

d. William Henry Harrison invaded Canada and defeated the British and the Indians in the Battle of the Thames.

e. The famous *Old Ironsides* was a U.S. ship that defeated British ships before Britain overcame the U.S.

48. Which of the following is true about the Treaty of Ghent?

a. The Treaty of Ghent was signed on December 24, 1814.

b. The European wars were over when the treaty was signed.

c. The Battle of New Orleans occurred after this treaty was signed.

d. The treaty restored all war cessions of land to both sides.

e. All of the above

49. Which of the following statements is *not* true of the Federalists during and after the War of 1812?

a. The Federalists in New England were adamantly against the war to the point that they considered seceding.

b. Delegates from New England states met in Hartford, Connecticut in 1814 and wrote a set of resolutions.

c. Federalists were a strong majority until the Treaty of Ghent and the Battle of New Orleans ended the war.

d. News of Jackson's victory in the Battle of New Orleans discredited the Federalists and the Hartford Convention.

e. When Federalists were humiliated by the Treaty of Ghent's return to prewar status, their party was disbanded.

50. Which of these is *least* closely related to the Monroe Doctrine?

a. Countries in South America had been revolting since 1810 against European imperialist rule.
b. After Napoleon's defeat in 1814, many Latin Americans declared independence from Europe.
c. Spain sold the remainder of its Florida territories not taken by Jackson to America in 1819.
d. Both British and American leaders were afraid Europeans would try to retake former colonies.
e. Addressing Congress, President Monroe said the Americas would not be colonized by Europe.

51. Which statement is *not* true regarding the years after the War of 1812 in America?

a. America experienced accelerated economic and social development during this time.
b. Overly rapid progress alternating with depression caused a negative popular mood.
c. There was a severe depression in 1819, a backlash against accelerated growth.
d. America was changing from an agricultural society into an industrial society.
e. The trend toward westward expansion in the United States gained more momentum.

52. Of the following decisions by Supreme Court Chief Justice John Marshall, which one represents the first time a state law was nullified for violating a constitutional principle?

a. Marbury v. Madison
b. Dartmouth v. Woodward
c. McCulloch v. Maryland
d. Fletcher v. Peck
e. Gibbons v. Ogden

53. Which of the following is *not* correct about the growth of America in the first half of the 19th century?

a. By 1840, two thirds of all Americans resided west of the Allegheny Mountains.
b. The population of America doubled every 25 years during this time period.
c. The trend of westward expansion increased as more people migrated west.
d. Immigration to America from other countries was not substantial prior to 1820.
e. Around 1820, immigration to the U.S. increased, mainly from the British Isles.

54. Which of the following was the first canal built in New York State?

a. The Cayuga-Seneca Canal
b. The Chambly Canal
c. The Oswego Canal
d. The Barge Canal
e. The Erie Canal

55. Which of the following is *not* correct concerning the growth of American labor unions?

a. The new factory system separated workers from owners, which tended to depersonalize workplaces.
b. The goal of attaining an 8-hour work day stimulated growth in labor organizing in the early 1800s.
c. The first organized workers' strike was in Paterson, New Jersey in 1828, and was by child laborers.
d. Recurring downturns in the economy tended to limit workers' demands for rights until the 1850s.
e. The period of growth in the organization of labor was curtailed by the depression of 1837.

56. Which of the following is *not* true regarding public schools in the early 19th century?

a. Virtually no public schools existed in America prior to around 1815.
b. Schools were mainly financed by private corporate or religious groups.
c. Thomas Jefferson's plan of a free school in Virginia was realized.
d. American schools were elitist, catering to the rich and to males in academics.
e. The New York Free School represented a very unusual instance of a school for the poor.

57. Which of these statements is incorrect about colleges and universities in the early 19th century?

a. The total numbers of colleges and universities increased significantly during this time period.
b. In the early 19th century, all existing institutions of higher learning were private, not public.
c. All of the institutions of higher learning during this time period charged expensive tuitions.
d. Early colleges and universities offered a variety of courses and gave professional training.
e. Less than one out of ten young men attended a college or university, and no women attended.

58. Washington Irving (1783-1859) was one of the most popular early American writers to earn international popularity. Of the following other successful American authors, which one was born in the 18th century?

a. James Fenimore Cooper
b. Nathaniel Hawthorne
c. Herman Melville
d. Henry Wadsworth Longfellow
e. Edgar Allan Poe

59. Which of the following written works did Thomas Paine publish *after* the American Revolution?

a. Common Sense
b. Rights of Man
c. The Age of Reason
d. (b) and (c)
e. None of the above

60. Which of the following is *not* true about the Second Great Awakening?

a. This movement was a reaction against the Enlightenment emphasis on rationalism.
b. This movement emphasized individualized, personalized, emotional religious faith.
c. This movement was characterized by the participation of large numbers of women.
d. This movement was characterized by the participation of large numbers of blacks.
e. This movement's individualistic nature contradicted nationalism and expansionism.

61. Which of the following is *not* true regarding the situation in the U.S. before and around the presidential election of 1824?

a. The majority of the states had removed property ownership as a prequalification for voting.
b. Free black men did not have access to the polls in Southern states, but most voted in the North.
c. The Massachusetts state constitution set a precedent in liberalizing voting requirements in 1820.
d. Before 1824, there was little interest in national elections, as voters were left out of the process.
e. In 1824, the legislative caucuses that previously made presidential nominations were not used.

62. Which of the following statements is *not* true about the period from 1829-1841 in America?

a. This period of time was referred to as the "Age of Jackson" and/or the Jacksonian Democracy.
b. Members of the Electoral College were mainly being elected by the state legislatures at this time.
c. Alexis de Tocqueville remarked on America's "equality of condition" found in no other country.
d. The electorate had become widened by this time so that all white males were able to vote.
e. While more constituents were able to vote in these years, blacks and women were still excluded.

63. Of the following, who was *not* a candidate for President of the USA in the 1824 election?

a. Henry Clay
b. William H. Crawford
c. John Quincy Adams
d. John C. Calhoun
e. Andrew Jackson

64. Which party designations are correct relative to the American presidential election of 1828?

a. John Quincy Adams's party called themselves National Republicans and Andrew Jackson's party called themselves Democratic Republicans.
b. John Quincy Adams's party called themselves Democratic Republicans and Andrew Jackson's party called themselves National Republicans.
c. John Quincy Adams's party called themselves Democrats and Andrew Jackson's party called themselves Republicans.
d. John Quincy Adams's party called themselves Republicans and Andrew Jackson's party called themselves Democrats.
e. John Quincy Adams's party and Andrew Jackson's party both referred to themselves as Republicans.

65. Who made the speech in 1830 that included the famous expression, "Liberty and union, now and forever, one and inseparable!"?

a. Henry Clay
b. Andrew Jackson
c. Daniel Webster
d. William Henry Harrison
e. Robert Young Hayne

66. Which of the following is *not* true regarding the Bank of the United States?

a. Andrew Jackson was opposed to the national bank and wanted to eliminate it.
b. Henry Clay and Daniel Webster pushed a bill for early re-charter of the Bank.
c. Congress passed a bill to re-charter the Bank, but Jackson vetoed the bill.
d. In 1832, Jackson redistributed federal funds from the Bank to state/local banks.
e. The recession of 1837 was not Bank-related, but was due to inflation and loose credit.

67. Which of the following does *not* accurately describe events in America between 1829 and 1840?

a. President Martin Van Buren convinced Congress to set up an Independent Treasury in 1840 to make up for the demise of the national bank.
b. The Whigs nominated William Henry Harrison, the war hero who defeated the Indians at Tippecanoe, to run for President in 1836 and 1840.
c. William Henry Harrison won the 1836 election, but he died a month after inauguration, making his the shortest term in presidential history.
d. Andrew Jackson's presidency, or the Age of Jackson, was the start of the two-party political system and conventions, things America still has today.
e. Having visited America to study its prison system, Frenchman Alexis de Tocqueville published his book *Democracy in America* in 1835.

68. Which of the following statements is *not* true regarding movements toward reform in America during the 1840s?

a. American society was undergoing changes, which made conditions unstable and uncertain.
b. During this period of time, the traditional values of American society were being challenged.
c. The Romantic Movement, a reaction to the Enlightenment, was supportive of reforms.
d. Challenges to tradition brought about a desire for increased stability, order, and control.
e. All of the above statements are true.

69. Of the following American authors, which was *not* from the Southern United States?

a. Edgar Allan Poe
b. William Gilmore Simms
c. Augustus Longstreet
d. Francis Parkman
e. All of the above authors were from the Southern United States.

70. Which of the following utopian communities was considered the earliest commune in America?

a. New Harmony in Indiana
b. Brook Farm in Massachusetts
c. Nashoba near Memphis, Tennessee
d. The Oneida Community in New York
e. The Amana Community in Iowa

71. Which of the following was *not* a source of social reform in America during the 19th century?

a. The Catholic Church for Irish and German immigrants
b. The Church of Jesus Christ of Latter Day Saints (Mormon)
c. The Transcendentalist movement begun in Concord, Massachusetts
d. The Protestant Revivalist movement and its many subsects
e. The American Society for the Promotion of Temperance

72. Of the following areas that experienced innovations as a result of organized social reform in the 19th century, which one met with the *most* difficulty in its early years?

a. Higher education
b. Free public schools
c. Mental institutions
d. Prison reforms
e. Abolitionist movement

73. Which of the following did *not* occur in America between 1790 and 1860?

a. By 1860, the U.S. population was eight times more than in 1790.
b. Birth rates dropped, increasing the median age of the population.
c. Previously high rates of immigration declined during this period.
d. The number of people residing in urban areas increased five-fold.
e. All of the above changes took place in America from 1790 to 1860.

74. Which of the following was *not* an immediate effect of rapid urban growth in the 1800s?

a. Poor sanitation conditions in the cities
b. Epidemics of diseases in the cities
c. Inadequate police and fire protection
d. Widespread urban political corruption
e. Inadequate housing and transportation

75. Which of the following was *not* an example of violence in cities that occurred as a result of rapid urbanization in America in the 1830s?

a. Democrats opposed Whigs in New York City so strenuously that the state militia was called in.
b. Both New York City and Philadelphia experienced a series of racial riots during the mid-1830s.
c. A Catholic convent was attacked and plundered by a violent mob in New York City in 1834.
d. There were 115 major incidents of mob violence reported in American cities during the 1830s.
e. All of the above occurred in American cities during the 1830s.

95

76. Which of the following is the *most* accurate description of the relationship between agriculture and industry in the 19th century?

a. With industrial and technological advances, farming was left behind in favor of industrial work.

b. With more urban workers needing food, farming became more important than industrial work.

c. Specialization and mechanization were applied more to agriculture at this time than to industry.

d. The development of both agriculture and industry was helped by technological innovations.

e. Specialization and mechanization were applied more to industry than to agriculture at this time.

77. Which of the following does *not* accurately describe life in the Northern United States from 1800-1860?

a. By 1860, the production of goods and services increased to twelve times that of 1800.

b. The purchasing power of the average working person increased by 100% during this time.

c. Everyday life became more comfortable thanks to big houses, indoor plumbing, and electricity.

d. For the first time, wage earners outnumbered independent self-employed workers.

e. All of the above statements accurately describe life in the Northern states from 1800-1860.

78. Which of the following statements is *not* true about the classes in the Southern states from 1800 to 1860?

a. The class of small, independent yeoman farmers represented the largest number of Southern whites.

b. The lowest class of severely poor Southern whites, or "crackers," numbered around one million.

c. In the planter class, those who owned large farms with 50 or more slaves were a small minority.

d. Three quarters of Southern whites within the planter class did not own any slaves at all.

e. Nearly half of all slave owners owned fewer than six slaves, and 12% owned 20 or more slaves.

79. Which of the following is true regarding Southern plantation slaves in the U.S. in the 1800s?

a. Whether Southern plantation slaves lived better or worse lives than Northern wage laborers remains a subject of debate among historians.

b. The consensus among historians about this time period is that Southern plantation slaves actually lived better lives than Northern wage laborers.

c. The consensus among historians about this time period is that Southern plantation slaves had worse lives than Northern wage laborers.

d. The lives of Southern plantation slaves were worse than those of comparable slaves who worked in South America during this period.

e. The lives of Southern plantation slaves were worse than those of comparable slaves who worked in the Caribbean during this period.

80. Which of the following statements does *not* characterize life in the Southern states from 1800-1860?

a. By 1860, half of all illiterate Americans resided in the South.
b. Southerners lived in cabins with one or two rooms, as did Northerners.
c. The staple foods of the Southern diet were corn, sweet potatoes, and pork.
d. Southerners had stopped settling disputes with duels by around 1800.
e. The Southern diet led to vitamin deficiencies, rickets, and pellagra.

81. Which of the following was *not* a Southern reaction to the abolitionist movement?

a. People defended slavery, citing scriptures as justifications.
b. People cited "scientific" evidence of black "inferiority."
c. Postal services charged extra to deliver anti-slavery mail.
d. All disagreement was squelched, causing a closed society.
e. Narrow mindedness made creative and academic writing wither.

82. Which of the following is *not* true of Southern actions in response to the question of slavery in the 1830s?

a. The last major Southern debate on slavery was held in the South Carolina legislature in 1836.
b. After Nat Turner's rebellion, a big legislative discussion stopped future talk of emancipation.
c. Southerners in the House passed the "gag rule," banning all talk of slavery on the House floor.
d. John C. Calhoun's "concurrent majority" would separate North and South with dual presidents.
e. Regular Southern conventions began in 1837 to discuss strategies to avoid Northern dominance.

83. Which of the following statements is *incorrect* about U.S. westward expansion and Manifest Destiny?

a. The idea that U.S. freedom and values should be shared with, even forced upon, as many people as possible had existed for many years.
b. The term "Manifest Destiny" and the idea it represented had been used for many years prior to the 1830s.
c. Many Americans believed that America as a nation should ultimately be extended to include Canada and Mexico.
d. Increased nationalism after the resolution of the War of 1812 and rapid population growth added to Manifest Destiny.
e. Reform movements and economic growth during the 1830s required markets and resources, which contributed to Manifest Destiny.

84. Regarding the Oregon country, in addition to the United States, which of the following other countries had *not* claimed the territory north of California and west of Louisiana at some point before the 1820s?

a. England
b. Spain
c. France
d. Russia
e. They had all claimed the territory at some point.

85. Which of the following statements is *not* true concerning the Whig Party, Henry Clay, and John Tyler?

a. President William Henry Harrison yielded to Henry Clay's influence to enforce Whig policies.
b. When Harrison died after a month in office, Vice President John Tyler succeeded as President.
c. Whigs chose Tyler to get Southern votes, but he was a constitutionalist in favor of states' rights.
d. Tyler, influenced by Clay, agreed with most of the Whig policies, but he disagreed with a few.
e. Tyler rejected the Whigs' whole program, and when Clay pushed it, he vetoed quite a few bills.

86. Which of the following is *incorrect* about the Webster-Ashburton Treaty?

a. Britain promised they would not stop or search American ships when patrolling the African coast to prevent the smuggling of slaves.
b. Britain and America arrived at a compromise to settle their conflict over mutual claims on the boundary between Canada and Maine.
c. Britain apologized for Canadian loyalists who burned the American ship the *Caroline*, which was taking supplies to Canadian rebels.
d. Britain promised not to interfere again as they had with the American ship the *Creole* by refusing to return slaves who had escaped.
e. Britain and America both agreed to cooperate in the future during their patrols of the African coast to stop the smuggling of slaves.

87. Which of the following statements is *not* accurate regarding the annexation of Texas and the election of 1844?

a. With no political party, President Tyler sought a following by proposing that Texas be annexed.
b. Mexico threatened to declare war if America annexed Texas because it was a Mexican territory.
c. Expansionist Democrats replaced anti-annexation Van Buren with James Polk at the convention.
d. Whig Henry Clay opposed annexation, but faltered and lost Northern votes to the Liberty Party.
e. When Polk won, lame-duck president Tyler got a joint resolution passed to annex Texas in 1845.

88. Which of the following was *not* a factor that contributed to the Mexican War?

a. During its many revolutions, Mexico could not protect American citizens, and did not pay their damages claims.
b. Mexico still resented America's annexation of Texas to the Union, and regarded it as a hostile action.
c. America claimed the Rio Grande as Texas's southern border, while Mexico claimed the Nueces River as the border.
d. Mexico was resentful of the American seizure of California in 1842, and was campaigning for its return.
e. Mexican politicians created anti-American bias in the people, so leaders feared revolt for conceding to the U.S.

89. Which of the following was *not* one of the prongs of President Polk's military strategy in attacking Mexico following the U.S. declaration of war against Mexico in 1846?

a. A land movement to California via New Mexico
b. A movement over the water to invade California
c. A movement over the water to go into Mexico
d. A land movement going south to invade Mexico
e. All of the above were prongs of the attack on Mexico.

90. Which of the following battles of the Mexican War was *not* won by General Zachary Taylor?

a. The Battle of Palo Alto
b. The Battle of Resaca de la Palma
c. The Battle of Monterey
d. The Battle of Buena Vista
e. The Battle of Sacramento

91. Who negotiated the treaty that put an end to the Mexican War?

a. USA President James K. Polk
b. State Dept. clerk Nicholas Trist
c. USA General Winfield Scott
d. U.S. Colonel Stephen W. Kearny
e. U.S. Commodore Robert Stockton

92. Which of the following is *not* true about the Compromise of 1850?

a. This eight-part compromise was originally proposed by Henry Clay.
b. John C. Calhoun felt the North must cater to the South and back off slavery.
c. President Taylor opposed it, but his successor Fillmore supported it.
d. Illinois Senator Stephen Douglas got it through Congress piecemeal.
e. Americans reacted ambivalently to it, and many were opposed to it.

93. Relative to the election of 1852, which of the following statements is *incorrect*?

a. The Democratic convention chose Lewis Cass, Stephen Douglas, and Franklin Pierce to run.
b. The Whig Party nominated Gen. Winfield Scott, a hero of the Mexican War but not a politician.
c. Northern and Southern Whigs disagreed over the Compromise of 1850, causing a rift in the party.
d. John P. Hale ran for the Free Soil Party, but had little success as people had tired of slavery issues.
e. Divisiveness in the Whig Party was causing it to fail as a party, making it easier for Pierce to win.

94. Of the following factors that contributed to U.S. economic development in the 1840s and 1850s, which was the *most* influential?

a. The improvement of water transportation by steamboats on the rivers and clipper ships on the seas

b. The advancement of agriculture in the North through the use of mechanical reapers and threshers

c. The flourishing of agriculture in the Southern states because of their success in farming "King Cotton"

d. The improvement of land transportation via the growth of railroads, which created a nationwide market

e. The textile industry's factory system, which made use of Howe's sewing machine and Singer's improved model

95. Which of the following is *not* an accurate statement related to the Kansas-Nebraska Act of 1854?

a. This bill was introduced by Illinois Senator Stephen A. Douglas to organize land west of Missouri and Iowa.

b. The passage of this act ended the period of sectional peace because of its repeal of the Missouri Compromise.

c. Douglas wanted a repeal of the Missouri Compromise in the act to allow possible slavery in these territories.

d. Douglas wanted to organize these territories to expedite the construction of a transcontinental railroad to benefit Illinois.

e. Whigs and Northern Democrats were against this bill, but Pierce's mostly Southern administration passed it.

96. Which of the following is *most* accurate regarding how the passage of the Kansas-Nebraska Act was related to the emergence of the Republican Party?

a. The passage of the Kansas-Nebraska Act strengthened the newly established Republican Party.

b. Anger over the passage of the Kansas-Nebraska Act sparked the formation of the Republicans.

c. The deteriorating Whigs and the divided Democrats allowed Republicans to prevail separately.

d. When the Republican Party formed, it soon became a major political power in North and South.

e. The newly formed Republican Party believed that slavery should be eradicated in all the states.

97. Which of the following statements is *false* regarding the 1856 Dred Scott case in the Supreme Court?

a. The Supreme Court's decision in the Dred Scott case definitively resolved the sectional disputes.

b. Scott was advised by abolitionists to sue for his freedom based on living in free areas for years.

c. Initially, the justices of the Supreme Court felt Scott could not sue, as a slave was not a citizen.

d. President-elect James Buchanan wanted the justices to finally settle the slavery controversy.

e. The Supreme Court ruled that Congress and territories did not have the right to ban slavery.

98. Which of the following led to the Panic of 1857?

a. Overspeculation in land and railroads
b. Flawed procedures in banking
c. The Crimean War in Europe
d. (a), (b), and (c)
e. None of the above

99. Which of the following is *not* true about the Lincoln-Douglas debates?

a. These debates were held as part of the campaign for Senator from Illinois.
b. The subject matter of the debates revolved around the issue of slavery.
c. Abraham Lincoln's success in these debates won him the Senate seat.
d. Abraham Lincoln's success in these debates brought him new fame.
e. Abraham Lincoln's success made the Republican Party stronger.

100. Which of the following states was not one of the original seven to secede from the Union and form the Confederacy?

a. South Carolina
b. Georgia
c. Texas
d. North Carolina
e. Florida

101. Which of the following was *not* a difference between the Constitution of the Confederate States and the United States Constitution?

a. It was allowed in the Constitution of the Confederate States to impose protective tariffs.
b. Slavery was recognized, and the right to move slaves to other states was guaranteed.
c. The president would serve a six-year term, and this term was not renewable.
d. The president had the right to veto individual items found in appropriations bills.
e. The sovereignty of each of the individual states was recognized specifically.

102. Which of the following statements is correct regarding President Buchanan and his role in the secession of the Confederate states from the Union?

a. President Buchanan was a lame-duck president by the time the Confederacy had its constitution.
b. President Buchanan announced that it was unconstitutional for states to secede from the Union.
c. President Buchanan said it was unconstitutional for the federal government to stop state secessions.
d. President Buchanan probably disagreed with the secessions, but did not think he should interfere.
e. All of the above statements are correct.

103. Which of the following is *not* true concerning Kentucky Senator John J. Crittenden's compromise proposals to save the Union during the secessions by southern states?

a. The proposals included an amendment to stop the federal government from interfering with slavery.

b. The proposals included extending the Missouri Compromise line out as far as the Pacific Ocean.

c. The proposals were to protect slavery in all the territories south of the extended compromise line.

d. Discussions broke down even though some Southerners were willing to consider compromising.

e. President-elect Lincoln told Republicans not to accept compromise, but to insist slavery not spread.

104. Of the following slave states, which seceded from the Union?

a. Delaware

b. Kentucky

c. Tennessee

d. Maryland

e. Missouri

105. Which of the following was not an advantage the North had over the South at the beginning of the Civil War?

a. The North was much wealthier than the South, and could better afford the costs of being at war.

b. The North had more experienced, qualified, and higher-ranking military officers than the South.

c. The North was better developed industrially, and could manufacture the necessary war material.

d. The North had nearly triple the manpower since slaves made up a third of the Southern population.

e. The North had a railroad system that was a great deal better than the South's smaller railroads.

106. Which of the following statements is *least* accurate regarding advantages the South had at the beginning of the Civil War?

a. The South was such a geographically large area that it was more of a challenge to defeat.

b. The Southern soldiers had the home advantage of fighting on their own familiar land.

c. The South's armies had the additional motivation of defending their own families and homes.

d. The South had the major advantage of its armies fighting defensive battles, which was easier.

e. The South had President Jefferson Davis's military experience, which was superior to Lincoln's.

107. Which of the following is *not* true about the Battle of Shiloh?

a. This battle was the bloodiest battle ever in the history of America up to that point in time.
b. General Beauregard joined General A.S. Johnston and took Ulysses S. Grant by surprise.
c. With other Northern victories, this battle allowed the Union to take all of the Mississippi River.
d. Despite being taken by surprise, Grant was not defeated by Beauregard and Johnston.
e. In this battle that lasted for two days, General A.S. Johnston was killed, along with many others.

108. Which of the following is *not* a correct statement regarding Britain, France, and Northern diplomacy in the Civil War?

a. Many Southerners thought that Britain and France would be glad the U.S. division weakened it.
b. Many Southerners thought that Britain and France would intervene for the South, needing cotton.
c. Britain had stockpiles of prewar cotton, and they imported it from Indian and Egypt as well.
d. British leaders felt it more important to import Southern cotton than Northern wheat from the U.S.
e. William Seward and Charles Francis Adams convinced Britain to be neutral, and France followed.

109. Which of the following does *not* describe how the North and South dealt with the expense of the Civil War?

a. Measures instituted by the South resulted in extreme inflation and then in confiscations.
b. The paper money that the Southern government issued made up for its scarce resources.
c. The North imposed high tariffs and the country's first income tax to help pay for the war.
d. The North's Treasury Dept. issued "greenbacks," which were helped by belief the North would win.
e. The Union passed the National Banking Act in 1863 to increase its available credit.

110. Which of the following is *not* true regarding the Emancipation Proclamation?

a. Overall, the public in the North was enthusiastic about Lincoln's issuance of the proclamation.
b. Radical Republicans who were abolitionists had been pressuring Lincoln to issue it for some time.
c. This proclamation freed all slaves in areas that were still in rebellion as of January 1, 1863.
d. The North had had many defeats in Virginia, so Seward advised Lincoln to wait for a victory first.
e. Lincoln waited to announce this proclamation until after victory at Antietam on September 17, 1863.

111. Which of the following statements is *not* correct concerning the 1864 election and the end of the Civil War in 1865?

a. By 1864, Jefferson Davis had decided to resort to including blacks in the Confederate armies.
b. Per Jefferson Davis's decision, freed black slaves were conscripted to the Confederate military.
c. During 1864, people were so tired of the war that even Lincoln felt he would lose the election.
d. Sherman's capture of Atlanta and his March to the Sea helped Lincoln win the election.
e. Lincoln was assassinated before he could receive news of the North's final victory in the war.

112. Which of the following was *not* true of Andrew Johnson's actions for the Reconstruction?

a. Johnson adhered quite closely to the policies of his predecessor, the late Abraham Lincoln.
b. Johnson's alignment with Lincoln's policies meant he made some only a little bit stricter.
c. Johnson required that the Thirteenth Amendment officially abolishing slavery be ratified.
d. Johnson required that all of the debts incurred by the Confederacy be paid.
e. Johnson required that secession be renounced, and recommended blacks be given the vote.

113. Which of the following is not accurate regarding America's purchase of Alaska from the Russians?

a. The Russian minister offered to sell Alaska to Secretary of State Seward in 1866.
b. The depletion of most of Alaska's available fur was a motivation for Russia to sell it.
c. Russians felt they would lose Alaska to Britain in a war, which looked likely then.
d. Seward, a strong expansionist, pushed the USA's purchase of Alaska through Congress.
e. In 1867, the United States purchased Alaska from Russia for a price of $5.5 million.

114. Resistance in some Southern states to President Johnson's Reconstruction plan took all except which of the following forms?

a. Refusing to ratify the Thirteenth Amendment
b. Refusing to renounce the Confederates' debt
c. Refusing to pass black codes on freed slaves
d. Refusing to grant voting privileges to blacks
e. Electing many past Confederates to Congress

115. Which of the following is *not* true about the 1868 election and the Fifteenth Amendment?

a. Due to his record as a Civil War hero, Ulysses S. Grant won the election by a landslide.
b. When the Republican Convention met in 1868, it was controlled by the Radicals.
c. The platform of the Republicans in 1868 recommended Radical Reconstruction.
d. Implications of election voting led Republicans to draw up the 15th Amendment.
e. Ratification by Southern states forced by Congress won the amendment approval.

116. Which of the following is *not* an accurate description of an outcome of the Reconstruction?

a. Corrupt political machines rose to power in both the North and South.
b. Property values in the South were reduced to half of prewar levels.
c. Southerners were distressed by the presence of the carpetbaggers.
d. Southerners were consternated by the existence of the scalawags.
e. The Ku Klux Klan used violence to stop pro-Reconstruction votes.

117. Which of the following was *not* one of the scandals associated with corruption that existed during Grant's presidency?

a. The Black Friday Scandal
b. The Salary Grab
c. The Whiskey Ring Fraud
d. The bribing of Belknap
e. All of the above scandals occurred during Grant's presidency.

118. Which of the following is true about economic issues during U.S. Grant's presidency?

a. Economic conservatives, business owners, and creditors were in favor of inflation.
b. People who had financial debts were more in favor of the deflation of currency.
c. The demonetization of silver by Congress in 1873 upset those favoring deflation.
d. Those favoring deflation wanted a return to the gold standard and no greenbacks.
e. The Specie Resumption Act of 1875 favored greenbacks over the gold standard.

119. Which of the following is *incorrect* concerning the election of 1876?

a. Democrats nominated Samuel J. Tilden, Governor of New York.
b. Democratic candidate Samuel J. Tilden had defeated the Tweed machine.
c. Democrats and Republicans were fraudulent, and so were both candidates.
d. Ohio Governor Rutherford B. Hayes was the selection of the Republicans.
e. Republican manipulations of the congressional commission got Hayes elected.

120. Which of the following statements is *not* true of the Compromise of 1877?

a. It was a response to a threat made by incensed Democrats in Congress.
b. It modified Reconstruction to appease both Republicans and Democrats.
c. Hayes promised he would take Southerners' interests into consideration.
d. Hayes promised he would remove all the federal troops left in the South.
e. Hayes agreed to end Reconstruction if Democrats accepted his election.

Answers and Explanations

1. E: The Treaty of Tordesillas was between Spain and Portugal. It was executed in 1491, not in the 1500s (a). The treaty did not set up a "Line of Demarcation" (b); this line was previously established 100 leagues west of the Cape Verde Islands by the Pope in response to demands by Ferdinand and Isabella of Spain to confirm their South American colonization. Since the line's division gave more territory to Spain than Portugal, but Portugal had a more powerful navy at the time, Spain and Portugal agreed through the Treaty of Tordesillas to move the Line of Demarcation farther west, not east (c). The treaty was not initiated by the Pope (d); he established the original Line of Demarcation. The treaty moved this line west, and Spain and Portugal agreed to this treaty. .

2. C: Hernando Cortes conquered the Mexican Aztecs in 1519. He had several advantages over the Indians, including horses, armor for his soldiers, and guns. In addition, Cortes' troops unknowingly transmitted smallpox to the Aztecs, which devastated their population as they had no immunity to this foreign illness. Vasco Nunez de Balboa (a) was the first European explorer to view the Pacific Ocean when he crossed the Isthmus of Panama in 1513. Juan Ponce de Leon (b) also visited and claimed Florida in Spain's name in 1513. Cabeza de Vaca (d) was one of only four men out of 400 to return from an expedition led by Panfilio de Narvaez in 1528, and was responsible for spreading the story of the Seven Cities of Cibola (the "cities of gold"). Hernando de Soto (e) led an expedition from 1539-1541 to the southeastern part of America.

3. B: Hernando de Soto led an expedition of 600 men to southeastern America between 1539 and 1541, getting as far west as Oklahoma and discovering the Mississippi River in the process. Francisco Vasquez de Coronado (a) and his men made an expedition to southwestern America between 1540 and 1542, traveling from Mexico across the Rio Grande and going to New Mexico, Arizona, Texas, Oklahoma, and Kansas. In the process, they became some of the first European explorers to see the Grand Canyon. Hernando Cortes (c) conquered the Aztecs of Mexico in 1519. Juan Ponce de Leon (d) explored Florida looking for the Fountain of Youth and for gold in 1513. At the time, he also claimed Florida for Spain. Panfilio de Narvaez (e) led an expedition to the Gulf Coast area of America in 1528. It failed, and only a few of the hundreds of men who participated in this expedition returned.

4. D: The conquistadores had to deal with labor shortages during their colonization of America in the 16th century. This was attributable to the fact that Spain during this time did not suffer from overpopulation (e), so only about 200,000 Spaniards migrated to America, not 300,000 (e). To address the shortage of labor, the Spanish first used Indian slaves. Only after the Indians were decimated by diseases brought from Europe and from being overworked did the Spanish begin to import slaves from Africa (b). The first system used by the Spanish was the *encomienda* system of large estates or manors, which was only later succeeded by the *hacienda* system (c), which was similar but not as harsh. It is not true that New Spain's society had no kind of class system (a). In fact, this society was rigidly divided into three strata. The highest class was Spanish natives (*peninsulares*), the middle class consisted of those born in America to Spanish parents (*creoles*), and the lowest class was made up of Mestizos, or Indians.

5. E: All of these explorers were involved in the search for a Northwest Passage (i.e. a route over water from North America to Asia). Giovannia da Verrazzano (a) of Italy sailed under the French flag in 1524 and went up the coast of America from what is now North Carolina to what is now Maine. John Cabot (b) of Italy, also known as Giovanni Caboto, was commissioned by England to look for a Northwest Passage in 1497, and was the first European to come to North America since the Vikings claimed the land in England's name. Jacques Cartier (c) made three expeditions to America beginning in 1534 on behalf of France. He explored and claimed the St. Lawrence River

106

area, progressing as far as Montreal in Canada. Ferdinand Magellan (d) of Portugal discovered a water route around the southern tip of South America in 1519. When he set sail five years after Verrazzano, Magellan hoped to follow in the earlier explorer's footsteps.

6. A: It is not true that England's defeat of the Spanish Armada in 1588 ended their war with Spain. It did establish England's naval dominance and strengthened England's future colonization of the New World, but the actual war between England and Spain did not end until 1604. It is true that Henry VIII's desire to divorce Catherine of Aragon strengthened English expansionism (b). Catherine was Spanish, and Henry split from the Catholic Church because it prohibited divorce. Henry's rejection of his Spanish wife and his subsequent support of the Protestant movement angered King Philip II of Spain and destroyed the formerly close ties between the two countries. When Elizabeth became Queen of England, she supported the Reformation as a Protestant, which also contributed to English colonization (c). Sir Francis Drake, one of the best known English sea captains during this time period, would attack and plunder Spanish ships that had plundered American Indians (d), adding to the enmity between Spain and England. Queen Elizabeth invested in Drake's voyages and gave him her support in claiming territories for England (e).

7. B: The Virginia Company of London was based in London, not Massachusetts. It had a charter to colonize American land between the Hudson and Cape Fear rivers (c). The other Virginia Company was the Virginia Company of Plymouth, which was based in the American colony of Plymouth, Massachusetts (a). It had a charter to colonize North America between the Potomac River and the northern boundary of Maine (d). Both Virginia Companies were joint-stock companies (e), which had often been used by England for trading with other countries.

8. E: It is not true that John Smith's governance helped Jamestown more than John Rolfe's discovery that a certain type of East Indian tobacco could be grown in Virginia. Smith's strong leadership from 1608-1609 gave great support to the struggling colony. However, when Smith's return to England left Jamestown without this support, the future of the colony was again in question. In 1612, however, when John Rolfe found that an East Indian tobacco strain popular in Europe could be farmed in Virginia, the discovery gave Jamestown and Virginia a lucrative crop. Therefore, both Smith's time in office and Rolfe's discovery were beneficial to Jamestown. Jamestown was established by the Virginia Company of London in 1607 (a), and it became the first permanent settlement by the English in North America (b). It is also true that Jamestown survived in spite of the fact that most of its early settlers died from starvation, disease, and Indian attacks (c). It is also true that many of Jamestown's settlers came from the English upper class and were unwilling to farm the land, while others came hoping to find gold or other treasures, and persisted in their search for these instead of working to make the land sustainable (d).

9. C: The Pilgrims were not Puritans seeking to escape religious persecution in England. They were actually English Separatists (d) who believed there was no fixing the Church of England, and thus chose to separate from it. They did embark on the *Mayflower* in 1620, and storms drove the ship to land at Cape Cod, Massachusetts (a). Their leader was William Bradford, and they had been given a charter by the London Company to settle America (b) south of the Hudson River. The Pilgrims knew that going ashore would leave them without any existing government, so while still on board the ship they created the Mayflower Compact (e) so that their New World colony would have a basis for government from its inception.

10. D: It is not true that Colonel Nicols granted very few civil or political rights to New York colonials. In fact, he gave them as many civil and political rights as possible to make up for the fact that James, Duke of York, who conquered New Amsterdam with his brother King Charles II's authorization (b), was strongly against representation for colonists, and prohibited any

representative assemblies in his renamed New York (c). Despite Nicols' allowing colonial citizens many other rights, they still wanted to govern themselves, especially Long Island's Puritans (e). James gave in to their demands in the 1680s, but upon his accession to the throne of England in 1685, he went back on his word. It is true that before the English conquered the New York territories, New Amsterdam on Manhattan Island was a trading settlement of the New Netherlands made by Dutch explorers to facilitate the Dutch West India Company's fur trade with the Indians (a).

11. A: Women settlers outnumbering male settlers was not something that contributed to the differences between life in the New England colonies and life in the Chesapeake colonies. In Virginia and Maryland, men greatly outnumbered women due to these colonies' large tobacco farms, which required men as workers. New England colonists did have life expectancies that were between 15 and 20 years longer than did Chesapeake colonists (b). Because Puritans lived longer, came to America with their families (most Chesapeake colonists came as individual indentured servants), and were a more homogeneous population, society in colonial New England was better organized and more stable than in the Chesapeake colonies (c). Puritans were also great believers in literacy because they felt it was so important to be able to read the Bible, so they had educational advantages over the colonies to the south (d). Because of the disproportionate sex ratio and the shorter life spans of Chesapeake settlers, their family and social lives were not as continuous or as stable as in New England. The fact that large tobacco farms such as those in Virginia and Maryland were not feasible in New England actually led to a better economy (e). A combination of smaller farms, cottage industries, trading, fishing and ship building industries, and the resulting emergence of Boston as a chief international seaport all contributed to local prosperity in New England.

12. D: While it is true that British mercantilism, used partly as a weapon against Holland, did contribute to three wars between Britain and Holland in the late 17th century, it is not true that mercantilism never contributed to colonial prosperity. It did contribute to the wealth of the New England colonies by supporting their active ship building industry. Conversely, mercantilism was harmful to the Chesapeake colonies because it lowered prices on tobacco crops, their main source of income. Mercantilism did make England richer and the American colonies poorer by raising prices for British goods for Americans and lowering prices on American goods (e). According to English mercantilism, economic enterprises should always be government controlled (a). As subjects of the British Empire, American colonies definitely contributed to the mercantilist system by farming many crops that the England could take advantage of (b) instead of having to import them from foreign countries. To enforce colonial supply of crops to England, Parliament passed the Navigation Acts from 1651 to 1673 (c).

13. E: It is not true that Penn initially established his colony without representative assembly. He began the settlement by guaranteeing colonists not only complete religious freedom, but also a representative assembly. It is true that Pennsylvania and Delaware, which was originally part of Pennsylvania, were established to give Quakers religious freedom (a), which they did not enjoy anywhere else in Britain or America. In addition to being pacifists, it is true that the Quakers were aggressively outspoken against the establishment and the class system (b). The Quakers were religious, but their religious beliefs were that each individual could communicate directly with God, so they did not find either the Bible or most human institutions important (c). The Quakers did originate in England around the time of the English Civil War as one of several radical religious groups (d).

14. B: King William's War, which was fought between 1689 and1697, included quite a few violent border attacks by Indians in America, but no major army battles. The Treaty of Ryswick ending this war did not make any changes in territories. Queen Anne's War (a), which lasted from 1702 to

1713, was fought against France and Spain. It was ended by the Treaty of Utrecht, which ceded much territory to England. King George's War (c), which lasted from 1739 to 1748, involved major army battles on American soil. American soldiers went on a number of expeditions with British troops. The Treaty of Aix-la-Chapelle ended this war. In it, England returned Louisbourg to France, trading it for territories on the Indian continent. The French and Indian War (d), which lasted from 1754 to 1763, featured many army battles on American soil. The 1763 Treaty of Paris ending this war ceded all of France's territories in Canada and North America to England. Since (b) is the correct answer, (e) is incorrect.

15. C: The charter to found Georgia was not granted in 1765. It was granted to General James Oglethorpe in 1732. In fact, by 1752, Oglethorpe's group felt that they had failed with this colony. The original purpose of the Georgia colony was indeed to create a buffer zone between South Carolina and Florida (a), which was a Spanish territory then. There were numerous wars being fought in the area between British and American troops and other imperialist countries. Oglethorpe was a British philanthropist, and he and his followers did found the Georgia colony (b). Oglethorpe and his group, as trustees who ran the colony for its first 21 years, laid down a great many rules in an effort to guide the colony's administration and development. This practice, however, meant that few people wanted to settle there. The few who did constantly complained about all of the rules (d). These settlers were made up of former British subjects who had lived in poverty in Britain (e) and migrated in the hopes of achieving greater success in the New World.

16. E: Among American political philosophers and writers who embraced the Enlightenment, Benjamin Franklin was the most famous. It is not true that this movement began in America and spread to Europe (a). On the contrary, it developed simultaneously in many European countries, and then spread to America. It is not true that the importance of God in the world was one of its central premises (b). The Enlightenment was a rationalist movement. According to its philosophy, the application of human critical thinking had more importance in solving problems than any divine intervention. It is not true that John Locke, a major British Enlightenment figure, believed governments should not be deposed for violating social or political rights (c). He believed the opposite: that if a government did not allow its citizens such rights, it was a valid reason to overthrow that government. This kind of thinking is also seen in the Enlightenment belief of challenging a society's traditional moral values, practices, and existing institutions rather than always upholding them (d).

17. D: Benjamin Franklin was not particularly associated with the Great Awakening, but was closely associated with the Enlightenment. William Tennent (a) and Gilbert Tennent (b) were Presbyterian ministers associated with the Great Awakening. Theodore Frelinghuysen (c) was a Dutch Reformed minister associated with this movement. Jonathan Edwards (e) was a Congregationalist minister whose sermon entitled "Sinners in the Hands of an Angry God" became very famous in American literature as well as in American religion and philosophy. (Note: A Great Awakening preacher who also had great influence in America was George Whitefield. Although he made many speeches to large crowds in America, he was actually British.)

18. B: After fighting began in American in 1754, the war spread to Europe in 1756, where it was called the Seven Years' War. In America, it was called the French and Indian War. George Washington, who was then a major in the Virginia militia, was sent to Pennsylvania to expunge the French, but he was not successful (a). He initially won a skirmish, but his troops were outnumbered, so they retreated and then surrendered. Meanwhile, delegates came from seven of the colonies to meet in Albany, N.Y. to confer on defense plans. The delegate who proposed the idea of an intercolonial government (c) was Benjamin Franklin, not Thomas Jefferson. Though other colonial delegates did not agree, Franklin's idea is considered significant because it set a precedent

for presenting a united front against a common enemy, something America did in later wars such as World Wars I and II. Major General Braddock of England was ambushed en route to Fort Duquesne (d), but he did not defeat the French and Indian fighters who ambushed his troops. Instead, Braddock and two thirds of the British troops were killed in this battle. In 1763, the Treaty of Paris ended the French and Indian War. As a result of this treaty, all of France's territories in Canada and the rest of North America were ceded to England (e).

19. A: The attitudes of American colonists after the 1763 Treaty of Paris ended the French and Indian War was not a direct contributor to the American Revolution. American colonists had a supportive attitude toward Great Britain then, and were proud of the part they played in winning the war. Their good will was not returned by British leaders (b), who looked down on American colonials and sought to increase their imperial power over them. Even in 1761, a sign of Americans' objections to having their liberty curtailed by the British was seen when Boston attorney James Otis argued in court against the Writs of Assistance (c), search warrants to enforce England's mercantilist trade restrictions, as violating the kinds of natural laws espoused during the Enlightenment. Lord George Grenville's aggressive program to defend the North American frontier in the wake of Chief Pontiac's attacks included stricter enforcement of the Navigation Acts, the Proclamation of 1763, the Sugar Act (or Revenue Act), the Currency Act, and most of all the Stamp Act (d). Colonists objected to these as taxation without representation. Other events followed in this taxation dispute, which further eroded Americans' relationship with British government, including the Townshend Acts, the Massachusetts Circular Letter, the Boston Massacre, the Tea Act, and the resulting Boston Tea Party. Finally, with Britain's passage of the Intolerable Acts and the Americans' First Continental Congress, which was followed by Britain's military aggression against American resistance, actual warfare began in 1775. While not all of the colonies wanted war or independence by then, things changed by 1776, and Jefferson's Declaration of Independence was formalized. James Otis, Samuel Adams, Patrick Henry, the Sons of Liberty, and the Stamp Act Congress (e) also contributed to the beginning of the American Revolution.

20. C: Colonists did find that tea shipped directly by the British East India Company cost less than smuggled Dutch tea, even with tax. The colonists, however, did not buy it. They refused, despite its lower cost, on the principle that the British were taxing colonists without representation (d). It is true that the British East India Company lost money as a result of colonists buying tea smuggled from Holland (a). They sought to remedy this problem by getting concessions from Parliament to ship tea directly to the colonies instead of going through England (b) as the Navigation Acts normally required. Boston Governor Thomas Hutchinson, who sided with Britain, stopped tea ships from leaving the harbor, which after 20 days would cause the tea to be sold at auction. At that time, British taxes on the tea would be paid. On the 19th night after Hutchinson's action, American protestors held the Boston Tea Party, dressing as Indians and dumping all the tea into the harbor to destroy it so it could not be taxed and sold. Many American colonists disagreed with the Boston Tea Party because it involved destroying private property. When Lord North and the British Parliament responded by passing the Coercive Acts and the Quebec Act, known collectively in America as the Intolerable Acts, Americans changed their minds (e), siding with the Bostonians against the British.

21. D: Paul Revere (a) and William Dawes (b) were both dispatch riders who set out on horseback from Massachusetts to spread news of British troop movements across the American countryside around the beginning of the War of Independence. John Parker (c) was the captain of the Minutemen militia, who were waiting for the British at Lexington, Massachusetts. Since (d) is correct, (e) is incorrect.

22. E: General William Howe (a), General Henry Clinton (b), and General John Burgoyne (c) were all British generals who came to Boston in May of 1775 to push General Gage to pursue further aggression against Americans. Since (e) is correct, (d), (a and c only) is incorrect.

23. E: Only (a) and (b) are correct. Ethan Allen (a) and Benedict Arnold (b) led the troops that captured Fort Ticonderoga in May of 1775. Following this victory, on December 31 of 1775, General Richard Montgomery (c) led an expedition to Montreal and Quebec to try to enlist the aid of Canada in America's resistance to Britain. This expedition met with another expedition led by Benedict Arnold. Their assault on Quebec was not successful. Montgomery was killed and Arnold was wounded. Since answer (e) is correct, answer (d) (a, b, and c) is incorrect.

24. C: The earliest event was the Second Continental Congress issuing the "Declaration of the Causes and Necessity for Taking up Arms" and sending the "Olive Branch Petition" to King George III, begging him to make peace with the American colonies. This took place in May of 1775. Following this, the King ignored the request for peace and approved the Prohibitory Act, declaring America to be in rebellion and thus not protected by him (d). This also took place in 1775. The next event chronologically in this list was (b). Thomas Paine published *Common Sense* in January of 1776, which urged Americans to vie immediately for independence from England. On June 7, 1776, (e) Richard Henry Lee of Virginia presented his resolutions for American independence and for a formal American government to Congress. On July 4, 1776, (a) America's Second Continental Congress officially accepted the Declaration of Independence.

25. B: Washington defeated Hessian (German) troops who fought for the British at Trenton, New Jersey, on December 25, 1776. His troops also defeated British troops at Princeton, New Jersey, on January 3, 1777. Prior to these victories, Washington's troops lost to the British at the Battle of Long Island, New York, on August 27, 1776, and at the Battle of Washington Heights, New York, on August 29 and August 30, 1776 (a). As Washington lost the New York battles and won the New Jersey battles, answer (c) is incorrect. Since the two victories in New Jersey (b) were not losses, answer (d) is incorrect. Since George Washington led battles at all four of these locations, answer (e) is incorrect.

26. A: At the Battle of Saratoga, aided greatly by Benedict Arnold's leadership, the troops of American General Horatio Gates defeated British General John Burgoyne's troops at Saratoga, New York, on October 17, 1777. After witnessing this victory by the Americans, France entered the war against Britain to support the Americans. Earlier, at Brandywine Creek (b), on September 1, 1777, George Washington was unable to stop British General William Howe from advancing to occupy Philadelphia. A bit earlier still, at the Battle of Oriskany (c) on August 6, 1777, British troops and Iroquois Indians led by Colonel Barry St. Leger defeated and killed America's General Nicholas Herkimer, but then had to retreat to Canada. Following this, in the middle of August 1777, the New England militia, commanded by General John Stark, defeated one of British General Burgoyne's detachments near Bennington, Vermont (d). (Note: the Battle of Saratoga was the last battle to take place out of the choices presented.) Since (a) is correct, answer (e) is incorrect.

27. D: Washington's troops received support from a French naval fleet that took over Chesapeake Bay to stop Cornwallis from attacking Yorktown via water. Washington's troops also received support from a French army that helped Washington's men stop Cornwallis's troops from advancing via land routes to Yorktown. Cornwallis surrendered to Washington on October 17, 1781. Answer (a) is incorrect because Cornwallis did not win this battle. Answer (b) is incorrect because Washington's army did not win the battle single handedly, but rather with help from French allies. Answer (c) is incorrect because although Cornwallis and Washington did go through a

three-week siege, the conclusion was not indecisive. It was decidedly in favor of the Americans. Because answer (d) is correct, answer (e) is incorrect.

28. E: The Treaty of Paris of 1783 did state that Britain and the other leading European countries now recognized the United States of America as an independent country. This treaty also set boundaries, but the southern tip of Florida was not the southern boundary (a). It was the northern boundary of Florida, which became a Spanish territory. Therefore, it is not true that Britain kept both Canada and Florida under this treaty (b). Canada did remain a British territory under its terms, but Britain had to cede Florida to Spain. The Treaty of Paris also gave private British creditors freedom to collect debts from Americans, not the reverse (c). The treaty also stipulated that property confiscated from loyalists during the war should be given back, not kept (d). Other terms of the Treaty of Paris included that the western boundary of the United States would be the Mississippi River.

29. C: Massachusetts did set a valuable example for other states by stipulating that its constitution should be created via a special convention rather than via the legislature. This way, the constitution would take precedence over the legislature, which would be subject to the rules of the constitution. It is not true that twelve states had new constitutions by the end of 1777 (a). By this time, ten of the states had new constitutions. It is not true that Connecticut and <u>Massachusetts</u> retained their colonial charters minus the British parts (b). Connecticut and <u>Rhode Island</u> were the states that preserved their colonial charters. They simply removed any parts referring to British rule. Massachusetts did not formalize its new constitution in <u>1778</u> (d). This state did not actually finish the process of adopting its new constitution until <u>1780</u>. Finally, it is not true that Pennsylvania began with a viable constitution featuring checks and balances (e). It is true that Maryland and Virginia did initially provide such workable constitutions. Pennsylvania, however, began with such a hyper-democratic document with so little in the way of checks and balances that officials found it impossible to manage and quickly got rid of it, eventually coming up with a more reasonable constitution.

30. A: It is incorrect that the Northwest Ordinance was passed by Congress in 1785. The Northwest Ordinance was passed in 1787. (Note: The Land Ordinance of 1785 is sometimes called the "Northwest Ordinance of 1785," which can be confusing. However, the Northwest Ordinance of 1787 is more commonly known as the Northwest Ordinance.) Three land ordinances were passed between 1784 and 1787 to expedite the settlement of land north of the Ohio River after Daniel Boone opened the Wilderness Road to Kentucky and Tennessee. The three ordinances were The Land Ordinance of 1784, the Land Ordinance of 1785, and the Northwest Ordinance of 1787. It is true that the Northwest Ordinance included a bill of rights for settlers (b). The Northwest Ordinance also prohibited slavery north of the Ohio River (c). In addition, the Northwest Ordinance had a provision that three to five territories could be created within its jurisdiction, and could gain admission to the union when their populations were large enough to become states (d). Because (a) is an incorrect statement, answer (e) is incorrect.

31. C: James Madison was the one who designed the Virginia Plan. Edmund Randolph, a more proficient public speaker, introduced this plan at Madison's request—not the other way around. It is true that the Convention delegates believed that humans are basically selfish by nature (a), which was why they instituted checks and balances in the constitution to keep the government or any part of it from abusing its powers or acquiring too much power. Benjamin Franklin was instrumental in the Great Compromise (b), which was reached with his help after the convention went into deadlock over choosing the Virginia Plan or the New Jersey Plan. The New Jersey Plan, designed by William Paterson, was offered as an alternative to the Virginia Plan (d), as it would give smaller states equal influence as larger states. The Great Compromise incorporated elements of both plans

by having the equal representation outlined in the New Jersey Plan in the Senate and the representation based on population outlined in the Virginia Plan in the House of Representatives. The Three-Fifths Compromise was reached to resolve differences between Northern and Southern states over the issue of slavery (e). Each slave was counted as three-fifths of a person for representation and taxation purposes.

32. D: George Washington was inaugurated as the first President of the United States in March of 1789, following the completion of each state's ratification of the Constitution. 1786 (a) was the year the Annapolis Convention met with the aim of changing the Articles of Confederation. Because only five states sent delegates, however, those officiating decided it would be better to arrange for a convention the following summer, which delegates representing all states would attend. This became known as the Constitutional Convention, which met in 1787 (b). The minimum requirement of ratification of the Constitution by nine of the thirteen states was achieved in 1788 (c). 1791 (e) was the year that the first ten amendments to the Constitution, or the Bill of Rights, became effective.

33. E: The amendment that is included in the Bill of Rights, which consists of the first ten amendments to the Constitution, is the Tenth Amendment. It states that all powers not specified as powers of the federal government are powers that the states keep (1791). The amendment that states cannot be sued by individuals (a) is the Eleventh Amendment (1798). The amendment abolishing slavery (b) is the Thirteenth Amendment (1865). The amendment for the direct election of senators (c) is the Seventeenth Amendment (1913). The amendment legalizing income tax (d) is the Sixteenth Amendment (1913).

34. B: Only the federal government has the power to give copyrights and patents to individuals or companies. The power to levy taxes, borrow money, and spend money (a) is a power shared by federal and state governments. The power to set the criteria that qualify individuals to vote (c) is a power given to state governments only. The power to ratify amendments proposed to the Constitution (d) is a power of only the state governments. The power to use police to manage public health and safety (e) is also a power of the state governments only.

35. A: The action that needs a three-fourths majority vote is state approval of a proposed constitutional amendment. Proposing a constitutional amendment (b) requires a two-thirds majority vote. Ratifying presidential appointments in the Senate (c) also requires a two-thirds majority vote. Introducing charges for impeachment in the House of Representatives (d) requires a simple majority vote. To override a veto by the President (e), a two-thirds majority vote is needed.

36. C: The Judiciary Act of 1789 did not include the appointment of nine justices of the Supreme Court. The original Supreme Court only had six justices. The Judiciary Act of 1789 did initially establish the Supreme Court (a). This act stated that Supreme Court Justices were to make rulings about whether state laws were constitutionally valid (b). The Judiciary Act also stipulated that a system of district courts be set up as courts of original jurisdiction (d), and it allowed for the establishment of three courts of appeal (e).

37. D: Jeffersonians were first known as Democratic-Republicans, and then became known as Republicans. Federalists supported Hamilton and their opponents supported Jefferson, not the other way around (a). Jeffersonians, first called Anti-Federalists by the Federalists, eventually became known as Republicans, not Democrats (b). Hamilton and the Federalists believed in a broad, loose interpretation of the Constitution, while Jeffersonians believed in following the Constitution more strictly, not the other way around (c). James Madison supported Thomas Jefferson's views, not Hamilton's (e).

38. B: In 1792, when the French Revolution turned into European war, American traders conducted business with both sides. It is not true that Washington allied with the French (a) at this time. Washington issued a Proclamation of Neutrality in 1792 when the French went to war with European countries. While they did trade with both sides, American merchants profited the most from the French West Indies, not the British West Indies (c). The Spanish navy did not retaliate against America for trading with the French (d). Though Spain was an ally of Britain, it was the British who most often seized American ships and forced their crews to serve the British navy. Edmond-Charles Genêt, or Citizen Genêt, a French ambassador to the United States during the French Revolution, defied Washington's policy of neutrality by encouraging the American people to support the French. Washington was embarrassed by this violation. He did not agree with it (e).

39. E: The Battle of Fallen Timbers, in which General Anthony Wayne defeated the Indian tribes, did not restore peace between settlers and Indians, nor did the Treaty of Greenville that resulted from this battle. Rather, this defeat and subsequent treaty removed all of the Indian tribes from the Ohio territory (d), ending the attacks on settlers in this area. It is accurate that (a) Indian tribes were retaliating against American settlers for impinging on their territory on the Northwestern border, and also (b) on the Southwestern border of the country. British officials in Canada did actually encourage Indian tribes in their attacks on the settlers (c) because of their own opposition to the Americans.

40. A: When the President sent federal troops, this caused the Whiskey Rebellion to end, which resolved the situation and added to the new government's credibility. It did not result in a setback for the government. It is true that the whiskey tax was central to Hamilton's revenue program (b). It is true that farmers in western states, including Pennsylvania, did not want to pay this tax (c). It is also true that in addition to objecting to the tax and refusing to pay it, a group of farmers in Pennsylvania terrorized tax collectors to make their point (d). It is true that Washington responded to the farmers' terrorism by sending around 15,000 soldiers to quell the Whiskey Rebellion (e) in 1794.

41. C: John Adams ran for President in 1796 as the Federalist candidate, and Thomas Jefferson ran for President against him as the Republican candidate. Therefore, it is not true that Adams was the Republican candidate (a), or that Jefferson was the Federalist candidate (b). It is also not true that Adams ran for President with Jefferson as his running mate (d). Even though Jefferson became the Vice President, he got this position because he received the second highest number of electoral votes after Adams. The current tradition of presidential candidates having running mates for V.P. was not yet established in 1796. It is not true that Jefferson ran with Adams as his running mate (e). Because Adams received the most electoral votes, he became President. Jefferson, with the next highest number of votes, became Vice President. This meant that two men from opposing parties served together, making for an uncomfortable situation.

42. D: The numbers of electoral votes were not tied between the Federalist candidates. However, the two Republican candidates did get an equal number of electoral votes (c), which caused the election decision to go to the House of Representatives, where there was a long impasse. Eventually, Federalist Alexander Hamilton transferred his support to Republican Jefferson (e), resulting in Jefferson being elected President and Aaron Burr being elected Vice President. It is true that Jefferson and Burr both ran as Republicans (a), and that John Adams and Charles Pinckney both ran as Federalists (b).

43. A: Marbury did sue Madison, but not to demand that Madison appoint him Justice of the Peace. Lame-duck President John Adams had already appointed Marbury to be a Justice of the Peace as one of his "midnight" judges or appointments, and these appointments were approved by the

Senate. However, for these appointments to take effect, the commissions had to be delivered to the appointees. John Marshall continued to act as Secretary of State at Adams's request after being appointed Chief Justice of the Supreme Court (e) until Jefferson took office and Madison succeeded as the next Secretary of State. Not all of the commissions for the "midnight" appointees could be delivered in time, and contrary to John Marshall's expectations, Madison did not deliver the rest of them. This was because Jefferson, upon becoming President, ordered Attorney General Levi Lincoln, who was acting as Secretary of State until Madison's arrival, not to deliver these commissions. When they were not delivered on time, Jefferson declared them void. Marbury did not sue to be appointed a Justice of the Peace, but rather to demand he receive his undelivered commission. It is correct that Marshall's statement that Marbury's claim was unconstitutional was the first time in U.S. history anything was declared unconstitutional by the Supreme Court (b). This case was a landmark, not only for this first, but also for establishing the precedent of judicial review (c), which states that the judicial branch can negate decisions made by other branches of the U.S. government. Additionally, this case helped to define the U.S. government's system of checks and balances (d) by demonstrating how the judicial branch could check the other two branches.

44. E: The Louisiana Purchase actually increased the U.S.'s territory by 100% overnight, not 50%. The Louisiana territory doubled the size of the nation. It is true that Jefferson initially sent a delegation to Paris to see if Napoleon would agree to sell only New Orleans to the United States (a). It is also true that Napoleon, who expected America to encroach on Louisiana, decided to avoid this by offering to sell the entire territory to the U.S. (b). It is likewise true that America only had authority to buy New Orleans. Nevertheless, the delegation accepted Napoleon's offer of all of Louisiana (c). Due to his belief in strict interpretation of the Constitution, Jefferson did require approval from Congress to make the purchase. When his advisors characterized the purchase as being within his purview based on the presidential power to make treaties, Congress agreed (d).

45. B: Hamilton did not object to U.S. western expansionism, and Burr did not support it. There were certain Federalists other than Hamilton who opposed expansion to the west as a threat to their position within the Union, and these opponents did attempt to organize a movement to secede (a). To get Aaron Burr to champion their cause, they offered to help him run for Governor of New York (c). Hamilton did lead the opposition against Burr's campaign (d). When Burr lost this election, he did challenge Hamilton to the duel during which Hamilton was killed (e).

46. D: The Non-Intercourse Act passed by Congress, which opened trade to all countries other than Britain and France, expired in 1810. It was succeeded by Macon's Bill No. 2 (a), which empowered the President to ban trade with any country that violated U.S. neutrality, and was thus more directly influential to the war. In 1810 and 1811, Indian tribes attacking U.S. settlements at the borders received encouragement from both British officials in Canada (b) and from Spain (c), one of Britain's allies. Henry Clay and John C. Calhoun were leaders of the War Hawks (e), a pro-war group. In 1811, they gained control of both the Senate and the House of Representatives, and pushed to declare war against Britain. By June 1, 1812, President Madison asked Congress to declare war, which it did.

47. A: The U.S. did carry out a three-pronged invasion of Canada early in the war, but they did not succeed on two fronts. Instead, they lost on all three. Americans did win sea battles against the British early in the war, but were soon beaten back to their homeports and then blockaded by powerful British warships (b). Admiral Perry did defeat the British on Lake Erie on September 10, 1813 (c). Perry's victory allowed William Henry Harrison to invade Canada (d) in October of 1813, where he defeated British and Indians in the Battle of the Thames. *Old Ironsides* was one of the ships that won early naval battles during the war (e) before Britain drove American ships to retreat.

48. E: All of the statements are true regarding the Treaty of Ghent. This treaty was signed on Christmas Eve of 1814 (a) in Ghent, Belgium, and agreed to the cessation of hostilities. Both Britain and America were anxious for peace by this time because the European wars had ended (b), so the main causes of America's disagreement with Britain were no longer important. Despite this peace treaty being signed, British forces invaded New Orleans (c) two weeks later on January 8, 1815, in an attempt to block the Mississippi River's mouth. They were, however, soundly defeated by Andrew Jackson's army. One provision of the Treaty of Ghent was to restore things to the way they were before fighting broke out, so both sides agreed in the treaty to return all land gained in the war to one another (d).

49. C: The Federalists were not a strong majority until the War of 1812 ended. Party numbers had been dwindling for some time, and when the Hartford Convention met, Federalists had already become a distinct minority. New England Federalists were opposed to the War of 1812 to the point that they considered seceding from the Union (a). Secession was one of the possibilities discussed in the resolutions they drafted at this convention (b) in an effort to protect their interests against the growing Southern and Western states. When it became known that Jackson had won the Battle of New Orleans, the Federalists and the resolutions they had proposed at the Hartford Convention were discredited (d). When the Treaty of Ghent restored all American and British possessions to antebellum status and established peace, the Federalists were disgraced and the party was disbanded (e) in most areas. The Federalist Party was no longer a political power after these events.

50. C: After Andrew Jackson claimed East Florida in 1817, Spain made the decision two years later to sell the rest of its Florida territories to America, anticipating that Americans would take this land anyway if they did not sell it to them. This is more related to American expansion than to the end of European colonization in the Americas, which is the subject of the Monroe Doctrine. South American countries had been rebelling for years against European imperialist rule (a) by Napoleonic governments. After Napoleon fell, a number of these Latin American countries declared independence and resisted the rule of the Bourbon and Hapsburg families brought back to power in France and Germany (b). In addition to the revolutions occurring in South America, there was concern on the parts of both British and American officials that the new European regimes would attempt to give former colonies in the New World back to the European royalty (c). Taking into account all of these factors, President Monroe made a statement in his yearly address to Congress that the Americas should no longer be considered potential colonies by any powers in Europe (e).

51. B: The popular mood in the country during these years was not negative, but quite positive. In fact, this period was often called the "Era of Good Feelings." The country did undergo very fast economic and social development (a). In was, in fact, so fast that there was a severe depression in 1819 as a result (c). However, this depression was temporary, and economic growth soon resumed. America, begun with an agricultural economy, was experiencing increasing industrialization (d) during this time, moving away from farming as the basis of its economy and toward urbanization and industry. At the same time, the country's rapid growth and prosperity stimulated the existing trend of westward expansion (e), speeding up and intensifying the movements of pioneers to the western parts of the continent.

52. D: The decision representing the first time a state law was nullified for violating a constitutional principle was Fletcher v. Peck (1810). In this case, the Georgia Assembly granted a great deal of land to the Yazoo Land Company in a deal that was later found to be corrupt, so the deal was repealed in a state legislative session. The Supreme Court ruled that the original agreement was a valid contract that could not be broken, regardless of the graft involved. The state repeal was voided, making it the first time a state law was made null for violating a principle of the constitution (that of valid contracts). The 1803 case of Marbury v. Madison (a) was the first time the Supreme

Court ruled whether federal laws were constitutional, establishing the power of judicial review and helping to define the U.S. government's system of checks and balances. The decision in the 1819 case of Dartmouth College v. Woodward (b) greatly restricted the powers of state governments to control corporations. The college's president wanted to revoke its charter to change Dartmouth's status from private to public. He was supported by Republicans, and the college trustees who disagreed were supported by Federalists. The Supreme Court ruled Dartmouth's original charter from colonial days was still a contract, and could not be revoked without both parties' agreement. This decision was important because the corporation was then the emergent business model. The 1819 case of McCulloch v. Maryland (c) received Marshall's ruling that a state does not have the right to control a federal agency. The state of Maryland had tried to impose a tax on Baltimore's branch of the Bank of the United States to keep Maryland's state banks competitive. The decision was based on the idea that such an action by a state would be against the "implied powers" of Congress to set up and run a national bank. In the 1824 case of Gibbons v. Ogden (e), the state of New York had given steamboat operator Ogden a monopoly on the waters between New York and New Jersey. Gibbons, a competitor, got a permit from Congress to run steamboats in the same area. Ogden then sued to keep his monopoly. When the New York state courts ruled in his favor, Gibbons appealed their decision. His appeal was presented to the Supreme Court, which ruled that navigation was a part of commerce, and that only Congress could regulate interstate commerce. This decision nullified the monopoly granted by the state.

53. A: By 1840, more than one third of all Americans lived west of the Alleghenies, but not two thirds. It is correct that in the first half of the 19th century, the American population doubled every 25 years (b). It is also correct that westward expansion increased as more people moved west (c) during these years. It is correct that there was not a lot of immigration to the U.S. from other countries before 1820 (d). It is also true that foreign immigration to America increased quickly around that time, with most immigrants coming from the British Isles (e).

54. E: The Erie Canal was officially opened on October 26, 1825, and connected the Hudson River to Lake Erie. The Cayuga-Seneca Canal (a) connecting the Erie Canal to Cayuga Lake and Seneca Lake was first used in 1828. The Chambly Canal (b) is a Canadian canal in Quebec that was opened in 1843. It is not a part of the New York State Canal System, as the other canals listed here are. The Oswego Canal (c), which connects the Erie Canal to Lake Ontario at Oswego, was opened in 1828. The Barge Canal (d) replaced the original Erie Canal in 1918 with a larger waterway. In 1992, the New York State Barge Canal was renamed the New York State Canal System, which incorporates all of the canals listed in this question except for the Chambly Canal (b), which is not in New York State.

55. B: Growth in labor organizing was stimulated by organizers wanting to achieve the goal of a shorter workday. However, what they were aiming for in the 1800s was a 10-hour day, not an 8-hour day, which was not realized until 1936. It is true that when the factory system supplanted the cottage industry, owners and workers became separate, and this depersonalized workplaces (a). Child laborers did conduct the first organized workers' strike in Paterson, N.J., in 1828 (c). Although the first strike did occur this early, there were not a lot of strikes or labor negotiations during this time period due to periodic downturns in the economy (d), which had the effect of keeping workers dependent and less likely to take action against management. The campaign to attain a 10-hour work day did stimulate a period of growth in labor organizing, but this growth period ended with the depression of 1837 (e).

56. C: Thomas Jefferson did describe a plan for Virginia to have a free school, but it was not realized. Jefferson's plan was never implemented. It is true that there were really no public schools worth mentioning in America before around 1815 (a). Once there were schools, they were mainly paid for

by private organizations – corporate ones in the Northeastern states and religious ones in the Southern and Mid-Atlantic states (b). America's early schools did cater to rich people, and specialized in providing academic instruction to males (d). The few schools for females in existence taught homemaking and fine arts rather than academic subjects. The New York Free School was a very unusual instance of an early American school that provided education for the poor (e). This school tried out the Lancastrian system, wherein older students tutor younger students, which not only employed a sound educational principle, but also helped the school to operate within its limited budget.

57. D: Early colleges and universities did not offer a variety of courses designed to provide professional training. In fact, the only professional training available at this time was in theology. Only a very few colleges and universities had courses in law or medicine, and these were only brief courses. The University of Pennsylvania offered a total of one year of medical training to become licensed to practice medicine. It is true that in the early 19th century the number of schools of higher learning increased significantly (a). At this time, all of these schools were private rather than public (b). Therefore, all of these schools charged high tuition fees (c) in order to stay afloat. Because of this, less than one in ten males attended a college or a university, and no females attended (e).

58. A: The contemporary of Washington Irving ("The Legend of Sleepy Hollow," "Rip van Winkle") who was also born in the 18th century was James Fenimore Cooper (1789-1851), best known for *The Last of the Mohicans* and *Leatherstocking Tales*. All the others were born in the 19th century. Nathaniel Hawthorne (b), best known for *The Scarlet Letter* and *The House of Seven Gables*, was born in 1804 and died in 1864. Herman Melville (c), best known for *Moby Dick*, was born in 1819 and died in 1891. Henry Wadsworth Longfellow (d), best known for the poems "Hiawatha," "Evangeline," and "Paul Revere's Ride," was born in 1807 and died in 1882. Edgar Allan Poe (e), best known for his poem "The Raven" and numerous short horror stories, was born in 1809 and died in 1849. He is also credited with inventing the detective fiction genre.

59. D: The written works Thomas Paine published *after* the American Revolution (1765-1783) were both (b) and (c). His *Rights of Man* (b) was published in 1791 in response to Edmund Burke's pamphlet *Reflections on the Revolution in France*, which criticized the French Revolution. Paine's *Rights of Man* defended the French Revolution. *The Age of Reason* (c) was a book Paine published in 1793-1794, which advocated deism and rationalism while criticizing traditional Christian beliefs and institutionalized religions. *Common Sense* (a) was a pamphlet Paine published in 1776, which was widely read and very influential to the American Revolution. Paine also published a series of pro-revolutionary pamphlets from 1776-1783 entitled *The American Crisis*.

60. E: It is not true that the Second Great Awakening's individualistic nature contradicted nationalism and expansionism. While it did have an individualistic nature, this evangelical movement, which started in 1801 at the first camp meeting in Cane Ridge, Kentucky, also created significant nationalistic feelings. These later resurfaced in the expansionist beliefs of Manifest Destiny. Therefore, the Second Great Awakening actually influenced nationalism and expansionism rather than contradicting them. In fact, the social implications of the Second Great Awakening later helped to ignite the major reform movements of the 1830s and 1840s. This movement was definitely a reaction to Enlightenment's focus on rationalism (a), and it did emphasize a type of religious faith that was individual, personal, and emotional (b). Both women (c) and black people (d) participated in this movement in large numbers.

61. B: Though it is true that free black men were not allowed to vote in the Southern states, it is not true that most of them voted in the North. In fact, in the majority of the Northern states, free black men were not allowed to vote, even in areas where they might have previously had this benefit

without a formal amendment to the constitution. During the early part of the Jacksonian era, the trend was to exclude blacks politically, socially, and economically. It is true that by 1824, most states in the Union had gotten rid of the qualification stating that a person must own property in order to vote (a). The liberalization this change represented was inspired by the 1820 example of the state constitution of Massachusetts (c), the first to remove the property qualification. It is true that up until this election, there was little popular interest in national elections because legislative caucuses made presidential nominations, keeping voters uninvolved in such choices (d). It is also true that these caucuses were disregarded in 1824 (e) in favor of letting the people decide.

62. B: During this time period, members of the Electoral College were no longer being elected by the state legislatures as they had been in earlier years, but rather by the people throughout the country. It is true that these years were called the "Age of Jackson," or the Jacksonian Democracy (a). In his visits to America, French historian and political philosopher Alexis de Tocqueville did notice a kind of equality in America that was not found in other nations (c). The electorate had been increased to enable all white males to have access to voting (d) at this time. Despite this advantage, black people and women were still not allowed to vote (e). Black people would be given the right to vote in 1870 by the 15th Amendment to the Constitution, and women would gain the right to vote in 1920 via the 19th Amendment.

63. D: The person who was not a presidential candidate in the 1824 election was John C. Calhoun. When John Quincy Adams was elected, Calhoun became his Vice President, but he had not run for President. Henry Clay (a) was Speaker of the House at the time, and ran for President with the "American System" as his platform. He was the only candidate to present an actual program for voters' consideration. Georgia's William H. Crawford (b) was Secretary of the Treasury at the time, and he was the choice for candidate by Congress's caucus. John Quincy Adams (c) was Secretary of State then, and this office historically tended to lead to the presidency. Tennessee's Andrew Jackson (e) ran based on his military victories in the War of 1812. Note: Jackson won 43% of the popular vote, but only 38% of the electoral vote due to the presence of four candidates. The House of Representatives voted on the three top candidates, eliminating Henry Clay. Clay gave his support to John Quincy Adams, who returned the favor by appointing Clay Secretary of State. Jackson and his followers criticized this as corrupt deal making, and used this claim as the basis for their campaign for the next election in 1828.

64. A: In the election of 1828, Adams's party called themselves National Republicans, while Jackson's party called themselves Democratic Republicans. Answer (b) is the reverse of the correct designations. American political parties at this time were not yet known as just Democrats or Republicans (c), (d). While both parties in this election were types of Republicans, they did not both refer to themselves as just Republicans (e), but differentiated their Republicanism as being either National (Adams) or Democratic (Jackson).

65. C: The orator who made the speech containing this famous phrase was Daniel Webster. In this speech, he was replying to a speech made by Robert Young Hayne (e), Senator from South Carolina, in the Webster-Hayne debate. In one of a series of disputes over Federal land policy, Hayne made a speech accusing the North of trying to limit westward expansion to its own advantage, and Webster's speech was a rebuttal to Hayne's in defense of New England. Henry Clay (a) was Secretary of State under President Andrew Jackson (b). When South Carolina passed its Ordinance of Nullification in 1832, Webster sided with Jackson's strategies of deploying troops to the state's borders and enacting the Force Bill. He did not, however, agree with Clay's compromise in 1833, which eventually resolved the situation. Webster did share with Clay a disagreement with Jackson's economic policies. William Henry Harrison (d), a war hero, was nominated by the Whig Party in

1839 as their presidential candidate. Webster had unsuccessfully run for President as a Whig in 1836. The Whigs offered Webster the Vice Presidency under Harrison, but Webster declined.

66. E: The panic of 1837 and the recession that began that year did result in part from loosened credit and economic inflation, but these events were also related to the Bank of the United States. President Jackson opposed the Bank (a), and tried to destroy it by removing federal funds and redistributing them to state and local banks (d). Another contributing factor was the government's subsidy of westward expansion. It was selling large amounts of land in the West to settlers for very low prices. Knowing Jackson wanted to get rid of the national Bank, Henry Clay and Daniel Webster teamed up 1832 in support of a bill to renew the bank's charter prematurely to its future expiration in 1836 (b). They succeeded in getting Congress to pass this bill, but then Jackson vetoed it (c), relegating the institution to lame-duck status.

67. C: William Henry Harrison was the Whig presidential nominee in both 1836 and 1840 (b), but he did not win the 1836 election. Martin Van Buren did. Harrison did win in 1840, and he did die 32 days after his inauguration, making his term the shortest in the history of the office. In his first term, President Van Buren did get Congress to create an Independent Treasury to manage federal funds in place of the defunct national bank (a). The "Age of Jackson" was the period when the present-day system of Democratic and Republican parties that hold national conventions first began (d). Alexis de Tocqueville did publish his famous book *Democracy in America* in 1835 (e), which described American society and its democratic process objectively, and in many cases even prophetically. This book is still a mainstay of many college courses on American government.

68. E: All of the statements regarding movements for reform in 1840s America are true. This was a period of change in society, meaning that conditions were unstable and people felt uncertainty (a). Additionally, many Americans during this time were challenging the old traditions and values (b). Romanticism began in Europe and spread to the New World as a reaction against the rationalism of the Enlightenment in both places. Romantics, preferring emotions over reason, had an optimistic belief in the basic goodness of humanity and in its ability to become better, which lent itself well to ideas of reform (c). At the same time that people were questioning established traditions, the natural instability resulting from change also increased people's perceptions of a need for greater control, order, and stabilizing influences (d). The movements for reform during this time were centered in the Northeastern states, particularly in the New England states.

69. D: The American author *not* from the South was Francis Parkman, a historian and nationalist from Massachusetts best known for *The Oregon Trail* and his huge seven-volume work *France and England in North America*. Edgar Allan Poe (a), famous for poems such as "The Raven," "Tamerlane," "Annabel Lee," and "The Bells," and for many short stories such as "The Black Cat," "The Cask of Amontillado," "The Fall of the House of Usher," "The Masque of the Red Death," "The Murders in the Rue Morgue" and "The Tell-Tale Heart," was born in Boston, Massachusetts. He moved to Richmond, Virginia, at the age of two years to live with the Allans after his parents died. Except for a period of five years during his childhood (from 1815-1820) when the family lived in England, Poe lived in Virginia for the rest of his life. William Gilmore Simms (b) of Charleston, South Carolina, was a poet, novelist, and historian whose work was focused on the South. He wrote a history of South Carolina (1842). His best known book is probably *The Partisan* (1835). Simms, who was pro-slavery, also wrote a reaction against Harriet Beecher Stowe's novel *Uncle Tom's Cabin* entitled *The Sword and the Distaff*, which was reprinted in 1854 under the title *Woodcraft*. Augustus Baldwin Longstreet (d) of Augusta, Georgia, was a Southern lawyer, minister, educator, and humorist who served as president of Louisiana's Centenary College, the University of Mississippi, and South Carolina College. Longstreet was most famous for publishing the book *Georgia Scenes* (1835), a

collection of articles originally published in newspapers. Since Francis Parkman (d) was from the North, (e) is incorrect.

70. B: The earliest utopian commune in America was Brook Farm in Massachusetts (b). Author Nathaniel Hawthorne lived at Brook Farm briefly and based his novel *The Blithedale Romance* on his experiences there. The community of New Harmony, Indiana, (a) was founded by Robert Owen, who denounced the institutions of religion, marriage, and private property. This proved unpopular with nearby communities, which led to the commune's demise within two years. The commune of Nashoba, near Memphis, Tennessee, (c) was created by Englishwoman Frances Wright as a haven for freed slaves. This community did not last long, as it was surrounded by slave-owning communities that opposed it. The Oneida Community (d) was a commune in New York State dedicated to the ideals of free love and open marriage. The Amana Community in Iowa (e) was an experiment in socialism, and featured a strictly organized society.

71. A: The Catholic Church was not considered a particularly important source of social reform in 19th century America. After 1830, many Catholics from Ireland and southern Germany immigrated to America. These newly arrived immigrants were against temperance, while Protestants were for it, and the Protestant Revivalist movement incorporated a strong anti-Catholic aspect. The Mormon Church (b) was the most successful example of all the experiments in utopian communalism. As proponents of romantic utopianism, which included the human ability to improve, the Mormons did serve as an impetus to reform. The Transcendentalist movement which began in Concord, Massachusetts, (c) was an offshoot of European Romanticism, and its ideas encouraged people to become more interested in reforming American society. Protestant Revivalism (d), which incorporated many different sects of Protestantism (e.g. Presbyterians, Cumberland Presbyterians, Baptists, Methodists, Adventists, Restorationists, etc.), was a strong influence to reform society. The Protestant Revivalists were also supportive of the Temperance Society (e), while Catholic immigrants were not. While not everybody agreed with temperance, it was a motivational factor in the reform of American society.

72. B: The area of reform that may be said to have met with the most difficulty in its early years is free public schools. The first reformers, such as Horace Mann and Henry Barnard, encountered apathy or resistance in their crusade to establish free public schools. Even though this movement gained momentum during the 1830s, there were still very few public schools in the Western states, even fewer in the Southern states, and none at all for blacks in the South. The movement for higher education (a) had some better early success thanks to a few innovations. The first state-funded women's college, Troy Female Seminary, was founded in 1839 in Troy, New York. In Ohio, Oberlin College became the first co-educational college in the country. In Watertown, Boston, the Perkins School for the Blind was the first school for the blind in the country. In 1887, Anne Sullivan, a graduate of Perkins, was sent by Perkins's director Michael Anagnos to Alabama to teach Helen Keller. She returned to the school with Helen Keller the following year. The area of mental institutions (c) experienced innovation in the form of campaigns to treat mentally ill people more humanely in hospitals designed for that purpose. Dorothea Dix was the most prominent leader in this crusade. Prison reform (d) experienced innovation in the form of building new penitentiaries intended to rehabilitate criminals rather than to simply punish them. The first new penitentiary was built in 1821 in Auburn, New York. The abolitionist movement (e) saw innovations through the work of William Lloyd Garrison, who began his paper *The Liberator* in 1831, founded the New England Anti-Slavery Society in 1832 and the American Anti-Slavery Society in 1833, and advocated immediate and complete emancipation, enlivening the abolitionist movement. Theodore Weld was also an abolitionist who proposed a slower emancipation, and escaped slave Frederick Douglass became an abolitionist orator and published the *North Star* newspaper. Many novels, such as

Harriet Beecher Stowe's *Uncle Tom's Cabin,* also lent support to this movement. Another movement that saw innovations in this era of social reform was the feminist movement.

73. C: Rates of immigration were not high before this time, and they did not decline. The opposite was true. Immigration was slow before the 1800s due to all of the fighting America did with England and France. Immigration increased from 1815 to 1837 when the wars ended and immigrants began seeking out economic opportunities. The population in America did increase eight-fold from 1790 to 1860 (a), growing from 4 million to 32 million. Birth rates did drop after 1800, particularly because of economic considerations, resulting in an older population with a median age of 20. It had previously been 16 (b). The U.S. population also moved from the country to the cities during this time. In 1790, only 5% of people lived in cities with populations of 2,500 or more. By 1860, 25% of people lived in cities that size (d). Since (c) is correct, (e) is incorrect.

74. D: Political corruption was not an immediate effect of the rapid urban growth during this time. The accelerated growth of cities in America did soon result in services being unable to keep up with that growth. The results of this included deficiencies in clean water delivery and garbage collection, causing poor sanitation (a). That poor sanitation led to outbreaks of cholera and typhus, as well as typhoid fever epidemics (b). Police and fire fighting services could not keep up with the population increases, and were often inadequate (c). With people moving to the cities at such a fast rate, there were also deficits in housing and public transportation (e).

75. D: All of these are examples of urban violence in 1830s America. Political differences between Democrats and Whigs in New York City escalated into such violent fighting that the state militia was called in to subdue the disagreeing parties (a). Race riots broke out in New York City and Philadelphia during this decade (b). An angry mob in New York even went so far as to raid a Catholic convent in 1834 (c). City records counted 115 major incidents of mob violence during this decade (d). All of these events were attributable to the very rapid influx of people to the cities, causing mob violence and street crime to grow out of control.

76. D: Advances in technology were applied not only to industrial production, but also to farming machinery. Farmers could then supply larger amounts of food to urban workers at lower prices. Farming was not abandoned in favor of industry (a). The many additional workers in cities needed food that they did not grow, so there was an even greater market for farming. This did not mean that farming took precedence over industry (b). Both fields increased during the 19th century, and they complemented one another. Specialization and mechanization were processes applied to both farming and industry. At this time, they were not applied more to farming (c) or industry (e).

77. C: In the Northern U.S. from 1800-1860, people did not have big houses. They usually lived in cabins with one or two rooms. They did not have indoor plumbing, but brought in water from springs, wells, or public water faucets. Lastly, they did not have electricity or central heating, but open fireplaces and lighting from candles and oil lamps. This time period was characterized by the fact that by 1860 production of goods and services grew to twelve times that of 1800 (a). It is also true that by 1860 the average American worker had double the purchasing power of workers in 1800 (b). Additionally, by 1860, those working for employers outnumbered the self-employed for the first time ever (d). Because (c) is correct, (e) is incorrect.

78. B: Extremely poor whites in the South numbered around half a million, not one million. These "crackers" had a poorer quality of life than even the slaves. The yeoman farmers, or independent owners of small farms, did make up the largest proportion of white Southerners (a). Located mostly in the upland part of the South and farming mainly corn, these people were in general less affluent than comparable Northerners. Planters with the biggest farms and 50 or more slaves actually

constituted a small minority of the population in the Southern states (c). Three quarters of the white people in the South did not own slaves (d). Of those who did, nearly half owned five or fewer slaves, and 12% owned 20 or more (e).

79. A: It is still a subject of debate among historians whether Southern plantation slaves had better or worse lives than Northern wage laborers during the first half of the 19th century. Historians do not agree that these slaves had better lives (b) or worse lives (c) than the Northern laborers. It is not true that these slaves were worse off than slaves in South America (d) or the Caribbean (e). Actually, they were better off than slaves in those areas.

80. D: Southerners continued to settle disagreements by fighting duels well into the 19th century, and did not cease this practice by 1800. It is true that of all illiterate Americans, half of them lived in the South by 1860 (a). During this time, most Southerners lived in cabins with one or two rooms, just as most Northerners did (b). In the South, staple foods included corn, sweet potatoes, and pork (c), and this diet resulted in vitamin deficiencies that caused diseases such as rickets and pellagra to become commonplace (e). Rickets can result from deficiencies of vitamin D and/or calcium and magnesium. Pellagra is usually caused by a deficiency of vitamin B_3 or niacin, which can happen if corn is eaten as a staple without first being treated with lime. This was the case in the 19th century South. The cause of pellagra was unknown until 1915, and corn was a staple food in the South in the 19th century.

81. C: Postal services did not charge extra to deliver anti-slavery mail as a reaction to the abolitionist movement. Rather, the postal services in the South would not even deliver such mail. People in the South did adopt a defensive position against abolitionism, including quoting the Bible in an attempt to justify slavery (a). They also trotted out "scientific" arguments about the innate "inferiority" of African black people (b), as if this would somehow make it acceptable to enslave other people, even if it were true. Dissension was not allowed, and the South became extremely repressive of any discussion, increasing the closing off of the South (d) from the North and West. In this repressive atmosphere, free thinking and open-minded inquiry were impossible, so creative and scholarly written expression withered and became severely limited (e). Writers like Edgar Allan Poe and William Gilmore Simms were rare exceptions to the rule.

82. A: It is not true that the last major Southern debate on slavery was held in the South Carolina legislature in 1836 (a). This debate occurred in 1832 in the Virginia legislature. It did follow Nat Turner's famous rebellion, and completely repressed any further attempts at emancipation (b). Four years later, in 1836, Southern congressmen in the House of Representatives managed to push the "gag rule" through, which prohibited any mention of slavery on the floor of the House (c). This rule was effective until 1844. John C. Calhoun, Senator of South Carolina from 1832-1843 and Secretary of State from 1844-1845, proposed his theory of "concurrent majority," which featured a dual presidency to effect independence of South from North and exempt the South from the rule of the majority (d). It is true that starting in 1837, Southerners regularly held conventions throughout the Southern states to talk about ways to get the South out from under the influence of the North (e).

83. B: The term "Manifest Destiny" had not been used for many years before the 1830s. This term was coined in 1844. However, it is true that the idea this term expressed had been around for many years before that (a). It is also true that many Americans believed Manifest Destiny would mean America would ultimately encompass Canada and Mexico (c). Factors contributing to Manifest Destiny included the rise in nationalism that followed the War of 1812 and the population growth that increased that nationalism (d). Other factors that contributed to Manifest Destiny included the

1830s' reform movements and the demand for additional markets and resources created by the growth of the economy (e).

84. E: Before the 1820s, the Oregon country had been claimed by the United States, England (a), Spain (b), France (c), and Russia (d). Since all of these nations had claimed these areas, (e) is the correct answer. The Adams-Onis Treaty in 1819 set the northern boundary of Spain's territories near the northern border of what is now California. Land north of that boundary and west of the Louisiana Territory's indefinite boundaries was claimed by all the countries listed over the years, but by the 1820s, all of this territory was ceded to England and America. They agreed on joint occupation of the disputed land.

85. D: Tyler did not agree with most Whig policies. Actually, he disagreed with all of them, rejecting their whole program, which included a national bank, federal funding of internal improvements such as canals and roads, and high tariffs for protection. When Clay insisted this program be passed, Tyler vetoed many of the Whigs' bills (e). This infuriated the Whig Party, and all but one member of the Cabinet resigned. The Whigs expelled Tyler from their party, and even tried unsuccessfully to impeach him. It is true that, when elected, President Harrison followed Clay's advice to vote for the Whigs' program (a). When Harrison died 32 days after being inaugurated, Vice President Tyler succeeded him (b). It is true that the Whigs had recruited Tyler to run on their ticket because he was a Southerner and they felt he would attract Southern votes. Tyler was also a strict constitutionalist and was in favor of states' rights (c), so he did not agree with the Whig policies of strong federal control.

86. A: It is incorrect that the British promised they would no longer stop and search American ships during their patrols of the African coast (a). Britain had at times done this in the course of their patrols to stop slave smuggling. However, this treaty did not include any specific provision against stopping and searching American ships. In this agreement, Britain and America did achieve a compromise regarding their conflicting claims to land along the border of Canada and Maine (b). Britain also apologized for Canadian loyalists having crossed the American border and burning the *Caroline* (c). Britain further agreed that they would not repeat their "officious interference," something they committed when they refused to return escaped slaves who had commandeered the *Creole* and taken it to the British territory of the Bahamas (d). Both countries agreed that they would cooperate with each other when patrolling the African coast to stop slave smuggling (e).

87. B: Texas was not a Mexican territory. Texas won independence from Mexico in 1836. Mexico did threaten to declare war if America annexed Texas, and those in Congress who were against slavery naturally opposed slavery in Texas as well. For both these reasons, Texas's request to be admitted to the Union was refused at that time. Expelled by the Whig Party and with no alliance with the Democrats, President Tyler did seek to gain his own following with his proposal to annex Texas (a). Democrat Martin Van Buren and Whig Henry Clay agreed against annexing Texas during campaigns for the 1844 election. At the Democratic convention, however, those in favor of westward expansion replaced Van Buren with James K. Polk (c), who was an expansionist. Henry Clay was against annexing Texas, but in the face of the pro-annexation popular mood in America, he backed off his stance a bit. His loss of resolve on this issue caused some Northerners who objected to annexation for anti-slavery reasons to switch their votes from the Whigs to the abolitionist Liberty Party (d). These votes lost by Clay allowed Polk to win the election. After Polk won and Tyler's presidency was in lame-duck status, Tyler succeeded in passing a joint resolution through Congress (a joint resolution needed a simple majority vote, which was easier than getting a two-thirds majority vote), resulting in the admission of Texas to the Union in 1845 (e).

88. D: America's seizure of California in 1842 was a temporary error by Commodore Thomas Catsby Jones, who was under the mistaken impression that war had already erupted between America and Mexico. When it was realized that this was not true, the U.S. apologized and returned California to Mexico. Therefore, Mexico would not have been campaigning for the return of a province that had already been returned. One influence on the war was that during Mexico's numerous revolutions, its government was unable to protect Americans in Mexico. Even when both countries agreed to arbitration for Americans' claims to damages, the Mexican government consistently refused to pay these damages (a). Another influence leading to war was that Mexico was still angry that the United States had added Texas as a state. They viewed this action as a hostile one (b). The fact that the U.S. and Mexico were in dispute over the southern border of Texas was an additional influence (c). A further influence that contributed to the Mexican War was the fact that Mexican politicians had incited such anti-American sentiment in the Mexican people. Officials in that country were afraid anything they did that could be interpreted as a concession to America would result in their being deposed by a people's revolution (e).

89. C: A sea movement to go into Mexico was *not* one of the prongs of Polk's military strategy. Polk's strategy in the Mexican War was made up of a three-pronged attack. This included an overland troop movement west through New Mexico and into California (a), a naval movement overseas, also going into California (b), and an overland troop movement south going into Mexico (d). Since (c) is correct, (e) is incorrect.

90. E: The Battle of Sacramento was not won by General Zachary Taylor. This battle was won on February 28, 1847 by Colonel Alexander W. Doniphan. As a result of this victory, he took possession of the city of Chihuahua. Taylor won the Battle of Palo Alto (a) on May 7, 1846. He won the Battle of Resaca de la Palma (b) on May 8, 1846. He won the Battle of Monterey (c) between September 20 and 24, 1846. He won the Battle of Buena Vista (d) between February 22 and 23, 1847.

91. B: The Treaty of Guadalupe-Hidalgo, signed on February 2, 1848, was negotiated by a clerk for the State Department, Nicholas Trist (b). This was done even though Trist had had his authority revoked and been ordered to return to Washington two months before that date. President Polk (a) did not negotiate this treaty and felt that its terms were too generous. He accepted it, however, and it was then ratified by the Senate. General Winfield Scott (c) was ordered by President Polk to capture Mexico City when Mexico's government refused negotiations even after the success of Polk's three-pronged attack. Scott defeated Mexican forces at Veracruz, Cerro Gordo, Churubusco, the fortress at Chapultepec, and finally at Mexico City. Colonel Stephen Kearny (d) had led the first prong of Polk's three-pronged attack, taking New Mexico and then advancing to California. In the second prong, Commodore Robert Stockton (e) brought his men ashore to join Kearny's men, and together they defeated Mexican soldiers at the Battle of San Gabriel in January of 1847, completing California's occupation.

92. E: It is not true that the American people were divided about the Compromise of 1850 or that many of them were against it once it had been adopted. After it was adopted, the majority of the American people were delighted with the Compromise of 1850, as it brought peace from regional disputes and resolved disagreements over slavery for a few years. However, there were many people in the government opposed to it before it was adopted, such as President Taylor, Northern abolitionists, and Southern extremists. However, when Taylor died and Vice President Millard Fillmore succeeded him, Fillmore was in favor of the compromise (c). Henry Clay had originally proposed this eight-part compromise (a). Thereafter it was the subject of intense controversy in Congress. John C. Calhoun felt the only possibility of preserving the Union was if the North gave the South everything it wanted and did not argue over the subject of slavery (b). Daniel Webster, who had been against slavery, broke with his own tradition and made a famous speech in defense of the

Compromise. With all of the disagreement over this compromise, Henry Clay departed from Washington in the summer, discouraged that it might never pass. Once Fillmore succeeded to office and supported compromise, Senator Stephen A. Douglas separated the eight parts of the compromise and enlisted the influence of various groups to get each part pushed through Congress separately (d), which finally allowed the Compromise to be passed.

93. A: In the election of 1850, it is incorrect that the Democrats selected Cass, Douglas, and Pierce all to run for President. Lewis Cass had been nominated previously by the Democrats in 1848, and Stephen Douglas had succeeded in getting Henry Clay's plan passed in the Compromise of 1850. At the 1852 Democratic Convention, the Democrats reached an impasse over whether to nominate Cass or Douglas. Unable to resolve this, they picked New Hampshire's Franklin Pierce instead, who was considered a "dark horse." The Whigs did nominate General Scott (b), who had captured Mexico City in the war but was not a politician (b). The Whig Party had been divided between its Northern and Southern members, who disagreed about slavery and therefore about the Compromise of 1850 (c). A third party, called the Free Soil Party, nominated New Hampshire's John P. Hale, but his candidacy was unsuccessful, showing how tired everybody was of the issue of slavery by then (d). Since General Scott had no experience or track record in politics and the Whig Party was starting to fall apart due to its division between Northerners and Southerners, Franklin Pierce was easily able to win the election (e).

94. D: While all of these contributed to the development of the American economy in the 1840s and 1850s, the most influential was the growth of the railroads, which created a nationwide market and connected the Midwest to the Northeast. This would not have happened with only water transportation. From 1840 to 1860, the total miles of railroad track increased tenfold. Other positive influences on the economy included the fast and steady industrialized growth of water transportation in the form of steamboats and clipper ships (a), the mechanization of farming in the North via Cyrus McCormick's invention of the mechanical reaper and the use of mechanical threshers (b), the prosperity brought to Southern plantations and farms by their producing the valuable commodity of cotton (c), and the factory system, which started in the textile industry with Elias Howe's invention of the sewing machine in 1846 and Isaac Singer's design of an improved model in 1851 (e). These inventions then extended to other industries.

95. C: It is not accurate that Douglas wanted a repeal of the Missouri Compromise included in the Kansas-Nebraska Act to allow the possibility of slavery in these territories. Douglas seemed neutral on the subject of slavery, and tended to avoid this sensitive topic. However, senators from the South pressured Douglas to include the repeal and provide that slavery in the Kansas-Nebraska territories be decided by popular sovereignty (i.e. by vote of territorial legislature). Douglas did introduce this bill to Congress to organize the land west of Missouri and Iowa (a). Douglas was motivated to propose the bill by the hope that it would enable a transcontinental railroad to be built along a central route, which would be beneficial to his Illinois constituency (d). Because Douglas was forced to add the repeal of the Missouri Compromise to the Kansas-Nebraska Act, its passage brought an end to the temporary period of sectional peace (b). Although what was left of the Whigs and Democrats from the North both opposed this act, President Pierce's administration was predominantly Southern and supported it, so it was passed into law (e).

96. B: The most accurate statement about how the Kansas-Nebraska Act was related to the birth of the Republican Party is that Northerners were outraged over the act's repeal of the Missouri Compromise. It is inaccurate that the passage of this act strengthened a newly established Republican Party (a), because the party did not yet exist and was formed as a direct reaction to the act's passage. It is not accurate that the deteriorating Whigs and the divided Democrats allowed Republicans to prevail separately (c). Many Northern Whigs left their crumbling party and many

Northern Democrats left their divided party, along with defectors from the short-lived Know-Nothing Party, to join the Republican Party, so the damage to the Whig and Democratic Parties benefited the Republican Party by adding to its numbers. While the Republican Party quickly became a major political power following its formation, this did not occur in both the North and South (d) but mainly in the North. Nevertheless, its confinement mainly to the North did not prevent the party from becoming politically powerful. While the Republican Party contained diverse aspects, it was unified by the belief that slavery should be banned in American territories and prevented from spreading, and that it be limited to the states where it was already present, rather than being eradicated from all states in the Union (e).

97. A: It is false that the Supreme Court decision in the Dred Scott case resolved sectional disputes over slavery. In fact, their decision actually exacerbated the controversy. In the case of *Dred Scott v. Sanford,* Dred Scott, who was a slave in Missouri, was advised by abolitionists to sue for his freedom because he had lived for several years with his owner, an Army doctor, in the free state of Illinois, and then in the free territory of Wisconsin (b). Initially, the justices wanted to rule that Scott could not sue because he was a slave and thus not a citizen (c). However, James Buchanan, who was about to be inaugurated as President, hoping to get the issue of slavery out of politics so it would not cause him problems in office, convinced the justices to make a more extreme ruling with the aim of settling the issue of slavery for good (d). At Buchanan's behest, the Court ruled that Scott was not qualified to sue in federal court, that living in a free state or territory for several years did not confer freedom on a slave, that the former Missouri Compromise had been unconstitutional as Congress had no authority to prohibit slavery in any territory, and that territorial governments, which got their authority from Congress, likewise did not have the authority to ban slavery (e). This ruling did not achieve what Buchanan wanted. Rather than settling the issue, it further divided opponents. Its extreme nature made Southerners less likely to consider compromising, and it fueled Northerners' suspicious views of the government as conspiring in favor of slavery. They did not approve of or accept the decision.

98. The answer is (d). All of the factors stated led to the Panic of 1857. With the growth of railroads and the expansion of territories, people speculated too much in these stocks (a). Some practices in banking were improper (b) and were also to blame. In addition, the Crimean War temporarily interrupted the influx of European money to investments in America (c). These factors combined to produce a short-lived but serious depression. Since these were all factors, (e) is incorrect.

99. C: Regarding the Lincoln-Douglas debates, it is not true that Lincoln's success in the debates won him the Senate seat. He lost by a very narrow margin. Though Douglas barely won re-election to the Senate by responding to Lincoln's logical argument that the idea of popular sovereignty contradicted the Dred Scott decision with a clever answer that became known as the "Freeport Doctrine," this debate still harmed his chances for the upcoming presidential campaign. The Lincoln-Douglas debates did emerge out of the senatorial campaign in Illinois (a), and the topics of the debates were focused on slavery (b). While he did not win the seat in the Senate, Lincoln's success in the debates did take him from being virtually unknown outside of Illinois to being nationally famous (d). His success also helped to strengthen the Republican Party (e) against compromising on issues related to slavery, since in the debates Lincoln argued against slavery as morally wrong, while Douglas avoided any moral stance at all.

100. D: The state that was not one of the original seven to secede from the Union and form the Confederacy was North Carolina. South Carolina (a) was the first state to secede from the Union on December 20, 1860. By February, 1861, the other six states to follow South Carolina in secession were Alabama, Georgia (b), Florida (e), Mississippi, Louisiana, and Texas (c). Virginia, Arkansas,

North Carolina (d), and Tennessee all seceded from the Union and joined the Confederacy after April 15, 1861.

101. A: The Constitution of the Confederate States included a provision that protective tariffs were not allowed, so this was *not* a difference from the U.S. Constitution. Protective tariffs were allowed in the U.S. Constitution. Unlike the U.S. Constitution, the Confederate Constitution specifically recognized slavery and guaranteed the right to move slaves from one state to another (b). The Confederate Constitution specified that the president of the Confederacy should serve a single term of six years that could not be renewed (c), whereas the U.S. Constitution provided for a four-year term and an incumbent could be re-elected to a second term. The Confederate Constitution also gave the Confederate president the right to veto individual items listed in an appropriations bill (d) rather than just the whole bill. The Confederate Constitution also specifically recognized state sovereignty (e).

102. E: Regarding the secession of southern states from the Union, all of the statements about President Buchanan are correct. By the time the Confederate states had taken up their own constitution, Buchanan was in lame-duck status (a). Buchanan stated that secession itself was unconstitutional (b), but he also stated that federal government's doing anything to stop secession would be unconstitutional as well (c). Because of this second statement, Buchanan did not do anything to interfere with the southern states' secessions, even though according to his first declaration, he probably disagreed with them (d).

103. D: Regarding Crittenden's compromise proposals, it is not true that some Southerners were willing to consider the compromises. Discussions did break down, but it was because *none* of the Southerners would consider any compromise not allowing slavery to spread. These proposals did include passing a constitutional amendment to keep the federal government from interfering with slavery (a) in states where it existed. They also included moving the line set by the former Missouri Compromise out to the Pacific Ocean (b) and protecting slavery in all the territories south of that extended line (c). Some Republicans in Congress were willing to consider these compromise proposals, but President-elect Abraham Lincoln strongly advised them to stay resolved against letting slavery spread any farther (e).

104. C: Of the remaining slave states that had not already seceded, the one that did secede after the surrender of Fort Sumter was Tennessee (along with Virginia, North Carolina, and Arkansas). The states that never did secede were (a) Delaware, which did not have many slaves and thus was not interested in seceding; (b) Kentucky, which first took a neutral position but then aligned with the North when the South disregarded its neutrality; (d) Maryland, which was about to secede but was stopped by Lincoln's declaring martial law; and (e) Missouri, which not only was preserved as a part of the Union by federal troops, but also had a large population of German immigrants living in St. Louis who supported the Union and opposed slavery.

105. B: The North did not have more experienced and qualified senior military officers; the South did. At the beginning of the war, the South got many senior officers from the U.S. Army, including Robert E. Lee, Joseph E. Johnston, and Albert Sidney Johnston. Good Northern officers like Ulysses S. Grant and William T. Sherman were younger and therefore did not move up to higher ranks until later in the war. The North did have the advantage of greater wealth (a) and greater industrialization (c), while the South's agricultural basis put it at a disadvantage for manufacturing war supplies and equipment. The North also had more people to contribute to their military effort because more immigrants came to the North than to the South during the war, and because the South would not allow slaves to be soldiers and a third of the South's population was made up of slaves (d). The railroad system in the North was also much more extensive and interconnected,

while in the South, there were fewer and smaller railroads (e). They were best suited for local transport of cotton, not nationwide transportation of large cargos of war material or soldiers.

106. E: While Jefferson Davis did indeed have greater military experience than Abraham Lincoln did, it turned out once the Civil War was in progress that despite his lesser military experience, Lincoln actually proved to be the better wartime leader. It was a distinct advantage for the South that it covered such a large geographical area, which would make subduing it a greater challenge for the North (a). The South also had an advantage in being able to fight on their own soil, meaning they were familiar with the terrain (b). Moreover, they were motivated by the fact that they were defending their own families, homes, and land (c). In addition, in the days of the Civil War, fighting defensively was much more advantageous to an army than fighting offensively (d).

107. C: With respect to the Battle of Shiloh, it is not true that the Union took all of the Mississippi River as of this battle (together with its other previous victories). This battle, in combination with previous Union victories, meant that the North took all *but* a piece of land 110 miles long between Vicksburg, Mississippi, and Port Hudson, Louisiana, which were both Confederate fortresses. Hence, by the end of the Battle of Shiloh, the North had taken all of the Mississippi River except for this area between Vicksburg and Port Hudson (which were captured almost a year later). It is true that the Battle of Shiloh was the bloodiest battle in U.S. history up until that point in time (a). It is true that though Grant forced Johnston to retreat to Corinth, Mississippi when he captured Southern strongholds Fort Henry and Fort Donelson, two months later General Beauregard arrived. He joined Johnston, adding to the reinforcements Johnston had just received, and together they took Grant's forces by surprise (b). Nevertheless, they failed to defeat Grant (d). In fact, Johnston himself was killed in the Battle of Shiloh, along with a great many troops (e).

108. D: The statement that is not correct is that leaders in Britain felt it more important to import cotton from the American South than wheat from the American North. Actually, British consideration of its need for America's Northern wheat crops is thought to have mitigated its likeliness to import cotton from the South instead, as it could not do both. It is correct, however, that Britain also had stocked up on cotton imported from the South before the war began, and additionally was able to import more cotton during the Civil War from India and Egypt (c), eliminating the necessity to import any from the Southern U.S. The fact that the British people opposed slavery added to Britain's motivation not to do business with the South. These facts were contrary to what many Southerners had believed, i.e. that Britain would need the South's cotton and therefore would intervene on the South's behalf, and that France would join them in this intervention (b). In addition, many Southerners did believe that both Britain and France would be happy that the North-South division of the U.S. by the war would make America weaker (a). Northern diplomats appointed by President Lincoln—Secretary of State William Seward and Ambassador to England Charles Francis Adams—were skillful at getting Britain to stay out of the war, so Britain maintained a neutral position, and France and other European nations followed suit (e).

109. B: The Southern government issued paper money, but printed so much of it that it was rendered practically worthless. This money, therefore, did not make up for the South's scarcity of resources. The paper money plus the scarce resources plus the war's upset of the economy all created extreme inflation in the South, and the Confederate government responded to this inflation by confiscating (a) or impressing goods such as produce and livestock, leading to even more scarcity of resources. The North had more money and resources than the South to finance the war, but the huge war expense still required the North to seek additional financial resources. Two solutions for the Union were to impose high tariffs and to create the country's first income tax (c). As a third solution, the Treasury Department issued paper money called "greenbacks," which were

fiat currency with no backing. "Greenbacks," however, were supported by widespread popular confidence that the North would win the war (d). A fourth measure the Union took to finance the war was to pass the National Banking Act in 1863 to create more credit, which it could use to help pay for the war (c).

110. A: The overall public opinion in the North about the Emancipation Proclamation was not one of enthusiasm since the Republican Party had sustained big losses in the 1862 elections to Congress. Though Northerners overall were not thrilled with the proclamation, Radical Republicans who were abolitionists before the war had been pushing Lincoln for quite some time to take an action like this proclamation (b). According to the proclamation, all slaves in areas still in rebellion as of January 1, 1863 were free (c). The North had experienced a series of defeats in Virginia battles, so to keep the proclamation's issuance from seeming like a desperate act, Secretary of State Seward advised Lincoln not to announce his issuance of the proclamation until there was a Northern victory (d). This occurred with the Battle of Antietam on September 17, 1863, after which Lincoln made the announcement (e).

111. B: Though Davis had decided to order the inclusion of blacks in the Confederate armies (a) to shore up the South's sagging defenses, the war was over before any blacks could be drafted. Before September of 1864, the great numbers of casualties and the apparent inconclusiveness of the war were discouraging to Northerners as well as Southerners, so much so that even Lincoln doubted he could win re-election that year (c). In September, however, William Tecumseh Sherman captured Atlanta and marched from there through Georgia to Savannah, leaving massive devastation in his wake. The news of this greatly increased morale in the North, and combined with other victories by the North, allowed Lincoln to win the election (d). It also helped the North finally win the war. While General Robert E. Lee surrendered to Ulysses S. Grant at Appomattox, Virginia, on April 9, 1865, it took a few more weeks for other Southern armies in different places to surrender. When Lincoln was shot on April 14, 1865, he died before being informed that the North had won the war (e).

112. D: Lincoln's Vice President Andrew Johnson, who succeeded to the presidency after Lincoln's assassination, did not require that Confederate debts be paid, but rather that they be forgiven. Some Southern states refused to comply with this stipulation. Johnson did follow Lincoln's policies very closely (a), making some of them only a little bit stricter (b) so that they were still more generous to the South than the Radical Republicans liked. He stipulated that the Thirteenth Amendment must be ratified (c), and even though some Southern states refused, it was ratified in December of 1865. He also required that the former Confederate states' secessions be renounced, and he furthermore advised that blacks should be allowed to vote (e).

113. E: It is not accurate that the U.S. bought Alaska for a price of $5.5 million. The price America paid Russia for Alaska in 1867 was $7.2 million. The Russian minister did offer to sell Alaska to Seward in 1866 (a). Russia was motivated to sell Alaska because the fur that had provided trade to this territory was by this time mostly exhausted (b). Russians were also motivated to sell Alaska because at that time, a war with England appeared imminent. If that happened, Russians felt they would lose Alaska to England (c). Secretary of State Seward was passionate about expansionism, and is credited with being chiefly responsible for pushing America's acquisition of Alaska through Congress (d). Seward also advised Congress that the sale would be a reward to Russia for its friendliness to the original American government during the Civil War, a time when England and France seemed friendlier towards the Confederate states.

114. C: Resistance in some Southern states to President Johnson's Reconstruction plan, which was not very radical in the first place, did not take the form of refusing to pass black codes. Black codes

restricted former slaves' freedoms, and Southern states resistant to the Reconstruction passed black codes. These resistors also refused to ratify the Thirteenth Amendment (a), which abolished slavery, to make it part of the Constitution (it was ratified by a majority anyway). They further refused to rescind Confederate debt (b) or to grant the vote to blacks (d). They also elected many former Confederates who had held high ranks into Congress and other positions of power in the South (e). These actions backfired in the sense that they gave Radical Republicans grounds to accuse the South of refusing to accept the outcome of the Civil War. They used these accusations to get Congress to leave Southern representatives out of its plans for the Reconstruction.

115. A: It is not true that Grant won the presidency by a landslide in 1868. He actually won by a very narrow margin—300,000 more popular votes than his opponent Horatio Seymour, a former New York governor. The Republican Convention that year was controlled by the Radical Republicans (b), who advocated Radical Reconstruction (c). The narrow margin by which Grant won, considering that around 700,000 blacks in Southern states under army occupation had voted in this election (and likely all of them had voted for Grant), meant that Grant did not get a majority of the white vote. Since Grant was a popular and strong candidate, Republicans saw as a result of this election that it would be politically pragmatic to give all blacks in both the South and North the right to vote. They drafted the Fifteenth Amendment, giving blacks the vote (d). Under these circumstances, it was ironic that this amendment was so disliked in the North that the only reason it got the required three-fourths majority vote was because Southern states were forced by Congress to ratify it (e).

116. B: Following the war, property values in the South were reduced not to half, but to a tenth of antebellum levels. Corrupt political machines (such as "Boss" Tweed's Tammany Hall in New York) rose to power in both the North and South during the Reconstruction (a). Northerners who traveled south to take part in Reconstruction governments, known as carpetbaggers, caused distress among Southerners (c) for maintaining widespread corruption in the governments, as did Southerners who supported Reconstruction rule, who were called scalawags (d). The Ku Klux Klan and similar groups used intimidation and violence to stop blacks and white Republicans from voting (e).

117. E: All of these were scandals associated with corruption during Grant's presidency. The Black Friday Scandal (a) involved two businessmen, Jim Fiske and Jay Gould, who concocted a scheme to corner the gold market. They recruited Grant's brother-in-law to tell Grant that it would benefit the farmers to stop sales of gold by the government. Not knowing any better, Grant agreed, and the resultant drastic bidding up of gold prices on "Black Friday" ruined a good many businessmen. In 1873, Congress voted for the President to receive a 100% increase in salary and for Congress to receive a 50% increase, both retroactive for two years. This "Salary Grab Act" (b) outraged the people. When the Democrats won the next congressional election, they repealed the act. The Whiskey Ring Fraud (c) was a conspiracy by whiskey distillers and Treasury Department officers to defraud the government out of a great deal of money obtained from the whiskey tax. President Grant's personal secretary was involved in this. Also, again not knowing any better, Grant had received gifts offered to him that were suspect. When the fraud was investigated, Grant tried to protect his secretary. W.W. Belknap, Secretary of War under Grant, took bribes (d) from dishonest agents who had a part in the Department of War's administration of Indian affairs. Belknap resigned to avoid being impeached when the fact that he had accepted bribes became known. Other scandals during the Grant administration included the Credit Mobilier Scandal and the Sanborn Contract Fraud.

118. D: Those who favored deflation wanted to take the greenbacks instituted in wartime out of circulation and return to the gold standard. Deflation was favored by economic conservatives, business people, and creditors over inflation (a). Conversely, debtors were in favor of inflation, not

deflation (b). This is because they had originally borrowed money backed by the gold standard, and it would be much easier on them if they could repay their debts with paper money that had depreciated in value and was worth less than the money they had borrowed. When Congress demonetized silver in 1873, this upset proponents of inflation, not deflation (c). More silver was available from silver mining in the West, so some people saw silver as implicated in inflation. Congress's demonetization of silver facilitated the return to a gold standard. This action by Congress angered those in favor of inflation. Congress continued in this direction in 1875 by passing the Specie Resumption Act, which required resumption of specie payments, which gave people the ability to redeem paper money for gold. This moved things closer towards eliminating greenbacks and returning to the gold standard, not the other way around (e).

119. C: Although the Democratic and Republican parties were indeed fraudulent in their tactics, neither of the candidates was. Both Tilden and Hayes were honest men. Both supported civil service reform, deflation, and gold-backed currency. Democrats nominated New York Governor Tilden (a) in their campaign against government corruption because he had put an end to the corrupt Boss Tweed political machine in New York (b). Republicans chose Ohio Governor Hayes (d) instead. Grant. Tilden won the popular vote, but needed one more electoral vote. Twenty votes were in dispute, as they came from Southern states still under federal military occupation that were run by Republicans. Congress formed a commission to resolve the situation. This commission, to be made up of five Senators, five Congressmen, and five Supreme Court justices, was supposed to have seven Republicans, seven Democrats, and one independent. The Republicans, however, manipulated the commission (e) by getting the legislature from the independent justice's state to elect him to a Senate seat. When this justice vacated his Supreme Court seat to assume office in the Senate, all the other justices left were Republicans. One of these Republican justices was selected for the commission instead of an independent (since the independent was gone). Therefore, all of the commission's votes for giving the 20 disputed votes to Hayes were eight to seven. This was how he won the election.

120. B: The Compromise of 1877 did not modify Reconstruction to appease both Republicans and Democrats. Rather, it involved Hayes promising to end Reconstruction in return for the Democrats' promising not to challenge his election (e). This was a response to the threat made by Democrats in Congress to overturn the election results (a), since it was obvious those results had been arrived at in an unethical manner. In addition to promising to end Reconstruction, Hayes agreed that he would consider the interests of Southerners (c), and would remove the remainder of the federal troops still occupying parts of the South (d). Note: It has been observed that the chief reason for the end of the Reconstruction was that the North lost interest in it. This was due to government corruption, economic depression ensuing from the Panic of 1873, and the fact that voters in the North had grown tired of endeavors to rebuild the South. It was also due to the fact that Radical Republicans who had promoted Reconstruction, like Thaddeus Stevens and Charles Sumner, had died. Therefore, it is presumed by historians that, while the Compromise of 1877 forced and formalized the end of the Reconstruction, it probably would have ended regardless due to lack of Northern motivation.

U. S. History Practice Test #2

1. Who was the president after Abraham Lincoln?

    a. Andrew Jackson
    b. Andrew Johnson
    c. Ulysses S. Grant
    d. Samuel J. Tilden
    e. Rutherford B. Hayes

2. Which of the following statements regarding the president's plans for Reconstruction in 1865 is incorrect?

    a. The president's plan kept former Confederate military and political officials from engaging in politics.
    b. The president's pardon of many former Confederate military and political officials let them take offices.
    c. The president's plans for Reconstruction allowed former Confederate officials only a minority of offices.
    d. The president's actions initially resulted in a majority of former Confederate officials being put in office.
    e. regarding new Southern members were rejected by Congress when it reconvened.

3. Which of the following took control of the government's Reconstruction policies after 1866?

    a. The president more than Congress
    b. Moderate Democrats in Congress
    c. Moderate Republicans in Congress
    d. Radical Republicans in Congress
    e. Conservative Democrats in Congress

4. Which of the following was not one of the provisions of the Fourteenth Amendment (1868)?

    a. The former Confederacy was enjoined to repay its debt.
    b. US citizenship was defined for the purpose of voting.
    c. Representation proportions were linked to voting rights.
    d. Rebels would not be permitted to hold political offices.
    e. These are all provisions of the Fourteenth Amendment.

5. Which of the following was not a provision of the Reconstruction Act of 1867?

    a. Confederate officials could not vote pending ratification of new state constitutions.
    b. The South was divided into five military districts until new governments could form.
    c. Black Americans could vote for constitutional conventions and all elections thereafter.
    d. Ratification of the Fourteenth Amendment and new constitutions by the Southern states.
    e. No citizens would be denied voting rights based on their race, color, or previous status of slave.

6. Which of the following events is not a social or economic outcome of the Reconstruction?

a. Howard University was established by the Freedman's Bureau.
b. American Missionary Association founded Atlanta University.
c. African Americans started to found black community churches.
d. Sharecroppers were aided by landowners to make some profits.
e. Falling prices for cotton led to depression in the Southern states.

7. Which of the following was not a factor in the dissolution of Reconstruction?

a. The advent of Liberal Republicans who disagreed with Radical Republicans
b. Congress' passage of the 1872 Amnesty Act, which pardoned Confederates
c. President Grant's stringent military policing of the former Confederate states
d. Democrats taking control of the House of Representatives
e. House Democrats resuming control of a majority of past Confederate states

8. Which state's vote in the election of 1876 was not disputed?

a. North Carolina
b. South Carolina
c. Louisiana
d. Florida
e. Oregon

9. Which statement is not true about the western US in the late 1800s?

a. The buffalo population was depleted by white settlers in the course of westward expansion.
b. The Native Americans' economic reliance on buffalo resulted in depletion of buffalo herds.
c. The depletion of buffalo on the western plains augmented conflicts of whites with Indians.
d. The Dawes Act of 1887 converted property ownership by Indians from tribal to individual.
e. The Dawes Act sought to reform white treatment of Indians, but in practice, this backfired.

10. Of the following, which was not one of the first industries to develop in the western US?

a. Gold mining
b. Silver mining
c. Lumber industry
d. Cattle industry
e. Sheepherding

11. Which of the following was not a factor that effectively ended the open-range cattle industry on the western Great Plains in the late 1880s?

a. The invention of barbed wire by Joseph Glidden in 1873
b. The incursion of farmers and shepherds to the Great Plains
c. The major blizzards that occurred between 1885 and 1887
d. The lower profits caused by cattlemen's mismanagement
e. The droughts occurring between blizzards in the period of 1885-1887

12. Which of the following laws was instrumental to spurring westward migration to the Great Plains between 1860 and 1880?

a. The Homestead Act
b. The Timber Culture Act
c. The Desert Land Act
d. None of these laws were instrumental to spurring westward migration to the Great Plains during that period.
e. All of these laws were instrumental to spurring westward migration to the Great Plains during that period.

13. When was the first American transcontinental railroad finished?

a. 1862
b. 1890
c. 1869
d. 1865
e. 1880

14. Of the following American railroads, which was/were primarily funded by the government?

a. The Santa Fe Railroad
b. The Great Northern Railroad
c. The Northern Pacific Railroad
d. The Southern Pacific Railroad
e. They all were government funded.

15. Which of the following industries did not experience major growth from the late 1800s to the early 1900s?

a. Beef
b. Steel
c. Oil
d. Cloth
e. Wood

16. Which statement does not accurately portray changes to the American labor force wrought by industrialization in the late 19th and early 20th centuries?

a. By 1880, there were almost five million individuals working in industrial jobs.
b. More than two million women were employed in factories or offices by 1880.
c. By the year 1890, 25% of children aged 10 to 15 years were in the workforce.
d. During these years it was common for workers to sustain injuries and illness.
e. Workers' compensation, disability, and retirement did not exist for workers.

17. Which of the following is true regarding business consolidation around the turn of the 19th and 20th centuries in American industries?

a. John D. Rockefeller used vertical integration with his Standard Oil Company.
b. Gustavus Swift was the first to use horizontal integration with meat packing.
c. Social Darwinists were opposed to consolidation as well as to deregulation.
d. Economists against consolidation favored more control of natural processes.
e. The Sherman Anti-Trust Act proved quite effective in preventing monopoly.

18. Which of the following statistics is not accurate with respect to the urbanization of America between 1870 and 1920?

    a. The number of Americans who lived in cities grew more than fivefold during this time.
    b. By 1920, almost half of the American population lived in cities with over 2500 people.
    c. Cities having populations greater than 100 000 went up by more than 3.5 times.
    d. Cities having populations greater than 500 000 increased to six-fold.

19. Around the turn of the 19th and 20th century, when city slums resulted from overcrowding due to immigration, in which of the following areas was the least improvement made?

    a. Housing
    b. Sewage
    c. Firefighting
    d. Street lights
    e. Water supply

20. Which of the following was not a development of city culture in America around the turn of the 19th and 20th century?

    a. Baseball had become America's favorite professional sport by the 1880s.
    b. Vaudeville shows rode trains from cities to small towns across America.
    c. Early directors like D. W. Griffith developed the motion picture industry.
    d. Pulitzer and Hearst gave mass popularity to newspapers and magazines.
    e. All of these were American urban cultural developments during this time.

21. What was not a characteristic of the "city machines" that arose as a result of rapid urban growth in the late 1800s?

    a. A high degree of organization
    b. A high degree of corruption
    c. A high degree of efficiency
    d. A high degree of wealth
    e. A high degree of power

22. Which of the following was not one of the structural reforms to city governments that began in the 1890s?

    a. City manager jobs
    b. City commissions
    c. Citywide elections
    d. Nonpartisan elections
    e. These were all reforms.

23. Of the following, which was not a national political issue for 1880s America?

    a. Civil service reform
    b. The gold standard
    c. Protective tariffs
    d. Women's suffrage
    e. Railroad regulation

24. Which is true about the US government between 1877 and 1901?

a. Congress had more influence during this time than the presidents had.
b. Most presidents had more control during this time than Congress had.
c. Democrats mostly dominated the Senate, House, and presidency at this time.
d. Republicans mostly had control of the presidency and Congress at this time.
e. The presidents and Congress tended to have an equal balance of power.

25. Which answer correctly lists the following US presidents in chronological order?

a. McKinley, Harrison, Arthur, Cleveland, Hayes, Garfield
b. Hayes, Arthur, McKinley, Garfield, Harrison, Cleveland
c. Garfield, Hayes, Cleveland, McKinley, Arthur, Harrison
d. Hayes, Garfield, Arthur, Cleveland, Harrison, McKinley
e. Cleveland, Garfield, Hayes, Harrison, McKinley, Arthur

26. Which of the following had the least influence on the formation of the national Populist Party between the 1860s and the 1890s?

a. A very large drop in wheat prices
b. The organization of the Granges
c. The formation of the Farmers' Alliances
d. The 1890 Kansas state elections
e. These all had an equal influence.

27. Which political party nominated William Jennings Bryan for president in the 1896 election?

a. The Democrats
b. The Republicans
c. The Populists
d. Both (b) and (c)
e. Both (a) and (c)

28. Which of the following was not an influence on the development of the Progressive Era in the early 20th century?

a. Alfred T. Mahan's book, The Influence of Sea Power upon History
b. Lincoln Steffens' book, The Shame of the Cities
c. Upton Sinclair's book, The Jungle
d. Author and reformer W.E.B. Du Bois' founding of the NAACP
e. Wisconsin Governor Robert M. LaFollette's state policy changes

29. Which of the following laws was not passed by President Theodore Roosevelt?

a. The Hepburn Act
b. The Meat Inspection Act
c. The Clayton Antitrust Act
d. The Pure Food and Drug Act
e. The National Reclamation Act

30. Which action by President William Howard Taft was not in the spirit of Progressive reform?

    a. His signing the Paine-Aldrich Tariff
    b. His support of the Mann-Elkins Act
    c. His enacting the Sixteenth Amendment
    d. His enacting the Seventeenth Amendment
    e. None of these actions supported reform.

31. Which of the following laws was not passed during Woodrow Wilson's presidency, 1913-1921?

    a. The Federal Reserve Act
    b. The Federal Farm Loan Act
    c. The Wilson-Gorman Tariff
    d. The Underwood Tariff
    e. The Adamson Act

32. Of the following, which did not signify an instance of early American expansionism after the Civil War?

    a. The purchase of Alaska from Russia as negotiated by Secretary of State Seward.
    b. President Grover Cleveland's stance with respect to the annexation of Hawaii
    c. Alfred T. Mahan's campaigning for the US to develop a larger navy
    d. The establishment of a US naval base in Samoa and eventual annexation of some of the islands
    e. Secretary of State Olney's and in preventing England from seizing Venezuela's land

33. Who was President of the United States during the Spanish-American War?

    a. McKinley
    b. Harrison
    c. Cleveland
    d. T. Roosevelt
    e. W. H. Taft

34. Which of the following correctly describes outcomes of the Spanish-American War?

    a. The territory of Guam was sold to the US.
    b. Spain ceded Guam and the Philippines to the US.
    c. Spain sold Guam, Cuba, and Puerto Rico to the US.
    d. US bought the Philippines and Cuba became independent
    e. Cuba, Guam, and Puerto Rico gained independence.

35. What is not a true statement regarding US-Philippine relations in the 19th and 20th centuries?

    a. Emilio Aguinaldo first declared the independence of the Philippines in January, 1899.
    b. Aguinaldo started an insurrection for Philippine independence that continued until 1902.
    c. America tried to Americanize the Philippines in the 1900s, but problems still occurred.
    d. In 1916, the US passed the Jones Act promising Philippine independence.
    e. The Jones Act of 1916 granted the Philippines independence, effective immediately.

36. Which of the following statements is accurate concerning the US and Cuba after the Spanish-American War?

a. The new Cuban constitution let the US government approve all of its treaties with other countries.
b. The US made Cuba put the Platt Amendment in its constitution, but this was only a formality.
c. Because Cuba was now independent, the US would not engage in military interventions there.
d. The US offered to send military aid to Cuba for political upheavals but Cuba refused.
e. The newly independent Cuba did not experience enough turbulence to need US intervention.

37. What did not contribute to ending America's neutrality in World War I?

a. Germany's declaration of a war zone surrounding the British Isles in February, 1913
b. Germany's declaration of a war on Russia after Archduke Ferdinand's assassination
c. Germany's sinking the British ship *Lusitania*, which killed 128 American passengers
d. Germany's declaration of unrestricted submarine warfare on all ships in the war zone
e. Germany's telegram to the Mexican government trying to recruit Mexico as an ally.

38. Which of the following did not help prepare the US for entry into World War I?

a. The National Defense Act
b. The Navy Act
c. The Revenue Act
d. The Selective Service Act
e. These all prepared the US for entry into World War I.

39. What federal agency was not an outcome of World War I?

a. The Food Administration
b. The Fuel Administration
c. Railroad Administration
d. These all were outcomes of World War I.
e. None were outcomes of World War I.

40. What was the "Great Migration" in the US around the time of World War I?

a. The immigration of millions of eastern and southern Europeans to America during the war
b. The departure of many Americans who disagreed with America's neutrality to other nations
c. The movement of half a million African Americans from South to North and to other states
d. The movement of millions of American women from managing households to factory work
e. The mass expatriations by Americans who were against the Espionage Act and Sedition Act

41. Of the following terms of peace following World War I, which was of paramount importance to President Woodrow Wilson?

a. Freedom of sea navigation
b. Open agreements of peace
c. National self-determination
d. Equality of trade conditions
e. Organizing a League of Nations

42. What event occurred after World War I but did not characterize the post-World War I general withdrawal from prewar progressive reform?

    a. Congress' lowering of taxes for corporations
    b. Passage of the Federal Highway Act in 1921
    c. The Fordney-McCumber Tariff Act of 1922
    d. Passage of the Sheppard-Towner Act in 1921
    e. Thirty percent drop in union memberships in the 1920s

43. Which of the following statements is true about agriculture under the Coolidge administration?

    a. The federal government's support of businesses included supporting agriculture.
    b. Congress' passage of the McNary-Haugen Acts was detrimental to the farmers.
    c. When Congress passed the McNary-Haugen Acts, Coolidge used his veto power.
    d. When Congress passed the McNary-Haugen Acts, Coolidge agreed with these.
    e. The McNary-Haugen Acts (1927, 1928) were not to give farmers price supports.

44. What is true regarding the federal government's position relative to immigration in the 1920s?

    a. Congress passed the Johnson Act in 1921 to encourage immigration to America.
    b. The Johnson Act based its quota on figures taken from the census made in 1910.
    c. The Johnson Act passed in 1921 stipulated that immigration meet a quota of 5%.
    d. The Johnson-Reid Act of 1924 based its quota on figures from the 1920 census.
    e. The Johnson-Reid Act of 1924 stipulated that immigration reach a quota of 6%.

45. Which of the following statements is correct regarding the American economy in the 1920s?

    a. America's gross national product went up 40% from 1919 to 1929.
    b. Three-quarters of the houses and apartments in America had electricity by this time.
    c. The number of people who owned cars in America quadrupled at this time.
    d. Twelve million American households had radios by the end of this decade.
    e. All of these statements are correct about the 1920s American economy.

46. Of changes to the US population in the 1920s, which of the following is not accurate?

    a. 1920 was the first time the majority of citizens lived in cities of more than 2500.
    b. Around six million citizens moved from farms to jobs in cities during the 1920s.
    c. During the 1920s, the population increased as the birth rates rose.
    d. The number of American women in the work force rose by around two million.
    e. The proportion of divorces compared to marriages increased during this decade.

47. Which of the following factors affecting American leisure pursuits in the 1920s is incorrect?

    a. Americans spent more money than previous generations on leisure pursuits.
    b. Americans had more time for leisure activities than did previous generations.
    c. Due to the influx in car ownership, Americans were more mobile.
    d. Movie theater attendance doubled.

48. Which of the following writers and musicians was not a member of the Harlem Renaissance?

a. Langston Hughes
b. George Gershwin
c. Alain Locke
d. Louis Armstrong
e. Bessie Smith

49. What was the subject matter of the 1925 Scopes trial?

a. Teaching Darwin's theory of evolution in public school
b. Violent crimes against minorities by the Ku Klux Klan
c. A murder trial of political anarchist Italian immigrants
d. Garvey's Universal Negro Improvement Association
e. None of the above

50. Which of the following did not contribute to the Great Depression, beginning in 1929?

a. Disproportionate distribution of new wealth during the 1920s
b. Unstable corporate structures and increased corporate debt
c. Stock over speculation and engaging in trades using borrowed money
d. Decreased trade with Europe coupled with European debt defaults
e. The extreme US economic reliance on too many industries

51. Of President Franklin Delano Roosevelt's first New Deal programs, which were eliminated by Supreme Court decisions not long after their inception?

a. The Civilian Conservation Corps and the Federal Emergency Relief Act
b. The National Recovery Administration and Agricultural Adjustment Act
c. The Public Works Administration and National Recovery Administration
d. The Commodity Credit Corporation and National Labor Relations Board
e. Emergency Banking Relief Bill and Securities and Exchange Commission

52. Of the following, who was (were) opposed to any part of Roosevelt's first New Deal?

a. Fr. Charles Coughlin
b. Dr. Francis Townsend
c. Senator Huey Long
d. The Supreme Court
e. All of the above

53. In FDR's second New Deal, which program was not authorized by the Emergency Relief Appropriation Act?

a. The Public Works Administration
b. The Works Progress Administration
c. The Resettlement Administration
d. Rural Electrification Administration
e. The National Youth Administration

54. Which of the following statements is correct?

a. The Social Security Act was created as a part of the First New Deal.
b. The Social Security Act was part of the First and Second New Deals.
c. The Social Security Act was not part of either New Deal.
d. The Social Security Act was created as part of the Second New Deal.
e. The Social Security Act was a New Deal program with minor impact.

55. Which of the following events did not occur during the Great Depression?

a. The Dust Bowl caused 350 000 farm families to move from the southern Great Plains to California.
b. The 1934 Indian Reorganization Act reversed the land ownership statutes of the 1887 Dawes Act.
c. The AFL and the CIO merged as labor unions improved and grew throughout the 1930s.
d. Executive Order 8802 called for Fair Employment Practices Committee to oversee defense jobs for blacks.
e. Secretary of Labor Frances Perkins became the first woman to occupy a position in the US Cabinet.

56. Which of the following is not a correct characteristic of "court-packing?"

a. FDR succeeded in filling the Supreme Court with justices he appointed in order to ensure approval of his programs.
b. FDR proposed to Congress that he be allowed to appoint more justices in the Supreme Court.
c. FDR's "court-packing" idea was a reaction to the termination of his programs by the Supreme Court.
d. FDR's proposal was effective in that after it the Supreme Court began approving New Deal acts.
e. FDR's proposal was rejected in Congress but it accomplished the results he desired nevertheless.

57. Which of the following did not occur following the Second New Deal in the late 1930s?

a. In 1937, FDR made limits on public spending in an effort to keep the budget balanced.
b. The Federal Reserve Board decided to increase interest rates.
c. The rate of unemployment increased by nearly 3 million by 1938.
d. Due to Presidential and Federal Reserve Board actions, the economy improved.
e. Roosevelt resumed deficit spending in response to unemployment.

58. Which of the following is not true about the US presidential election in 1940?

a. America's attention was beginning to focus on the war in Europe.
b. The American economy was bolstered by defense industry jobs created to support the war in Europe.
c. President Roosevelt promised not to send Americans to foreign wars as part of his reelection campaign. Reelection
d. President Roosevelt ran for reelection in 1940 against the Republican candidate Wendell Willkie.
e. When FDR won the election in1940, he was only the second after Washington to serve three terms.

59. Which of the following is not accurate regarding the US attitude toward war and peace during the 1920s?

a. Following the experiences of World War I, Americans were generally adverse to war activity.
b. The Women's Peace Union and other organizations promoted peaceful alternatives to fighting wars.
c. Secretary of State Hughes advocated naval expansion at the 1921-1922 Washington Conference.
d. US, England, France, Italy and Japan agreed to naval reduction, including destruction of ships.
e. The US pioneered the Kellogg-Briand Pact, eventually signed by 62 countries, denouncing war.

60. Which of the following statements regarding the world economy after World War I is correct?

a. Both the US and Europe were in serious debt following the war.
b. The passage of the Dawes Plan (1924) gave Germany more time to repay debts.
c. As the US stock market appreciated, Americans lent more money to Germans.
d. The 1929 Young Plan was successful in resolving international debt problems.
e. When some countries defaulted on loans, President Hoover demanded payment.

61. Which statement about US tariffs after World War I is not true?

a. The US was the largest exporter of products in the world after World War I.
b. The US raised protective tariffs by passing the Hawley-Smoot Act in 1930.
c. The US lowered protective tariffs by the Fordney-McCumber Act in 1922.
d. Secretary of State Hull lowered tariffs using the 1934 Reciprocal Trade Agreement Act.
e. In 1934, the Export-Import Bank stimulated trade via international loans.

62. Which of the following Latin American countries did not have dictatorships supported by the US after World War I?

a. Dominican Republic
b. Honduras
c. Nicaragua
d. Cuba
e. All of the above had dictatorships supported by the US.

63. Which statement is incorrect with regard to the US position on war before and at the onset of World War II in Europe?

a. The US Congress had passed a Neutrality Act in 1935, which prohibited shipping arms to countries at war.
b. The US Congress had passed a Neutrality Act in 1936, which prohibited lending money to nations at war.
c. The US Congress had passed a Neutrality Act in 193, which prohibited Americans from riding ships owned by warring countries.
d. The US Congress did not make changes to its neutrality policies when war broke out in Europe.

64. Which of the following statements about the beginning of World War II is not correct?

a. Hitler attained power in Germany in 1933, and he occupied the Rhineland in 1936.
b. Hitler recruited Italy and Japan to be Germany's allies after occupying the Rhineland.
c. Hitler invaded Czechoslovakia during 1938-1939 and then took over the country.
d. After his occupation of Czechoslovakia, Hitler invaded Poland on September 1, 1939.
e. Reacting to Hitler's military aggression, France and Poland declared war on Germany.

65. Which statement is true concerning the US position relative to Asian aggression in the 1930s?

a. The first sign of Japanese aspirations to world power was its 1931 invasion of Manchuria.
b. In the "Stimson Doctrine" the Secretary of State recognized Japan's action as belligerent.
c. President Roosevelt officially recognized the Sino-Japanese War when it started in 1937.
d. Japan's apology for sinking the US *Panay*, demanded by FDR, resolved Asian tensions.
e. In 1939, America reaffirmed a 1911 trade treaty between the US and Japan.

66. What event was not an aspect of or catalyst to America's support efforts for England in World War II before the US entered the war?

a. Signing the Tripartite Pact with England and France
b. France's fall to Germany and the apparently imminent defeat of England
c. The sale of surplus military supplies to England and France in 1940
d. America's exchange with England of US destroyers for naval bases

67. Before entering World War II, which of the following events did not occur as a result of America's desire to aid England's war efforts?

a. Congress passed the Selective Training and Service Act for a peacetime draft.
b. FDR pushed the Lend-Lease Act through Congress to send armaments to England.
c. Roosevelt and Churchill signed the Atlantic Charter agreeing to war purposes.
d. Congress revised neutrality acts to ship England arms in armed US ships.
e. All of these events transpired as part of America's aid to England's war efforts.

68. Which statement correctly pairs actions and reactions leading to US entry to World War II?

a. FDR froze Japan's US assets after Japan signed a three-way agreement with Germany and Italy.
b. FDR placed an embargo on certain shipments to Japan after Japan invaded French Indochina.
c. Japan declared war on the US following the attack on the naval base at Pearl Harbor.
d. The US Congress voted to declare war on Japan following the attack on Pearl Harbor.
e. Germany and Italy declared war on the US, and in turn the US declared war on Japan.

69. Which of the following events contributed least to Germany's surrender in World War II?

a. Germany's invasion of the Soviet Union
b. Soviet victory at the Battle of Stalingrad
c. The US and British invasion of Italy
d. Allied invasion of Normandy, then Paris
e. The Soviet arrival at the Elbe via Poland

70. Which of the following Pacific events brought an end to World War II?

a. The US sank Japanese aircraft carriers at Midway.
b. The US won the Battle of the Philippine Sea.
c. The US bombed Hiroshima and Nagasaki.
d. The US defeated Japan at Okinawa.
e. None of these events ended the war.

71. Of the following international diplomatic conferences, which one made US-Soviet differences apparent?

a. The Potsdam conference
b. The conference at Yalta
c. Dumbarton Oaks conference
d. The Tehran conference
e. The Casablanca conference

72. Of the following demonstrations of Soviet disagreements with the US after World War II, which was the first to transpire?

a. The Soviet Union backed Communist control of Hungary and Romania.
b. The Soviet Union endorsed Communist control of Czechoslovakia.
c. The Soviets did not allow conservatives to serve in the Communist government imposed on Poland.
d. Soviets refused to take part in the international Baruch Plan because they mistrusted American motives.
e. Winston Churchill referred to the division developing in Europe as an "iron curtain."

73. Which of the following was responsible for creating the CIA and DOD?

a. Truman Doctrine
b. National Security Act
c. Marshall Plan
d. North Atlantic Treaty Organization (NATO)
e. None of the above created the CIA and DOD.

74. Which of the following is not true regarding the Korean War?

a. Fighting between Chinese Nationalists and Communists existed before World War II.
b. Truman's administration would not recognize Mao's new People's Republic of China.
c. The United Nations Security Council approved the US bid for military intervention.
d. General MacArthur's invasion of Inchon on September 15, 1950, was not successful.
e. Armistice discussions began in July, 1951, but the war did not end until July, 1953.

75. Of the following events, which one took place last?

a. USSR launched the satellite *Sputnik*
b. China produced an atomic bomb
c. Soviet detonation of a hydrogen bomb
d. US detonation of a hydrogen bomb
e. The US organization of NASA

76. Which statement about relations between the Middle East and the US and Europe in the 1950s is incorrect?

a. President Nasser of Egypt refused to align with the US in the Cold War.
b. President Eisenhower removed US funding from the Aswan Dam in 1956.
c. President Nasser nationalized the Suez Canal, which was owned by England.
d. In 1956, Egypt attacked Israel, and England and France joined in the war.
e. In 1957, President Eisenhower stated the US would support Middle Eastern efforts against Communism.

77. Which of the following did not happen during President John F. Kennedy's administration?

a. The Soviet Union lifted its moratorium on above-ground nuclear testing.
b. The US production of nuclear weapons proliferated greatly.
c. The Limited Test Ban Treaty caused the nuclear arms race to grind to a halt.
d. The President refused to participate in negotiations regarding Berlin's status.
e. The USSR built the Berlin Wall between East Berlin and West Berlin.

78. Which _most_ correctly describes the group that invaded the Bay of Pigs in 1961?

a. Members of the US CIA
b. A group of Cuban exiles
c. The people of Cuba
d. The US
e. CIA-sponsored Cuban exiles

79. Which statement is not true about the Cuban Missile Crisis?

a. JFK launched an invasion of Cuba to remove Soviet missiles.
b. JFK demanded publicly that the USSR remove its missiles.
c. JFK announced a global alert for the American armed forces.
d. JFK sent ships to the Caribbean to intercept Soviet shipments.
e. JFK agreed not to invade Cuba if the USSR removed its missiles.

80. Of the following events, which was the earliest precursor to the Vietnam War?

a. The Truman administration financially supporting French imperialism
b. Vietminh rebellion against the French
c. The Eisenhower administration's financial support of the French cause
d. The French signing of the Geneva Accords, which divided the country
e. The US support of a military coup ousting South Vietnamese Diem

81. Which of the following was not part of President Nixon's policy of "Vietnamization?"

a. The US contributed monetary assistance to the South Vietnamese.
b. South Vietnam would be given more responsibility for the war in this policy.
c. President Nixon began removing US troops from the country in increments.
d. President Nixon accelerated the US bombing of North Vietnam in this policy.
e. All of these things were elements of President Nixon's "Vietnamization" policy.

82. Which of the following statements concerning events leading up to and including the Vietnam cease-fire is not true?

a. The ongoing peace talks made sufficient progress to culminate in a cease-fire.
b. President Nixon directed the US to heavily bomb North Vietnam in 1972.
c. North Vietnam and the US signed a cease-fire soon after bombing was escalated.
d. The cease-fire required US to withdraw all troops from Vietnam in 60 days.
e. The cease-fire required coalition government with Vietcong of South Vietnam.

83. Which of the following statements regarding détente during Nixon's administration (1970s) is not correct?

a. President Nixon's unprecedented 1972 announcement, "I will go to China," shocked America.
b. Nixon's China visit set the stage for diplomatic recognition and also aided relations with the USSR.
c. Nixon's visit led to the US recognition of China and a Soviet trade agreement, both in 1973.
d. The Strategic Arms Limitations Talks Treaty with Russia was aided by Nixon's visit to China.
e. The Soviet Union and US signed agreements for grain trade and missile limits the same year.

84. During President Jimmy Carter's administration, which of the following actions did he not take relative to the Cold War?

a. Carter instigated the SALT-II Treaty limiting bombers and long-range missiles.
b. When the Soviets invaded Afghanistan in 1979, Carter acted to reinforce the SALT-II Treaty.
c. When the Soviets invaded Afghanistan in 1979, Carter stopped wheat shipments to Russia.
d. When Soviets invaded Afghanistan in 1979, Carter boycotted the Moscow summer Olympics.
e. When the Soviets invaded Afghanistan in 1979, Carter secretly supported Afghani resistance.

85. Which of the following was least associated with actions President Ronald Reagan took against Communism in his administration?

a. His reinforcement of America's military weaponry
b. His Strategic Defense Initiative for space defenses
c. His Reagan Doctrine supporting freedom fighters
d. His withdrawal of Cuban troops from Angola
e. His missile-banning agreement with Gorbachev

86. Which statement is not true about President Reagan's actions in Latin America?

a. Early in his first term, Reagan assisted El Salvador's leaders in resistance against leftist rebels.
b. The US trained "Contras" to depose Nicaragua's leftist government of Sandinistas.
c. Congress voted to stop aiding the Contras in 1984, and those actions remained in effect through 1988.
d. Reagan's administration covertly sold arms to Iran and gave the profits to the Contras.
e. Reagan deployed troops to depose a leftist regime on the Caribbean island of Grenada.

87. Which of the following statements regarding events in the Middle East that took place during the Reagan administration is not correct?

a. Israel invaded Lebanon to get rid of the Palestine Liberation Organization's camps there.
b. When a terrorist bombing killed 240 US Marines, Reagan escalated military action.
c. Lebanon was already in the midst of a civil war when Israeli troops invaded the country.
d. President Reagan deployed US Marines to Lebanon in 1982 on a peacekeeping mission.
e. After the Palestinian Intifada began, Reagan initiated talks with Arafat to promote peace.

88. Which answer does not correctly describe an event leading to the dissolution of the Soviet Union and the end of the Cold War?

a. Older generation Communists successfully staged a coup against Mikhail Gorbachev.
b. Soviet leader Gorbachev initiated Perestroika to restructure the Soviet economy.
c. Soviet leader Gorbachev instituted Glasnost to publicize the Soviet government.
d. The Berlin Wall came down, leading to reunification of East and West Germany.
e. In two years, Communist governments fell in seven Eastern European countries.

89. Of the following countries whose Communist governments fell during the disintegration of the Soviet Union, which one did not collapse during the same year as the others?

a. Poland
b. Hungary
c. Romania
d. Albania
e. Bulgaria

90. Which of the following was not a part of President George H.W. Bush's "New World Order," initiated between 1989-1992 and following the end of the Cold War?

a. The START I and START II treaties signed by the US and Russia
b. Government reform in Nicaragua and the end of civil war in El Salvador
c. The signing of NAFTA by three countries and its ratification by the Senate
d. The US intervention in the Persian Gulf War ended fighting
e. All of these were actions taken by the Bush administration from 1989-1992.

91. Of the following, which did not have a negative impact on the US economy after World War II?

a. The Servicemen's Readjustment Act of 1944
b. The demobilization of the US armed forces
c. A decrease in defense manufacturing
d. An increase in inflation rates
e. The decrease in union members' work hours

92. Which of the following is true about the Eightieth Congress during the Truman administration?

a. Congress approved the Taft-Hartley Act in 1947 after President Truman agreed to it.
b. The Taft-Hartley Act allowed workplaces to restrict employees to union members.
c. Congress raised farm aid and passed bills for health insurance and minimum wages.
d. Truman promoted his "Fair Deal," but bipartisan Southern congressmen foiled it.
e. American voters' approval of Congressional acts ensured the reelection of Truman.

93. Of the following, which person or group was *not* instrumental in postwar advancement of civil rights and desegregation?

a. The President
b. The Supreme Court
c. The Congress
d. The NAACP

94. In the 1940s and 1950s, which of the following did not exacerbate American paranoia about Communism?

a. Soviet and Chinese political climates
b. The Alger Hiss and Klaus Fuchs trials
c. Senator Joseph McCarthy's witch hunt
d. The Internal Security Act passed in 1950
e. These all exacerbated fear of Communism.

95. In President Eisenhower's "Dynamic Conservatism," which of his programs was less successful than the others listed here?

a. The enlargement of Social Security
b. Keeping the federal budget balanced
c. The passage of the 1954 Housing Act
d. The 1954 St. Lawrence Seaway project
e. The passage of the Highway Act of 1956

96. During the Civil Rights era of the 1950s, which of the following events furthered the civil rights cause?

a. The Supreme Court's decision in Brown v. Board of Education of Topeka
b. Governor Orval Faubus' actions relative to Little Rock High School
c. Eisenhower's use of National Guard paratroopers to protect students
d. The city of Little Rock's actions with regard to its high schools in 1958-1959
e. Both answer a. and c. furthered the cause of civil rights.

97. Of the following people or groups, which was not associated with the 1957 Montgomery Bus Boycott?

a. Rosa Parks
b. Martin Luther King, Jr.
c. The SNCC
d. The Supreme Court
e. The SCLC

98. Which statement about factors related to the growth of the US economy between 1945 and 1970 is incorrect?

a. The Baby Boom's greatly increased birth rates contributed to economic growth during this time.
b. The reduction in military spending after World War II contributed to the stronger US economy.
c. Government programs and growing affluence nearly quadrupled college enrollments in 20 years.
d. Increased mobility and bigger families caused fast suburban expansion, especially in the Sunbelt.
e. Infant deaths were reduced by a third and the lifespan increased by four years during this time period.

99. Which of the following does not accurately describe changes in the American entertainment industry in the years after World War II?

a. The number of TV sets in American households increased more than 5,000 times from 1946-1960.

b. In the face of competition from TV, radio stations shifted programming from dramas to music.

c. Nonconformist movements, like the Beat movement, in music and literature emerged.

d. With America's newfound affluence and mobility, movie attendance rose greatly from 1960-1970.

e. All of these accurately describe changes in the American entertainment industry after World War II.

100. Which of the following statements regarding exceptions to postwar prosperity in 1960s America is not true?

a. As of 1962, almost 15% of Americans had incomes at the government-defined poverty level.

b. The government-defined poverty level in 1962 was under $4,000 a year for a family of four.

c. Blacks in city ghettoes and Mexican American migrant workers made up major impoverished populations.

d. Native American Indians and whites living in Appalachia comprised major impoverished populations.

e. Elderly Americans who did not qualify for Social Security benefits comprised a major impoverished population.

101. Of the programs enacted by President Lyndon B. Johnson's administration, which was most closely related to John F. Kennedy's legacy?

a. The Economic Opportunity Act

b. The Civil Rights Act

c. The Great Society program

d. All of these were equally related to JFK's legacy.

e. None of these were related to JFK's legacy.

102. In LBJ's Great Society program, which of the following was not included?

a. Medicare

b. Voting rights

c. Federal aid to education

d. Ending the Vietnam War

e. The US Department of Housing and Urban Development

103. Which is not correct regarding black activism during the 1960s?

a. There was a riot in the Los Angeles ghetto of Watts in 1965.

b. There was a riot involving black activists in Newark, New Jersey, after the Watts riot.

c. The Mississippi Freedom Democrats unseated that state's delegation at the convention.

d. There was a riot involving black activists in Detroit, Michigan, after the riot in Watts.

e. The Black Panthers and Black Muslims became more active during this time period.

104. Of the following events, which did not have an impact on or was not associated with the "New Left" of protesting youth in the 1960s?

a. The organization of the Students for a Democratic Society (SDS)
b. The organization of the Berkeley Free Speech Movement at UC
c. The assassinations of Martin Luther King, Jr. and Bobby Kennedy
d. The violence that erupted at the Chicago Democratic convention
e. All of these were associated with or had an impact on the New Left.

105. Which of the following is not true about affirmative action?

a. In the case of *Bakke v. University of California,* the Supreme Court upheld affirmative action.
b. Affirmative action in the 1960s tried to raise black representation to approximate racial balance.
c. White critics contended that affirmative action backfired by engendering reverse discrimination.
d. Following *Bakke v. University of California,* Supreme Court rulings mitigated affirmative action.
e. All of these statements are true with respect to events associated with affirmative action programs.

106. Which of the following statements is not correct concerning feminism in the 1970s and 1980s?

a. President Ronald Reagan appointed Sandra Day O'Connor as the first female Supreme Court justice.
b. The administration of Republican President Ronald Reagan was generally against feminist goals.
c. The Equal Rights Amendment, which supported the goals of feminism, was passed by Congress in 1972.
d. The Equal Rights Amendment was ratified by Congress in 1983.

107. Which of the following statements regarding immigration to America during the 1980s is not true?

a. Twice as many immigrants came to America during the 1980s than during the 1970s.
b. Latin Americans comprised the largest proportion of immigrants to America in the 1980s.
c. Most immigrants to the US in the 1980s were Latin American, Asian, and Caribbean.
d. The 1986 Immigration Reform and Control Act impeded illegal Mexican immigration.
e. All of these statements are true with respect to immigration to America during the 1980s.

108. Which of the following regarding AIDS during the 1980s is not correct?

a. Cases of this new syndrome were first discovered in 1984.
b. The infection causing AIDS spread quickly in intravenous drug users.
c. Initially, AIDS spread quickly among male homosexuals.
d. Cases of AIDS multiplied at an average of more than 8,000 each year.
e. More than half of the reported cases of AIDS ended in death by 1988.

109. Of the following factors, which is not true regarding the US presidential election of 1992?

a. George Bush's handling of the Persian Gulf War earned him high approval ratings.
b. Bill Clinton received 47% of the votes while George Bush received 35% of votes.
c. Problems with America's domestic economy worked against Bush in the election.
d. Bill Clinton's campaign platform as a less liberal Democrat helped him in the race.
e. Texan H. Ross Perot's third-party candidacy diverted some votes away from Bush.

110. Which of the following is not true of issues in America during the Clinton administration?

a. Due to objections, Clinton amended his suspension of the ban on gays in the military to a "don't ask-don't tell" policy.
b. The Family and Medical Leave Act was passed in 1993, reforming employee policies in the event of family emergencies.
c. President Clinton proposed the provision of universal health care coverage, but it was rejected by Congress.
d. Clinton's plan to remedy the federal deficit via raising taxes and reducing federal spending was passed by Congress.

111. Which of the following statements regarding laws passed during the Clinton administration to control crime is not correct?

a. The Brady Handgun Violence Prevention Act stipulated a five-day waiting period to buy a handgun.
b. Following the shooting and consequent disability of James Brady, the "Brady Bill" passed without opposition.
c. The Brady Handgun Violence Prevention Act allocated funds for a background-checking computer system.
d. In 1994, Congress passed Clinton's bill to fund 100 000 additional police officer hires with over $8 billion.
e. Clinton's 1994 crime bill provided for building more prisons and banned 19 weapons.

112. Which is true about the Welfare Reform Act passed during the Clinton administration?

a. The Welfare Reform Act was proposed by President Clinton and modified by the Republicans.
b. This act transferred responsibility for welfare programs from federal government to the states.
c. The Welfare Reform Act provided for federal block grants to states for their welfare programs.
d. This act stated that heads of welfare households would lose benefits if they did not get a job in two years.

113. Which of the following was not instrumental in enabling Republicans to take control of the House and the Senate in the 1994 Congressional elections during the Clinton administration?

a. Alleged impropriety in the "Whitewater" deal
b. Rumors alleging sexual misconduct by Clinton
c. Debates on healthcare and gays in the military
d. The 1994 Republican "Contract with America"
e. All of the above were factors that helped the Republicans gain control of Congress.

114. Which of the following statements regarding the 1998 impeachment of President Clinton is not correct?

a. The grounds for impeachment were perjury and obstruction of justice.
b. The House of Representatives voted for the impeachment of Clinton.
c. The Senate voted to impeach before Clinton was acquitted of charges.
d. Clinton first denied a relationship with Lewinsky, and then admitted to it.
e. Following this incident Speaker of the House Newt Gingrich resigned.

115. Which of the following is not true about the use of computers in America?

a. Mainframe computers existed in America beginning in 1946.
b. The invention of microprocessors in the 1970s enabled the creation of a PC.
c. The PC allowed the widespread use of computers by private citizens.
d. PCs allowed the home use, but had less impact on businesses.
e. The Internet's origin was the Department of Defense's Arpanet in the 1960s.

116. Of the following, which statement about the US economy in the 1990s is correct?

a. By the year 2000, the US economy was increasing at a rate of 5% a year.
b. The rate of unemployment in America at this time dropped to 6%.
c. The rates of productivity and of inflation in the US were about the same.
d. The US stock market's total value had doubled in only six years.
e. The federal government had a surplus of $40 billion in the 1998 fiscal year.

117. Which of the following statements regarding the Branch Davidians in 1993 is not true?

a. The Branch Davidians were a Seventh Day Adventist sect living on a compound located near Waco, Texas.
b. The Bureau of Alcohol, Tobacco, and Firearms got a search warrant for the Branch Davidian compound.
c. When attempts to look for weapon stockpiles led to gunfire and deaths, the FBI attacked the compound.
d. The incident at the Branch Davidian compound in Waco developed into a siege that lasted for two weeks.
e. The siege at the Branch Davidian compound ended with many deaths, including that of sect leader David Koresh.

118. Which statement regarding US international trade policy in the 1990s is incorrect?

a. In 1994, the General Agreement on Tariffs and Trade (GATT) was approved by Congress.
b. The GATT included 57 countries who agreed they would remove or reduce many of their tariffs.
c. The GATT created the World Trade Organization (WTO) to settle international trade differences.
d. The NAFTA (North American Free Trade Agreement), ratified in 1994, had originally been set up by George H.W. Bush's administration.
e. The NAFTA had Clinton's support and was ratified.

119. Which of the following statements about the presidential election of 2000 is not true?

a. In this election, Democratic candidate Al Gore won the majority of the popular votes.
b. Votes for Green Party candidate Ralph Nader diverted some votes from Gore.
c. The state of Florida's electoral votes determined who won.
d. Confusion over the Florida ballots and recounts of the votes delayed the final tally.
e. When Gore demanded another recount in Florida, it yielded the exact same results.

120. Which of the following statements is not true regarding the events of September 11, 2001, in the US?

a. Shortly after that date the US defeated the Taliban and captured Al-Qaeda leader Osama bin Laden.
b. On September 11, 2001, Muslim terrorists flew two hijacked airplanes into the World Trade Center in New York.
c. On September 11, 2001, Muslim terrorists flew a hijacked passenger airliner into the Pentagon in Arlington, Virginia.
d. An airplane hijacked by Muslim terrorists crashed in Pennsylvania after passengers resisted the terrorists.
e. Following the terrorist events of September 11, 2001, President Bush announced a "war against terrorism."

Answers and Explanations

1. B: Andrew Johnson (b), vice president to Lincoln's, succeeded to the presidency after Lincoln was assassinated by John Wilkes Booth in 1865. Andrew Jackson (a) was the seventh president, from 1829-1837. Ulysses S. Grant (c) was elected president in 1868, following Johnson. Samuel J. Tilden (d) ran in the 1876 election and won the popular vote but was one electoral vote shy of the win. The election was disputed, and the dispute was resolved by a congressional electoral commission, which unethically manipulated the vote in support of the Republican candidate, Rutherford B. Hayes (e.

2. C: President Johnson's plan did not allow former Confederate officials to run for political offices. However, Johnson pardoned many former Confederates, who were eventually elected to Congress (b) in large enough numbers to form a majority (d). Many of the pardons occurred during a congressional recess, and when Congress reconvened, its members did not allow the newly elected Southerners to be seated (e). Instead, Congress appointed a joint committee for the review of policies regarding Reconstruction.

3. D: Radical Republicans in Congress (d) took over Reconstruction policymaking after 1866, when the president vetoed two bills, which were later passed. Therefore, President Johnson was not primarily in charge of the Reconstruction (a). Among members of Congress, Democrats (b), (e) disagreed with both conservative and moderate (c) Republican members. Both the president and the Democrats refused to work with conservative or moderate Republicans, and thus, radical Republicans (d) were able to assume control of Reconstruction policy.

4. A: Repayment of Confederate debt (a) was not a provision of the Fourteenth Amendment (1868). Rather, this amendment declared the Confederate debt incurred during the Civil War to be null and void. Provisions of the amendment also included: the definition of a citizen (b) as any person born or naturalized in the US, including African Americans; a stipulation that representation be based upon the population of male citizens who were able and allowed to vote (c); and a clause prohibiting rebels, who, by their rebellion, violated their previous oath in support of the US Constitution, from holding political office (d). Because (a) is not a provision of the Fourteenth Amendment, answer (e), these are all provisions of the Fourteenth Amendment is not correct.

5. E: Black Americans were given a guarantee of their right to vote in constitutional convention elections and all elections after (c) by the Reconstruction Act of 1867, but it was the Fifteenth Amendment that specifically proscribed denial of voting rights because of race, color, or former slavery. The Reconstruction Act of 1867 did not allow Confederates to vote until the new state constitutions were ratified (a), and it also subdivided the South into five military districts pending the formation of new governments (b). It further stipulated that Southern states must ratify the Fourteenth Amendment and also ratify their new state constitutions (d), which had to receive congressional approval.

6. D: Sharecroppers were given land, seeds, and farming supplies by landowners, but these landowners did not help sharecroppers profit; to the contrary, the landowners eventually manipulated their arrangement to the point that sharecroppers did not turn any profits but instead were always in debt. Social and economic changes brought on by Reconstruction included the Freedman's Bureau's administration of more than 4 000 schools and the foundation of Howard University (a); the foundation by the American Missionary Association of Atlanta University (b) and Fisk University; community building by black Americans in the form of starting their own churches (c); and depression of the agricultural economies in Southern states caused by dropping cotton prices (e) during the late 1800s.

7. C: President Grant did not institute or continue stringent military policing in the former Confederate states. In fact, he preferred to avoid confrontations with the Southern states so much so that by 1874 the numbers of federal troops stationed in the South had decreased to 4000, not counting Texas, where their primary job was to deal with Indians. The development of Liberal Republicans (a) was a factor, since unlike the Radical Republicans, the Liberal Republicans were against the federal government's intervention in Southern states and were therefore against Reconstruction efforts that promoted such intervention. The Amnesty Act, which Congress passed in 1872, pardoned the majority of previous Confederates (b) and bolstered the Democratic Party. The Democrats grew strong enough that by 1874, they had achieved control of the House of Representatives (d). By 1876, the House majority of Democrats had also taken back eight of the eleven Confederate states (e). All of these events [other than (c)] weakened the radical Republican support for Reconstruction.

8. A: The votes of South Carolina (b), Louisiana (c), Florida (d), and Oregon (e) were all disputed. After Congress removed the only Independent Supreme Court Justice on the electoral commission, which had been formed to resolve the dispute, the remaining commission members were all Republican and voted for Rutherford Hayes rather than for Democrat Samuel Tilden, Thus, Hayes received the disputed votes and won the election. In the Compromise of 1877, Hayes agreed to make concessions to the Southern states in exchange for congressional Democrats' forgiving the unethical presidential election decision.

9. B: While the American Indians did rely on the buffalo as their primary source of subsistence, they did not seriously deplete the buffalo's numbers. It was the white settlers of the western plains, during westward expansion, who killed millions of buffalo, reducing the herds to a few hundred by the late 19th century (a). This drastic depletion of the buffalo did add to conflict between whites and Indians (c) and contributed to conflicts between tribes. White reformers who campaigned against the treatment of Native Americans supported the 1887 passage of the Dawes Act, which included changing Indian property ownership from tribal ownership to individual ownership (d). While the intentions of the act were good, it backfired (e) as a large part of land previously designated as Indian reservations came under white control, and individual Indian land combined with white domination destroyed tribal authority and unity.

10. E: Sheepherding (e) was not one of the first industries to develop in the Western US; rather, sheepherding, along with farming, eventually supplanted the cattle industry. Initial developments in Western expansion included mining for gold (a) and silver (b), which could only be accomplished by large mining companies once individual prospectors had exhausted the shallow veins of ore. The 1878 Timber and Stone Act advanced the lumber industry (c) by allowing individuals to buy low-priced land, whereupon large companies funded these individuals and then transferred the individual land purchases to their corporations. With the large grasslands in the West, cattle (d) initially became a big industry as well as mining and lumber. However, cattlemen were soon deprived of grazing land by famers and sheepherders (e) who also settled the Great Plains.

11. D: Mismanagement by cattlemen (d) was not a factor causing lower profits that contributed to the end of the open-range cattle industry on the Western Great Plains. Lower profits were caused by Joseph Glidden's invention of barbed wire (a), which restricted open-range grazing, and the invasion of the plains by farmers and shepherds (b), which took grazing land away from cattle. In addition to the decrease in profits caused by these factors, the blizzards that occurred between 1885 and 1887 (c), and the droughts that took place in between these two major blizzards (e), further undermined the cattle industry until it was effectively ended.

12. E All the laws (e) named were instrumental in spurring westward migration to the Great Plains. The Homestead Act (a), passed in 1862, gave settlers 160 acres of land at no monetary cost in exchange for a commitment to cultivating the land for five years. The Timber Culture Act (b), passed in 1873, gave the settlers 160 acres more of land in exchange for planting trees on one quarter of the acreage. The Desert Land Act (c), passed in 1877, allowed buyers who would irrigate the land to buy 640 acres for only 25 cents an acre. Thus, (e), all of these laws were instrumental to spurring westward migration to the Great Plains during that period, is correct.

13. C: The first transcontinental railroad was finished in 1869 (c) on May 10. Construction on the railroad was begun in 1862 (a) but not completed until seven years later. After completion, economic depression prevented more railroad building until the 1880s (e) and 1890s (b). In 1865 (d), there were 35 000 miles of railroad track in the country; by 1890 (b), there were 200 000 miles. The first transcontinental railroad connected the Central Pacific Railroad, which began in Sacramento, California, to the Union Pacific Railroad, which began in Omaha, Nebraska, in Utah.

14. B: The Great Northern Railroad (b) was the only railroad that was not chiefly financed through government subsidies. The Santa Fe (a), Northern Pacific (c), and Southern Pacific (d) were constructed with government funding. Therefore (e), they all were government funded, is incorrect. All of the railroads listed were built in the 1880s and 1890s.

15. A: The industry that did not experience major growth from the late 1800s to the early 1900s was (a) beef. The cattle industry was devastated by a combination of competition from farmers and shepherds for land, the advent of barbed wire, and destructive weather conditions in the late 1880s (see Question #11). The steel industry (b) grew more than tenfold from 1880 to 1914, sparked by the rise of the railroads, which also stimulated the growth of the petroleum or oil (c) industry from virtual nonexistence to becoming one of the country's biggest enterprises. The construction of several hundred textile mills in the cotton states meant that by 1920, the South surpassed the New England states in the production of cloth (d). During this period of industrialization, other industries that profited greatly included those of lumber or wood (e), iron, coal, and of course, the railroads.

16. C: The statement that does not accurately portray conditions in industrializing America in the late 19th and early 20th centuries is (c).: By 1890, there were not 25% of children aged 10-15 years in the workforce, but rather 18% of children aged 10-15 years were working. There were almost five million people working in industry by 1880 (a), and 2.5 million women worked either in factories or in offices by that year (b). Conditions for industrial workers during this time were very dangerous, so work-related injuries and illnesses were quite common (d). Moreover, at this time there were no programs such as disability insurance, workmen's compensation, or retirement pensions (e). This time period also saw the first formations of labor unions, but it would be some time before the activities of these unions would lead to new legislation instituting such protection for workers.

17. D: The only true statement is (d): Economists who opposed business consolidation believed that society would only progress if the government took greater control over processes that naturally developed out of economic activities. Among those who believed the opposite were Social Darwinists, who were in favor of consolidation (c) deregulation, as they felt the government should not interfere with competition and free enterprise. Types of consolidation include horizontal integration, which was used by John D. Rockefeller—not vertical integration (a)—to allow his Standard Oil Company to corner 90% of the petroleum industry; and vertical integration, which Gustavus Swift used in the meat packing industry—not horizontal integration (b). Horizontal integration involves eliminating one's competitors by either buying them out or driving them out of

business, as practiced by Rockefeller. Vertical integration involves taking over all the parts of a particular industry, such as raw materials, manufacturing, and transportation, as practiced by Swift. In response to the critics of business consolidation, Congress eventually passed the Sherman Anti-Trust Act in 1890, but it was not particularly effective against business monopoly (e). Due to imprecise wording in this law, whenever the government tried to dismantle a monopoly, the courts were usually able to rule against these attempts and defeat them.

18. B: The statistic that is not accurate with respect to American urbanization between 1870 and 1920 is (b).: By 1920, *more than* half of the population, or 51%, lived in cities with more than 2 500 inhabitants, rather than *almost* half. Americans living in cities did grow more than fivefold during this period (a): their numbers went from 10 million in 1870, to 54 million in 1920 (5.4 times as many). Cities with populations greater than 100000 increased more than 3.6 times (c) during this period, from 15 cities to 68. And during these years, cities with populations over 500 000 grew to six times as many as before (d), changing from two cities to twelve cities this large.

19. A: Farmers moved from rural America to the cities to escape debts and low crop prices; at the same time, many immigrants from southern and Eastern Europe arrived in American cities. The influx of immigrants coupled with overcrowded housing resulted in city slums. . Reformers, such as Jacob Riis, author of *How the Other Half Lives* (published in1890), exposed these living conditions and expressed the need for improved housing. However, housing (a) was the one area of those listed that saw the least improvement. More progress was made to improve American urban infrastructure, such as sewer systems (b), fire fighting (c), street lighting (d), water supply (e), and pavement of streets and sidewalks.

20. E: All of these were American urban cultural developments during this time. The Cincinnati Red Stockings (now the Cincinnati Reds) made a tour of the country in 1869. Baseball became quite popular and was America's chief sport by the 1880s (a). Vaudeville made its way from cities to various small towns throughout the country with the help of the railroad. (b). DW Griffith made the landmark film *Birth of a Nation* in 1913, advancing the progress of the motion picture industry (c). Joseph Pulitzer used the rotary press to publish the *New York World.* The press enabled less expensive, mass-production of newspapers. Pulitzer is also known as a pioneer of the sensational publishing movement known as "yellow journalism." William Randolph Hearst followed Pulitzer's example and created an empire of newspapers and magazines (d).

21. C: A high degree of efficiency, (c), was not a characteristic of the "city machines" of the late 1800s. The city machines were political organizations that were highly organized (a) but also notoriously corrupt (b). The city machines' "bosses" did attain substantial wealth (d) and power (e) through their corruption. These officials typically received bribes and kickbacks for public works agreements. They also traded jobs and legal services to citizens, mostly new immigrants, for votes to keep them in office. Despite their organized character, the city machines were not known for being efficient, since self-interest of the bosses and their cronies came before interest in the public good. Reformers spoke out against the city machines, resulting in the introduction of different forms of government and other changes in the 1890s.

22. E: All the answers listed (e) were structural reforms introduced for city governance in the 1890s. As an alternative to overly powerful, corrupt "bosses," the position of city manager (a) was introduced to help run city administrations. Another form of government introduced was the formation of commissions (b) to organize and manage the cities. Elections at the city level (c) were also instituted to give residents a vote instead of being stuck with whatever "boss" had garnered enough power by making deals to maintain control of the city. Citywide elections were also made

nonpartisan (d) so that party politics could no longer keep the same administration in power, as corruption tools, such as bribery and graft had served to keep "bosses" in power.

23. B: The gold standard (b) was not a national political issue in the 1880s as it had been restored by 1878. Silver, not gold, was a national political issue in the 1880s. After an 1873 law prohibited government purchase or coining of silver, farmers lobbied for monetizing silver in order to push inflation in their favor. Both the Bland-Allison Act (1878) and Sherman Silver Purchase Act (1890) attempted to address the concerns. However, neither of these bills proved sufficient to make proponents of silver happy. Civil service reform (a) was also a national political issue in the 1880s due to the corruption of Grant's administration and in response to the assassination of President Garfield in 1881. The assassin was motivated by being denied a civil service job. Congress responded by passing the Pendleton Civil Service Act in 1882. This law established a set of tests by which applicants could compete for civil service jobs. Only about 10% of government jobs were covered by these tests, but the Pendleton act was a clear start to reform in instituting fair and objective criteria for employment in some civil service positions. Another national political issue at this time was tariffs (c). High protective tariffs on commodities resulted in a federal treasury surplus. Republicans were for these tariffs, but Democrats contended the tariffs unfairly gave advantages to manufacturers and disadvantages to farmers. The Democrats were unable to relieve these inequities, since the McKinley Tariff, passed in 1890, and the Dingley Tariff, passed in 1897, increased tax rates further. The issue of women's suffrage (d) was also a national political concern at this time. The National Woman Suffrage Association joined with the American Woman Suffrage Association in 1890, and the combined organization, National American Woman Suffrage Association, campaigned for women's rights to vote and for legal reforms to benefit women. While full suffrage was note granted until 1920, women were granted the rights to vote in school elections in 19 states and to vote on tax and bond issues in three states by 1890. During this time, regulation of the railroads (e) was a national political issue as well. Railroads varied their shipping prices. As might be expected, larger shippers got better deals. Farmers and other small groups demanded that the government regulate railroads. The Interstate Commerce Act, passed in 1887, banned a number of discriminatory practices and formed the Interstate Commerce Commission for oversight of railroads. Unfortunately, this act was significantly diluted by court rulings.

24. A: Between 1877 and 1901, the six presidents who held office did not have much influence on American politics when compared to Congress. Therefore answer (b) is incorrect. Congress and the presidency were not controlled most of the time by either the Democratic (c) or Republican (d) parties. There were only three spans of two years each when one party controlled both houses of Congress and the presidency. Since (a) is correct, (e) is incorrect.

25. D: The correct chronological order of the presidents who served between 1877-1901 is (d): Hayes, Garfield, Arthur, Cleveland, Harrison, and McKinley. Rutherford B. Hayes held office from 1877-1881. James Garfield was President in 1881; he was assassinated in the same year he was inaugurated. Chester Allan Arthur succeeded Garfield in 1881 and held office until 1885. In 1885, Grover Cleveland was elected and served until 1889. Benjamin Harrison was President from 1889-1893. In 1893, Grover Cleveland was elected to a second term and served from 1893-1897. William McKinley then held office from 1897-1901. After serving the four-year term, McKinley was reelected in 1900, but he was assassinated in 1901. Answers (a), (b), (c), and (e) are not in the correct chronological order.

26. B: The farmers' organization of the Granges (b) had the least influence, relatively, on the formation of the Populist (People's) Party as a national party. Granges began as social organizations. Between 1860-1880, Granges formed sales cooperatives and lobbied for legislation to regulate storage and transport of grain. However, their efforts were largely unsuccessful. By the

159

1880s, the Granges returned to their original form as social organizations. Though they did not succeed politically, Granges were formed in reaction to a dramatic decline in wheat prices (a), and the Farmers' Alliances (c) were formed for the same reason. However, the Farmers' Alliances were more successful politically. They influenced the government to build "sub treasuries" or warehouses to store crops in return for credit. Moreover, members of a Farmers' Alliance formed the Populist Party that won the Kansas state elections (d) in 1890, which bolstered to the party to a national position.

27. E: Both (a), the Democrats, and (c), the Populists, backed William Jennings Bryan as the presidential candidate. The Republicans (b) nominated Ohio Governor, William McKinley, as their candidate. Therefore answer (d), both (b) and (c), is incorrect as the Republicans did not nominate Bryan. Answers (a), (b), and (c) individually are incorrect as answer (e) [both (a) and (c)] is correct.

28. A: Alfred T. Mahan's book, The Influence of Sea Power upon History (a), did not influence the development of the Progressive Era in the early 20th century. Mahan published this book in 1890 to promote the idea of a larger US navy toward the goal of expansionism. Lincoln Steffens' book, *The Shame of the Cities* (b), published in 1904, was an exposé of the political "city machines" and helped to stimulate political reform. Upton Sinclair's 1906 book, *The Jungle* (c), supported socialism and criticized capitalism while exposing food contamination in the meat packing industry as well as poor treatment and conditions for workers. The passage of the Pure Food and Drug Act and the Meat Inspection Act in the same year that *The Jungle* was published were both strongly influenced by Sinclair's work, so this book directly contributed to the Progressive Era's reforms. W.E.B. Du Bois' and others' founding of the National Association for the Advancement of Colored People, the NAACP (d), was an effort to reform policies of segregation and was a hallmark of the Progressive Era. The Progressive Era's atmosphere of reform also enabled the leadership of progressive politicians at the state level. One such leader was Wisconsin Governor LaFollette (e), who passed legislation to affect tax reform, to regulate railroads, and to implement direct political primaries.

29. D: The Clayton Anti-Trust Act (c) was passed by President Woodrow Wilson's administration in 1914. Theodore Roosevelt was President from 1901-1909. Roosevelt passed the Hepburn Act (a) in 1906, giving the Interstate Commerce Commission more power to determine railroad charges. Also, in 1906, he passed the Meat Inspection Act (b) to oversee the meat packing industry after Upton Sinclair's book, *The Jungle,* exposed its practices and caused public outrage. The same year, Roosevelt's administration also passed the Pure Food and Drug Act (d) making drug labeling mandatory. In 1902, Roosevelt had passed the National Reclamation Act, or Newlands Reclamation Act (e), to fund irrigation of Western land and expand our national forests by almost 150,000 acres.

30. A: President Taft's signing of the Payne-Aldrich Tariff Act (a) was not in the Progressive spirit of reform. Though Taft considered himself a Progressive, in 1909, he passed this tariff, which included compromises allowing protective tariffs that were favored by conservatives in the Republican Party and were too high for manufacturers, farmers, and reformers. He also allowed eliminated certain land protections, which alienated conservationists. Taft's support of the Mann-Elkins Act (b), passed in1910, was more in the Progressive spirit of reform as it allowed him to bring eighty antitrust suits, gave the Interstate Commerce Commission more regulatory power, and protected more land against public use than even Roosevelt's administration. Taft's administration also enacted the Sixteenth Amendment (c), which legalized income tax, and the Seventeenth Amendment (d), which established direct senatorial elections, both in 1913. Since some of these actions supported reform, (e) is incorrect.

31. C: The law not passed during Woodrow Wilson's 1913-1921 presidency was (c), the Wilson-Gorman Tariff, also known as the Revenue Act. The Wilson-Gorman Tariff was passed in 1894, and

charged very high duties on Cuban sugar imports. This seriously hurt Cuba's economy and contributed to the Spanish-American War. President Woodrow Wilson's administration passed the Federal Reserve Act (a) in 1913 to establish a centralized system of banking. In 1916, Wilson passed the Federal Farm Loan Act (b) to support agriculture by financially helping farmers. In 1913, he passed the Underwood Tariff (d), which made tariffs lower and established graduated income taxes. In 1916, the Wilson administration also passed the Adamson Act (e), which legalized an eight-hour work day for railroad employees. In addition to these four, Wilson also enacted the Clayton Anti-Trust Act and the Federal Trade Commission Act, both in 1914, which allowed government more regulation of business. He later passed the Eighteenth Amendment and the Volstead Act, which directed alcohol prohibition; and the Nineteenth Amendment, which gave women the right to vote. All of these laws were reform actions.

32. B: President Grover Cleveland's stance with respect to the annexation of Hawaii (b) was not an instance of early US expansionism because Cleveland was against annexing Hawaii. A group of American planters deposed Queen Liliuokalani in 1893, and Cleveland wanted to restore the Hawaiian monarchy. The planters refused to comply with President Cleveland's wishes and pursued annexation, succeeding in 1898 during the Spanish-American War. Hawaii's annexation is an example of early US expansionism rather than President Cleveland's opposition to it. Secretary of State Seward's initiative to purchase Alaska from Russia (a) was an example of early expansionism. Alfred T. Mahan, author of *The Influence of Sea Power upon History* (1890), campaigned for the US to develop a larger navy (c), and his book was widely influential: During the 1880s, shipbuilders took advantage of the advances in steel production and steam power to create the "New Navy." In 1878, the US established a naval base in Samoa and within ten years, had annexed part of the Samoan islands (d), which is another example of early expansion. In 1895, England disputed the border between British Guiana and Venezuela, and threatened to seize Venezuelan territory when US Secretary of State James Olney invoked the Monroe Doctrine and warned British officials against their course of action. America and Britain settled the matter in 1896. This was also an indirect example of early expansionism as it prevented regression to British imperialism in the Americas.

33. A: William McKinley (a) was President from 1897-1901. The Spanish-American War was in 1898. Benjamin Harrison (b) was President from 1889-1893. Grover Cleveland (c) was President from 1885-1889 and from 1893-1897. Theodore Roosevelt (d) was President from 1901-1909. William Howard Taft (e) held office from 1909-1913.

34. D: The US bought the Philippines from Spain for $20 million, and Cuba became independent. Guam was ceded to the US, not sold, so (a) is incorrect. Since the US bought the Philippines, (b) is incorrect. Since Spain sold only the Philippines to America while Guam was ceded to the US and Cuba both became independent, (c) is incorrect. Since the Philippines were sold to and Guam ceded to America, neither country received independence along with Cuba, so (e) is incorrect.

35. E: Though the Jones Act did promise independence to the Philippines (d), it was not effective immediately. In fact, this promise was not fulfilled until after World War II ended; Philippine independence was made official on July 4, 1946. It is true that Emilio Aguinaldo announced the independence of the Philippines in January 1899 (a), and that the insurrection he started then continued until 1902 (b). It is also true that America tried to annex the Philippines during the 1900s, and despite these efforts, problems still occurred there (c).

36. A: Although Cuba had been formally granted independence, the US forced Cuba to include the Platt Amendment in its new constitution. This amendment allowed the US government to approve Cuba's foreign treaties. Therefore, the Platt Amendment was not merely a formality (b) as it gave

the US control over any treaties Cuba would want to make with other countries. It is not true that the US would not provide military intervention in Cuba (c), that Cuba refused to accept such intervention (d), or that Cuba did not need such intervention (e). In fact, there was enough political upheaval in Cuba over the twenty years following its independence that the US sent troops there three times during that period.

37. B: Germany's declaration of war on Russia in 1914, following the assassination of Archduke Ferdinand (b), did not contribute to ending American neutrality in World War I. Once Germany declared war, England, France, Italy, Russia, and Japan joined as the Allied Powers against the Central Powers of Germany and Austria-Hungary, and US President Woodrow Wilson declared America's neutrality. When Germany designated the area surrounding the British Isles as a war zone in February 1913 (a), and warned all ships from neutral countries to stay out of the zone, an end to American neutrality was prompted. President Wilson's responded to Germany's declaration by proclaiming that America would hold Germany responsible for any American losses of life or property. When Germany sank the British passenger vessel *Lusitania,* 128 American passengers were killed (c). This further eroded Wilson's resolve to remain neutral. In February 1917, Germany declared unrestricted submarine warfare on any ship in the war zone (d); this signified that ships from any country would face German attack. President Wilson's reaction to this declaration was to cease diplomatic relations with Germany. Meanwhile, England intercepted a telegram from Germany to Mexico asking Mexico to join forces with Germany. This infuriated the American public. President Wilson then asked for a declaration of war on Germany on April 2, 1917, which Congress approved.

38. E: All of these laws prepared the US (e) for entry into World War I. The National Defense Act (a), in 1916, expanded America's armed forces, and the Navy Act (b), also in 1916, expanded the US Navy. Also, in 1916, the Revenue Act (c) created new taxes to finance the growth of America's military. The Selective Service Act (d), passed in1917, instituted the military draft.

39. D: All of the agencies listed (d) were federal agencies formed in response to World War I, and the institution of said agencies expanded the American federal government. The Food Administration (a) oversaw distribution and pricing of food. The Fuel Administration (b) managed distribution, pricing, and use of fuel for transportation. The Railroad Administration (c) worked with issues of railway transportation. Additional federal agencies included the War Industries Board, the War Shipping Board, and the National War Labor Board. Since (d) is correct, (e) is incorrect.

40. C: The "Great Migration" (1910-1940) refers to the migration of more than a million African Americans from southern states to northern, Midwestern, and western states (c). Approximately, half a million migrants moved to northern states. Migrants sought employment in industrial cities and escape from segregation and racism. The "Great Migration" did not include or refer to European immigration to America during WWI (a); Americans leaving the country over US neutrality (b); the movement of women to factory employment (d); or migrations expatriates instigated by the Espionage Act (1917) and the Sedition Act (1918).

41. E: President Wilson expressed the points most important to him for world peace in his Fourteen Points speech to Congress in 1918. Of paramount importance to Wilson was the fourteenth point, the establishment of a League of Nations (e) to maintain international peace. Other points included the freedom of all countries to navigate the seas (a) in war or in peace; the open and public agreement to peace treaties (b) as opposed to secret or private diplomacy; the self-determination of each nation (c); and equal conditions of trade (d) for all nations agreeing to peace. Note: The Treaty of Versailles included the provision of a League of Nations, but this treaty was denied by the US

Senate. The League of Nations existed from 1919-1946, but the US was never a member. The League of Nations had some early successes but was unable to avert aggression by Germany and other Axis powers in the 1930s, and when World War II broke out this proved a failure of the League of Nations to prevent future world wars. After World War II, the United Nations was formed in place of the League of Nations.)

42. D: The event which took place after WWI but did not exemplify the general postwar withdrawal from earlier progressive reform was (d), the passage in 1921 of the Sheppard-Towner Act. Also known as the Sheppard-Towner Maternity and Infancy Protection Act, this act provided for federal funding to support maternity and child care by creating maternity and pediatric clinics. As such, it not only echoed prewar progressive reform movements but also reflected the fact that women were gaining political influence. The fact that Congress lowered taxes for corporations (a) and rich people in 1921 did characterize the postwar withdrawal from progressive reform. The Harding and Coolidge administrations generally supported business interests and opposed intervening in the economy. When railroad workers and miners went on significant strikes in 1922, the Harding administration suppressed them (b). Such actions and a general pro-corporate, anti-union atmosphere caused union memberships to drop by a third during the 1920s (e). Also, in 1922, the Fordney-McCumber Tariff Act (c) raised tariff rates, again favoring large businesses, not farmers.

43. C: When Congress passed the McNary-Haugen Acts, Coolidge vetoed them. Therefore, it is not true that he agreed with these bills (d). This veto showed that the federal government under Coolidge supported big business, but this support did not extend to include agriculture (a). The McNary-Haugen Acts would not have been detrimental to the farmers (b) if Coolidge had not vetoed them because they were written to give the farmers pricing supports; therefore (e) is incorrect.

44. B: The Johnson Act did base its immigration quota on figures from the US census taken in 1910. This act was passed in1921; however, it was not enacted to encourage immigration to America (a) but rather to limit it as the government was concerned about immigration's impact on society. The Johnson Act did not establish an immigration quota of 5% (c) but rather of 3%. This act was further amended by the Johnson-Reid Act, passed in 1924, but the population figures were not taken from the 1920 census (d) but from the 1890 census. The outdated statistics resulted in a lowered immigration quota of 2% (from 3%) rather than an increase to 6%.

45. A: From 1919 to 1929, America's GNP rose by 40%. By the 1920s, only two-thirds of American households had electricity (b). The number of car owners did not quadruple at this time (c); however, it nearly tripled over the decade, from 8 million to 23 million. American households with radios did not reach 12 million by the end of the decade (d), but more than 10 million households did acquire radios by the end of the 1920s. Since only answer (a) is correct, answer (e) is incorrect.

46. C: During this decade birth rates fell; more women were working and more marriages ended in divorce. The other statistics are accurate.

47. D: During the 1920s, Americans *more than* doubled their attendance to movie theaters, with 40 million going to movies in 1922 and 100 million attending in 1930. . The other statements are correct.

48. B: George Gershwin, composer and pianist, did not contribute to the Harlem Renaissance. While Gershwin did much to popularize jazz by incorporating it into his classical compositions, and while he was a contemporary of the others, he was a white, Jewish American. Members of the Harlem Renaissance were by definition African American. Some of these included poet Langston Hughes (a), essayist Alain Locke (c), jazz musician Louis Armstrong (d), and singer Bessie Smith (e).

49. A: The subject matter of the 1925 Scopes trial, sometimes referred to as the "Scopes monkey trial," was (a) teaching evolution in public school. Young teacher John T. Scopes believed his students had the right to learn about an important theory, supported by paleontological evidence, but highly religious and provincial people in his Tennessee town objected so ardently to his teachings that the state prosecuted Scopes. Though the state won its case, the countrywide newspaper coverage portrayed those opposed to the theory as ignorant and impeding intellectual progress. The Ku Klux Klan (b) re-emerged in the face of changing American culture, adding approximately five million members by 1923, but its popularity had dwindled by the end of the 1920s. A trial for the murder of two Italian immigrants who held anarchist political views (c) was the Massachusetts Sacco and Vanzetti trial, in 1921. There were many accusations that the trial was rigged and Sacco and Vanzetti did not commit murder but were being targeted for their political views; regardless, the two were executed by the state in 1927. Marcus Garvey founded the Universal Negro Improvement Association (d) in the early 1920s, which advocated African American capitalism, black pride, and separatism. Initially the organization was popular enough to garner more than 500 000 members, but it lost strength mid-decade due to financial setbacks and legal actions taken against Garvey. Since (a) is the correct answer, (e) is incorrect.

50. E: The US economy did not rely too heavily on too many different industries (e), and such reliance was not a contributing factor to the Great Depression. Rather the US economy relied too heavily on too *few* industries, while not giving enough business to others, such as the coal industry and family-run farms. Factors that did contribute to the depression included: (a), the fact that increased income in the 1920s was made mostly by the wealthy, causing products made by the working class to be priced beyond the means of the workers; (b), indebted corporations were structurally unstable and could not stay afloat in the face of profit losses; (c), stock market over speculation, which was out of proportion to the industries' actual gains, and stock purchases made with borrowed money; and (d) greater American profits resulting in fewer investments in European businesses, which in turn led to European war-debt default. Additionally, the Federal Reserve cut back on available money, and together all of these things led to the Great Depression.

51. B: The programs included in FDR's first New Deal that were eliminated by Supreme Court decisions include, (b), The National Recovery Administration (NRA), created by the National Industrial Recovery Act (NIRA) in 1933 and ended by the Supreme Court in 1935; and the Agricultural Adjustment Act (AAA), passed in 1933 and reversed by the Supreme Court in 1936. The NRA tried to stabilize the economy by fixing prices to reduce competition, which many economists doubted would work. Thus, the Supreme Court ruling ending the program was not disputed.

The AAA compensated farmers for planting fewer crops in an effort to counter overproduction. However, the act came under great opposition and the Supreme Court ruled that regulating agricultural production was unconstitutional.

The CCC sought to relieve unemployment by recruiting young men to plant trees and construct buildings, while the FERA gave state and local governments money to aid relief efforts (a).

The PWA was created by the NIRA to oversee road and public building construction, and the TVA built dams and power plants to control floods and supply water power. These projects ultimately helped to stabilize the entire Tennessee region's economy (c). The TVA still exists today.

The Commodity Credit Corporation was created to make loans to farmers, and the National Labor Relations Board, created by the Wagner Act, supported union organizing, helped resolve labor disputes, and protected the right of collective bargaining by unions (d).

The Emergency Banking Relief Bill (e) provided for bank reopenings under the aegis of the Treasury Department after an emergency congressional session known as the "Hundred Days."

The Securities and Exchange Commission (SEC) (e), established to regulate the stock market, still exists today.

While some of these programs were temporary and others still remain, (b), the NRA and the AAA, were the only two revoked by Supreme Court decisions.

52. E: All of these individuals, (e), were opposed to parts of FDR's first New Deal. Fr. Charles Coughlin (a) was a Detroit priest who initially approved of the New Deal but was against the AAA's methods of restricting crop growth. Dr. Francis Townsend (b), a Californian, made an alternative proposition of the Old Age Revolving Pensions Plan, and Louisiana Senator Huey Long (c) made a proposition in 1934 to "Share Our Wealth Society" for redistribution of wealth. These people formed the American Liberty League in 1934 and criticized the New Deal, which they claimed destroyed "individual initiative" by providing emergency relief measures. The US Supreme Court (d) showed its opposition of two New Deal programs, the National Recovery Administration and the Agricultural Adjustment Act, and eliminated both of these in 1935 and 1936, respectively.

53. A: The Public Works Administration (a), or PWA, was not authorized under the Emergency Relief Appropriation Act of the Second New Deal. The PWA was created under the First New Deal by the National Industrial Recovery Act (NIRA), in 1933. Under the Second New Deal (1934-1935), the ERAA established the Works Progress Administration (b), which funded highway and bridge construction projects as well as countrywide cultural event. The ERAA also founded the Resettlement Administration (c) to help poor families in rural and urban areas relocate to government-planned communities.

The REA eventually became the Rural Utilities Service (RUS), which is a US Department of Agriculture (USDA) agency that still operates today.

The National Youth Administration (e) designed work-study programs for minors in relief families so that they could live at home, work part-time jobs and receive job training.

54. D: The Social Security Act was created under FDR's Second New Deal in 1935 The Social Security Act was probably the most innovative, even revolutionary, reform measure of all of the New Deal programs in its provision of government-funded insurance benefits to citizens who are retired, unemployed, disabled, or dependent.

55. C: The AFL and the CIO both existed during this period, and both grew stronger as labor unions grew throughout the decade. However, these two organizations did not merge in the 1930s but, rather, in 1955. During the 1930s, a drought in the southern Great Plains followed by high winds created the Dust Bowl, which prompted more than 350,000 farming families to migrate west to California (a).

The Indian Reorganization Act in 1934 restored tribal ownership of land to the American Indians, effectively reversing the Dawes Act passed in 1887 (b), which had changed Indian land ownership from tribal ownership to individual ownership—a well-intentioned but disastrous move that destroyed Indian tribal authority.

World War II broke out in Europe, defense industry jobs proliferated.   After word of a proposed march on Washington to dispute racial discrimination in terms of hiring practices was received by the President, FDR issued Executive Order 8802, which established the Fair Employment Practices Committee.

Women's political influence increased when Frances Perkins was appointed Secretary of Labor in 1933 and became the first woman ever to have a position in the US Cabinet (e).

56. A: The inaccurate statement is (a), FDR's "court-packing" proposal succeeded in filling the Supreme Court with justices he appointed and who would approve his programs. The other answers are correct.

57. D: The economy did not improve in the 1930s (d). Rather, due to actions by the President and the Federal Reserve Board, there was a downturn in the economy. One such action was the president's limitation of public spending in an attempt to keep a balanced budget (a). Another action was the Federal Reserve Board's increase of interest rates (b). These actions not only caused economic downturn; they also resulted in higher unemployment rates—unemployment increased substantially by 1938 (c). In an effort to remedy this turn of events, the president removed his limits on public spending and reverted to deficit spending, but this did not make much of an impact on the unemployment rate (e).

58. E: When FDR won the 1940 election, he was the only US president to serve three consecutive terms. In fact, he was elected to a fourth term but died shortly thereafter. No other American president has held office for 12 consecutive years. Presidential terms were not limited to two consecutive terms until the Twenty-Second Amendment was passed in 1951.

59 C: At the 1921-1922 Washington Conference, Secretary of State Charles Evans Hughes advocated for naval reduction, not naval expansion. Other countries agreed with the proposal, and England, France, Italy and Japan agreed to reduce the sizes of their navies. In fact, England, the US, and Japan actually destroyed some of their ships (d) to meet the required ratio.

60. B: The Dawes Plan, passed in 1924, gave Germany an extension of its original debt repayment period. Neither the US or Europe were in serious debt following the war (a). In fact, Europe was indebted to the US, and the US did not owe. . When the US stock market appreciated, American lent less money to Germany (c). As the stock market at home became more appealing to investors, American loans to Germany had dropped by 1928. The Young Plan, passed in 1929, was an attempt to resolve this situation, but it was not successful (d). When several countries were unable to make reparations by 1931, due to economic difficulties, President Hoover did not demand payment (e) but, rather, announced a moratorium on any more payments of war debts as he realized these were impossible under the current conditions.

61. C: The US did not lower its protective tariffs with the Fordney-McCumber Act in 1922; this law actually raised protective tariffs. Additionally, the US raised its protective tariffs again in 1930 with the Hawley-Smoot Act (b). These laws both increased our protective tariffs in spite of the fact that America was the largest exporter in the world at the time (a). However, in FDR's new administration, Secretary of State Cordell Hull promoted international trade as a means of stimulating the economy. . Accordingly, Hull and FDR's administration passed the Reciprocal Trade Agreement Act in 1934 to lower tariffs (d) via individual agreements with other countries. Another stimulus to international trade, also in 1934, was the creation of the Export-Import Bank, which offered loans for other countries to buy American commodities (e).

62. B: Honduras (b) did not have a dictatorship supported by the US after World War I. US did deploy troops to Honduras in 1924 to quell unrest, and US businesses had control of Honduras'

economy between 1914 and 1929. However, America did not support a Honduran dictator during this time.

63. D: When World War II began in Europe in 1939, Congress did make a change to its neutrality acts by revising the Neutrality Act of 1935, which prevented the US from sending arms to countries at war (a). The revision allowed the sale of arms to countries at war, but only if buyer paid cash and transported the arms. The Neutrality Act of 1936 prohibited US loans to countries at war (b). The Neutrality Act of 1937 not only prohibited Americans from traveling on ships owned by warring countries (c), but it also allowed warring nations the opportunity to buy nonmilitary supplies from the US if the goods were paid for in cash and transported by the buyer.

64. E: Poland did not declare war on Germany. By the time other countries declared war, Poland was occupied by Germany. In reaction to Hitler's military aggression in Europe, France and England declared war on Germany, on September 3, 1939. Hitler did rise to power in Germany in 1933, and three years later he occupied the Rhineland (a). He then made alliances with Italy and Japan (b). After obtaining these allies, Hitler took over Czechoslovakia in 1938-1939 (c), and he invaded Poland in 1939 (d). It was after this last invasion that England and France declared war on Germany.

65. B: The true statement is (a): Japan did invade Manchuria in 1931, signaling its desire to gain international power. It is not true that the Stimson Doctrine recognized Japan's invasion of Manchuria as a belligerent act or otherwise; in this doctrine Secretary of State Henry L. Stimson stated that the US would *not* recognize any appropriations of land in Asia by Japan. When the Sino-Japanese War began in 1938, FDR did *not* officially recognize it (c), which enabled China to buy arms for its defense. When Japan sank the US gunboat *Panay,* FDR demanded an apology and Japan complied. However, this did not resolve tensions in Asia (d). By 1939, the US revoked a treaty to trade with Japan signed in 1911; it did not reaffirm this treaty (e).

66. B: The signing of the Tripartite Pact (a) was not part of US support for England. This pact was not signed by the US, England, or France. It was signed by Japan, Germany, and Italy (the warring foes). As such it had nothing to do with US aid to England. When France fell to Germany's attacks in 1940 and it appeared that England would soon follow (b), these events did contribute to Roosevelt's decision to help England. His first action was to sell US military surplus supplies to both England and France (c). A few months later, FDR made an exchange with Britain of destroyer ships for naval bases (d).

67. E: All of these events (e) were among US efforts to aid England in World War II prior to America's entry into the war. When Congress approved the Selective Training and Service Act in 1940, it was the first ever draft during peacetime in America's history (a). In 1941, FDR pushed his Lend-Lease Act through Congress, allowing America to send arms to England (b). Several months later FDR and British Prime Minister Winston Churchill signed the Atlantic Charter confirming their agreement to purposes of war (c). Shortly thereafter an undeclared nautical war with Germany erupted. In response, Congress made a revision to its Neutrality Acts that allowed America to arm its merchant vessels and use them to ship war supplies to England (d).

68. D: The only correct pairing of actions and reactions leading to US entry to World War II is (d): After Japan bombed the US naval base at Pearl Harbor in Hawaii, Congress voted to declare war on Japan. FDR froze Japan's US assets, not after Japan signed an agreement with Germany and Italy (a), but after Japan invaded French Indochina. FDR put an embargo on shipments of airplane fuel and scrap metal to Japan, not after Japan invaded French Indochina (b), but after Japan signed the Tripartite Pact with Germany and Italy. Japan did not declare war on the US after the attack on Pearl

Harbor (c); the US declared war on Japan after the attack. Germany and Italy did not first declare war on the US (e); the US declared war on Japan, and in turn, Germany and Italy declared war on the US.

69. A: The event that contributed least to Germany's surrender in WWII was (a) Germany's invasion of the Soviet Union in June of 1941. While the ultimate outcome of Germany's invasion was its defeat, this was not a direct result of the invasion per se. After Germany's invasion of Russia, the Soviets defeated the Germans at the Battle of Stalingrad (b) in 1942-1943. This defeat did contribute to Germany's eventual surrender more than Germany's invasion of the Soviet Union did. Later in 1943, both American and British troops invaded Italy (c), which surrendered in less than a month. This struck another blow to the Axis powers. In June 1944, the Allies invaded Normandy and proceeded through France to Paris (d), adding to Allied progress in the war. The Allied forces crossed the Rhine River the following March. In the meantime, Soviet troops had crossed Poland and joined with the American army at the Elbe River (e) in April. In May, Germany surrendered to the Allies.

70. C: The event in the Pacific that brought an end to World War II was (c) the US bombing of Hiroshima and Nagasaki. When America sank four of Japan's aircraft carriers at Midway (a) in June of 1942, this was considered to be the turning point of the war in the Pacific. Subsequently America defeated Japan in the Battle of the Philippine Sea (b) in October of 1944. Very violent battles at Iwo Jima and Okinawa did not signal American victory (d) but rather led US leadership to a realization that attacking the Japanese mainland would result in extreme numbers of American casualties. President Harry S. Truman, who had just succeeded to office after FDR died, was notified of the successful testing of an atomic bomb. Truman later approved the use of the atomic bomb as a means to end the war. US bombers dropped an atom bomb on the city of Hiroshima on August 6, and on the city of Nagasaki on August 9, 1945 (c). Japan surrendered on August 14.

71. A: The postwar conference that brought US-Soviet differences to light was (a) the Potsdam conference in July of 1945. The conference at Yalta (b), in February of 1945, resulted in the division of Germany into Allied-controlled zones. The Dumbarton Oaks conference (c) (1944) established a Security Council, on which with the US, England, Soviet Union, France, and China served as the five permanent members. Each of the permanent members had veto power, and a General Assembly, with limited power, was also established. The Tehran conference (d) included FDR's proposal for a new international organization to take the place of the League of Nations. This idea would later be realized in the form of the United Nations. Earlier in 1943, at the Casablanca Conference (e), President Roosevelt and Prime Minister Churchill agreed to a policy of unconditional surrender for all enemies of the Allied powers.

72. C: The earliest instance of Soviet-US differences was (c): The USSR establishment of a communist government in Poland, which prohibited conservative participation and occurred in 1945. The next event (1946) was British Prime Minister Winston Churchill's speech to Americans in Fulton, Missouri, in which he described the division developing between Eastern and Western Europe as an "iron curtain" (e). In 1947, the Soviets backed the Communist control of Hungary and Romania (a). In 1948, the Soviets also supported communist rule in Czechoslovakia (b). Later the USSR refused to participate in the Baruch Plan (d), which aimed to set up an international agency to manage the use of atomic energy. This action demonstrated an unwillingness to cooperate with other nations in the interest of peace. These events signified the beginning of the Cold War.

73. B: The National Security Act (b) was the legislation responsible for creating the Central Intelligence Agency (CIA) and the Department of Defense (DOD) in 1948. The Truman Doctrine (a) was President Truman's 1947 policy preventing domination by communists through

"containment," a term coined by George F. Kennan of the State Department. The Marshall Plan (c), also in 1947, was Secretary of State George C. Marshall's plan for funding the reconstruction of Europe, both to foster prosperity and provide a preferable alternative to Communism there. NATO (d) was developed following the signing of the North Atlantic Treaty in 1949 and constituted an alliance for defense among the US, Canada, and a majority of the countries in Western Europe.

74. D: It is not true that (d) General Douglas MacArthur's invasion of Inchon was unsuccessful. While previous US interventions did not succeed in Korea, MacArthur's attack at Inchon on September 15, 1950, forced North Korean troops to retreat behind the 38th parallel, the temporary division set up after the war, which the North Koreans had breached on June 25, 1950.   The other answers are true.

75. B: China' production of an atomic bomb in 1964. The USSR launched *Sputnik* (a), the first man-made satellite, into space in 1957. The USSR detonated a hydrogen bomb (c) in 1953, the year after the US detonated its first hydrogen bomb (d) in 1952. The US formed the national Aeronautics and Space Administration (NASA) in 1958 (e) to facilitate competition in the arms and space races.

76. D: In 1956, Egypt did not attack Israel. On October 29, 1956, Israel attacked Egypt. England and France did join this war within two days. It is true that Egyptian President Gamal Abdul Nasser refused to take America's side in the Cold War (a). In reaction to his refusal, President Eisenhower's administration pulled its funding from the Aswan Dam project in Egypt (b). Nasser then nationalized the British-owned Suez Canal (c). Eisenhower further declared in 1957 that America would provide aid to any country in the Middle East facing Communist control (e). Pursuant to Eisenhower's declaration, the US invaded Lebanon in 1958 to resolve a conflict in government.

77. C: The Limited Test Ban Treaty, which banned all above ground nuclear testing, did not occur during Kennedy's administration. The US and others continued to build and test nuclear weapons. The Soviet Union did lift its moratorium on above-ground nuclear testing (a) in the autumn of 1961. Around the same time, the US produced a great many more nuclear weapons (b). President Kennedy refused to take sides regarding the division of Berlin, Germany (d), where the Soviets built a wall separating the Soviet-created German Democratic Republic in East Germany from the Federal Republic of Germany created by the Allies in West Germany (e).

78. E: Cuban exiles sponsored by the CIA, (e), is the most correct description of the Bay of Pigs (1961) invaders. It was not members of the CIA themselves (a). It was a group of Cuban exiles (b), but this answer is not as correct as (e), which further specifies that these Cuban exiles were sponsored by the CIA. They were also trained by the CIA and supported by US armed forces. The people of Cuba (c) did not invade nor did they support the invasion. In fact, the invasion was quashed by Cuban armed forces within three days. While the US assisted Cuban exile invaders and persistently aggravated Cuba, it is not as precise to say that the US (d) invaded the Bay of Pigs.

79. A: JFK launched an invasion of Cuba to remove Soviet missiles, is not a true statement regarding the Cuban Missile Crisis. Once informed of Soviet missile installations on Cuba, JFK publicly demanded that Russia remove these missiles (b). He also put the American armed forces on global alert(c). He further sent ships to the Caribbean to intercept shipments of Soviet arms (d) headed for Cuba. Following negotiations, on October 28,1962, Soviet premier Nikita Khrushchev agreed to remove his missiles from Cuba in exchange for JFK's promise not to invade Cuba (e).

80. B: The Communist Ho Chi Minh led the Vietminh rebellion against French efforts to colonize Vietnam in 1946. Truman's administration gave monetary support to French colonizers (a) starting in 1950. Following Truman's office, Eisenhower's administration also financially supported French

imperialism (c). France signed the Geneva Accords, creating a temporary division between North and South Vietnam (d), in 1954. North Vietnam was given to Ho Chi Minh while South Vietnam was given to Bao Dai, who was backed by the French. Initially the US supported Ngo Dinh Diem in deposing Bao Dai because American leaders thought this would prevent Vietnam falling under Communist control. However, once in power, Diem became corrupt and dictatorial, leading to South Vietnamese resistance against his reign. By 1963, the US government had become so disenchanted with the South Vietnamese regime that it supported a military coup resulting in Diem's death (e).

81. E: All of these factors were parts of President Richard M. Nixon's policy of "Vietnamization" after he took office in 1969. He directed that the US would give South Vietnam financial support (a) to assume more responsibility for the war (b). In gradual steps, Nixon started pulling American troops out of Vietnam (c), simultaneously stepping up the US bombing of North Vietnam (d).

82. A: Peace talks made sufficient progress towards a cease-fire in Vietnam is not true. Actually, the peace talks were stalled. As a response to the lack of progress, President Nixon gave orders to heavily bomb North Vietnam (b), December of 1972. Due to the escalated bombing, North Vietnam signed the cease-fire in January of 1973(c). US troop withdraw from Vietnam within 60 days (d) was part of the cease-fire agreement. Another part of the agreement was that South Vietnam set up a coalition government that included the Vietcong (e).

83. C: Nixon's visit to China did lead to US diplomatic recognition of that country and a trade agreement with the Soviets, but not in 1973. Nixon went to China in 1972; the US officially recognized China in 1979. The trade agreement with Russia was made in 1972. It is true, therefore, that Nixon's visit not only prepared the way for diplomatic recognition of China but also moved the Soviets toward cooperation with the US (b). It is also true that when Nixon announced in 1972, "I will go to China," Americans were surprised (a) as US had not had diplomatic relations with China for many years. His announcement made global headlines. During Nixon's trip to China, Russia and the US signed the Strategic Arms Limitations Talks (SALT) Treaty (d), which set limits on the number of antiballistic missiles allowed each country. This treaty was signed in 1972, and in the same year the US and Russia signed a trade agreement allowing wheat purchases by the USSR from the US(e).

84. B: Carter did not reinforce the SALT-II Treaty during the Cold War. Rather, the treaty was garnered via negotiations during the SALT talks (a). However, upon the Soviet invasion of Afghanistan, the Senate passage of the treaty was threatened, and Carter withdrew it from the Senate following the Afghan invasion. Carter did not order a stoppage of US wheat shipments to Russia (c); a boycott of the summer Olympics in Moscow (d); or surreptitious aid to the anti-Soviet resistance in Afghanistan (e) in response to the invasion.

85. D: The action least associated with Reagan's anti-Communist measures was (d), his withdrawal of Cuban troops from Angola in 1988. This troop withdrawal was in answer to pressure to force an end to South Africa's apartheid policies, which segregated blacks from whites. The US levied economic sanctions against South Africa in 1986, after "constructive engagement" efforts failed to end apartheid. In 1988, the Reagan administration negotiated to allow black majority rule in Namibia and to remove Cuban troops from Angola. Therefore answer (d) is a reflection of anti-apartheid actions rather than anti-Communist actions. In efforts to protect the US from Communism, Reagan reinforced our systems of military weaponry (a). He introduced the Strategic Defense Initiative to establish antimissile systems in space (b). In addition, he announced his "Reagan Doctrine," which granted American support to freedom fighters who resisted communist rule (c). In 1987, Reagan made an agreement with Russia's Mikhail Gorbachev to ban intermediate-range, land-based missiles in Europe (e).

86. C: Statement (c), Congress voted to end aid to the Contras in 1984 and this policy remained in effect 1988 is not true regarding Reagan's actions in Latin America. Congress reversed its 1984 decision in 1986 and once again provided aid, as well as training (b), to the Contras (counter-revolutionaries). Shortly after assuming office, Reagan aided El Salvador's government in combating leftist uprisings (a). Reagan's administration also sold arms in secret to Iran and used the sales profits to support the Contras (d). When these covert sales were exposed, a major "Iran-Contra" scandal erupted in America. In 1983, Reagan also deployed US troops to Grenada, a Caribbean island, to depose a leftist regime (e). This military action also caused controversy in America.

87. B: Reagan escalated military action in response to a terrorist bombing that killed 240 US Marines, is not true. Reagan sent the Marines to Lebanon in 1982 as part of a peacekeeping effort (d) after Israel invaded Lebanon on a mission to eradicate its PLO camps (a). At the time, Lebanon was already engaged in a civil war (c). When the terrorist attack killed 240 Marines, Reagan withdrew the rest of the troops rather than escalate the action. In 1988, an uprising of Palestinians known as the First Intifada started on the Jordan River's much-contested West Bank. In response to this uprising, Reagan initiated peace talks with the PLO's leader, Yasser Arafat (e). However, the goal of peace in the Middle East never materialized.

88. A: Communists adhering to more traditional thought did stage a coup against Gorbachev, but it was not successful. Its failure proved the ineffectiveness of the Central Committee, the Communist Party, and the Soviet government. Gorbachev's actions at this time were not to preserve the communist union but to reform the government and the economy, and they ultimately led to the USSR dissolution. He initiated Perestroika, which, literally translated, means "restructuring," to reform the economy (b). He also instituted Glasnost, open government processes, to make Russian politics transparent to all (c), in an effort to decrease communist and Soviet government corruption. These new policies introduced by Gorbachev started a chain reaction of events in Eastern Europe that Soviets could not control. These included the collapse of East Germany's communist government in 1989, whereupon the Berlin Wall was dismantled, leading to East and West Germany's reunification in 1990 (d). These events also included the ends of Communist governments in seven Eastern European countries, all in a period of only two years (e). In 1989, communist leadership ended in Poland, Hungary, Czechoslovakia, and Romania. In 1990, Bulgaria's and Albania's communist governments also fell, and that year Lithuania detached itself from the Soviet Union, at which point the Union fell apart. Following the failed coup attempt, the Soviet Union was dismantled.

89. D: The country whose Communist regime did not collapse during the same year as the others was (d): Albania, whose communist government fell in 1990. Lithuania also broke away from the Soviet Union in 1990. The Communist governments of Poland (a), Hungary (b), Romania (c) and Bulgaria (e) all fell in 1989.

90. E: All of these were actions taken by the Bush administration between 1989-1992, is correct. In 1991, the US and Russia signed the START I treaty, and in 1992, they signed the START II treaty (a). Both of these treaties were agreements by both countries to decrease their arsenals of nuclear weapons. In 1989, the US invaded Panama and overthrew Dictator Manuel Noriega while supporting the National Opposition Union there, which won the 1990 election against the Sandinista Front; and in 1992, US diplomacy ended the civil war in El Salvador (b). Also, in 1992, the US signed the North American Free Trade Agreement (NAFTA) with Canada and Mexico, and the US Senate ratified it in 1994, (c). This agreement provided for trading relations among these countries that were mostly free of tariffs. The Persian Gulf War resulted from Iraq's invasion of Kuwait in 1990. Bush intervened with the US Air Force in January of 1991, and within a month he

mobilized the Army, Marine Corps, Navy, and Coast Guard to Saudi Arabia, subsequently invading Iraq. At Bush's encouragement, other countries also sent troops there. These combined forces moved the Iraqis out of Kuwait in four days. The UN Security Council approved a cease-fire in April 1991; a hundred days after the ground forces were deployed. Additional actions by Bush during this period included sending troops to Somalia in 1992 to manage the distribution of humanitarian aid and assigning a UN peacekeeping force in 1993 to assume this duty.

91. A: The event that did not have a negative impact on the postwar US economy was (a) the Servicemen's Readjustment Act of 1944, or Public Law 78-346. More familiarly called the GI Bill, this law gave financial aid for education to former soldiers. More than a million war veterans went to college on the GI Bill. This was one economic advantage among a number of disadvantages. Demobilization of the armed forces (b) took place quickly, such that from 1945 to 1947, the numbers in the military were reduced to one quarter of their previous count, from 12 million to 3 million, putting a great strain on the economy. With war supplies no longer needed, the defense manufacturing industry was reduced (c), so by 1946, rates of unemployment had risen to more than 2.5 million people. The Office of Price Administration removed wartime controls on prices, and Americans began spending money they had saved during the war, resulting in an increase in inflation (d) to 18% by 1946. Many unionized laborers found their work hours and wages, reduced after the war (e), leading to a proliferation of union strikes. When the United Mine Workers went on strike in 1946, President Truman ordered a temporary seizure by the government of the coal mines and threatened repeats of this action.

92. D: After being re-elected in 1948, Truman continued to promote his "Fair Deal," but Southern members of Congress from both Democratic and Republican parties prevented most of the programs from passing into law. When Congress passed the Taft-Hartley Act in 1947, it was not with Truman's agreement (a); Congress passed this law after Truman vetoed it. The Taft-Hartley act did not allow workplace to restrict their employees to union members (b); this act outlawed such "closed shops," which mitigated the power of labor unions. Congress did not raise the amount of aid to farmers or pass bills for health insurance and minimum wages (c); conversely, Congress reduced financial support for farming and turned down bills to providing health insurance and establishing a minimum wage. In fact, Truman's reelection was somewhat unexpected because many Americans did not approve of Congress' actions (e). Most voters were displeased by Congress' limitation of labor unions, lack of support for farmers, refusal to enact provisions for health coverage, and its refusal to establish a minimum wage.

93. C: The person or group *not* instrumental in advancing civil rights and desegregation after WWII was (c), Congress. As African American soldiers came home from the war, racial discord increased. President Harry Truman (a) appointed a Presidential Committee on Civil Rights in 1946. This committee published a report recommending that segregation and lynching be outlawed by the federal government. However, Congress ignored this report and took no action. Truman then used his presidential powers to enforce desegregation of the military and policies of "fair employment" in federal civil service jobs. The National Association for the Advancement of Colored People (NAACP) (d) brought lawsuits against racist and discriminatory practices, and in resolving these suits, the Supreme Court (b) further eroded segregation. For example, the Supreme Court ruled that primaries allowing only whites would be illegal, and it ended the segregation of interstate bus lines.

94. E: All of these (e) events exacerbated Americans' paranoia of Communism during the 1940s and 1950s. During this time, the Soviet Union was pressured Eastern European countries, and China was under Communist control (a). In 1950, former State Department official Alger Hiss denied to a grand jury that he had given classified information to a communist spy during the 1930s and was convicted of lying; while Klaus Fuchs, who worked at Los Alamos on the atomic bomb project, was

convicted by the British court for giving information regarding nuclear science to agents of the Soviet Union (b). Perhaps most instrumental to provoking paranoia was Senator Joseph McCarthy's announcement in 1950 that over 200 State Department employees were Communist and that a list of these people existed (c). While it was ultimately proven that McCarthy had no evidence substantiating his claim, the four years before this was established were wrought with suspicion and frantic searches to expose Communists in America. The Internal Security Act passed by Congress in 1950 (d) mandated that members of "Communist-front" groups must register with the government.

95. B: In his program, "Dynamic Conservatism," Eisenhower tried to build on and modify the New Deal. Among his efforts, the least successful was (b), keeping the federal budget balanced. Though balancing the budget was one of Eisenhower's goals, he only accomplished this three out of eight years in office. He was more successful in extending Social Security (a) in 1954, and in passing the Housing Act the same year (c), which financed the building of homes for families with low incomes. Eisenhower's administration also succeeded in public works programs. For example, the St. Lawrence Seaway project, in 1954, (d) built a canal to connect Lake Erie in America with Montreal in Canada. And in 1956, the Highway Act (e) financed building the Interstate Highway System.

96. E: Both answer (a) and answer (c) furthered the civil rights cause, but (b) and (d) impeded this cause. In the case of *Brown v. Board of Education of Topeka* (a), the Supreme Court's 1954 ruling stated that schools segregated by race are by nature not equal. This ruling was monumental in the NAACP's fight against school segregation. Orval Faubus, Governor of Arkansas, tried to prevent Little Rock High School's integration in 1957 (b). The situation escalated such that President Eisenhower gave the Arkansas National Guard nationalized status and sent paratroopers to protect the high school students from harm (c). These actions furthered civil rights by showing the government's defense of school integration. The city of Little Rock, Arkansas and its high schools violated civil rights during that time period (d) and closed the high schools to prevent integration.

97. C: The person or group not associated with the 1957 Montgomery Bus Boycott was (c) the SNCC. The Student Nonviolent Coordinating Committee (SNCC) was formed in 1960 as a result of a growing sit-in movement. This movement began after African American students in North Carolina refused to allow themselves to be thrown out of a Woolworth's lunch counter on racial premises. Since the Civil Rights Act passed in 1957 by Congress was not effective, African Americans deemed more assertive action necessary, as exemplified in the North Carolina Woolworth's incident. This incident initiated the sit-in movement which then spread to additional cities and ultimately led to the formation of the SNCC. Since the SNCC formed in 1960, it could not have been involved in the 1957 Montgomery Bus Boycott.

First a black woman named Rosa Parks (a) refused to give up her seat on the bus to a white man. As others rallied to show their support for Ms. Parks and against racism, the Reverend Martin Luther King Jr. (b) became the leader of the boycott movement. That same year, the Supreme Court (d) ruled that the laws in Alabama governing desegregation were unconstitutional. This decision upheld the boycott and Dr. King's leadership. As a result, also in 1957, King was made president of the Southern Christian Leadership Conference (SCLC).

98. B: There was not a reduction in military spending after the war. Although the manufacturing demand for war supplies and the size of the military decreased, the government had increased military spending from $10 billion in 1947 to more than $50 billion by 1953—a more than fivefold increase. This increase strengthened the American economy. Other factors contributing to the strengthened economy included the significantly higher birth rates during the Baby Boom (a) from 1946 to 1957, which stimulated the growth of the building and automotive industries by increased

demand. Government programs, such as the GI Bill (the Servicemen's Readjustment Act of 1944), other veterans' benefits, and the National Defense Education Act all encouraged college enrollments, which increased by nearly four times (c). Additionally, larger families, increased mobility and low-interest loans offered to veterans led to suburban development and growth (d) as well as an increased home construction. Improvements in public health were also results of the new affluence; the rate of infant deaths decreased significantly, and as a result, from 1946-1957, the American life span rose from 67 to 71 years (e). Moreover, Dr. Jonas Salk developed the polio vaccine in 1955, which virtually wiped out poliomyelitis, preventing many deaths and disabilities in children.

99. D: The answer that does not accurately describe changes in the American entertainment industry in the years after World War II is (d): Movie attendance did not increase from 1960-1970. In those ten years, movie audiences decreased by a third, from 60 million per week to 40 million per week. As household televisions became commonplace – approximately 8,000 households had TV sets in 1946, whereas 46 million households had TV sets in 1960 – fewer people sought out movie entertainment. Movies were not the only casualty of competition with television. Rather, radio stations also lost their audiences for radio dramas, including soap operas, and adjusted to this loss by substituting more music, especially the emerging rock & roll music (b), to target the youth culture. Another aspect of youth culture was nonconformity, which found expression in the themes of new movies and in such social phenomena as the Beat movement (c). The Beat movement included Beat poets such as Allen Ginsberg, novelists such as Jack Kerouac, and many jazz musicians. Ginsberg's 1956 epic poem *Howl* and Kerouac's masterful 1957 novel *On the Road* both attracted powerful cult followings and profoundly influenced the subculture and rebellions of youth in the 1960s.

100. A: As of 1962, almost **25%** (not 15%) of Americans had poverty-level incomes (less than $4,000 a year for a family of four) (b). The least prosperous segments of the population were black people living in ghettoes of the inner cities; Mexican American migrant farm workers; Native American Indians; white people living in Appalachia; and elderly Americans who could not get Social Security benefits. The proportion of poor people in an affluent nation was brought to light by Michael Harrington in his 1962 book *The Other America*.

101. B: Of the programs enacted by Johnson, the one most closely related to JFK's legacy was (b), the Civil Rights Act, which Johnson pushed through Congress using allusions to Kennedy's and his goals. While Kennedy received congressional backing for a raise in minimum wage and public housing improvements, his efforts regarding civil rights were thwarted by conservative Republicans and Southern Democrats in Congress. However, as the Civil Rights movement progressed through the campaigns of the Freedom Riders, Kennedy developed a strong commitment to the cause.

The Economic Opportunity Act gave almost $1 billion to wage Johnson's War on Poverty. The Great Society (c) was Johnson's name for his comprehensive reform program which included a variety of legislation (see also question #102).

102. D: The war ended during Nixon's administration. The Great Society program included legislation to create Medicare (a), eliminate obstacles hindering the right to vote (b), provide federal funding for education (c), and establish the Department of Housing and Urban Development (HUD). The Great Society also included a number of programs aimed at alleviating poverty. Johnson's social reform accomplishments were overshadowed by the Vietnam War during his last two years in office.

103. C: The Mississippi Freedom Democratic Party did attend the 1964 Democratic convention; however, they were unable garner Johnson's support to unseat the regular delegation from Mississippi. A riot did break out in Watts in 1965 (a), and in the following three years, more riots occurred in Newark, N.J. (b) and in Detroit, Michigan (d). These riots were manifestations of the frustrations experienced by blacks regarding racial inequities in American society. Another demonstration of black unrest was the increasing activity of the Black Panthers and the Black Muslims in the 1960s (e). Both were militant organizations demanding civil rights reforms.

104. E: All of these (e) events were associated with and/or had an impact on the emergence of the New Left, young people who were politically and socially disenchanted with America. In 1962, in Port Huron, Michigan, the SDS (a), spearheaded by Tom Hayden, Alan Huber, and others, held its first convention and was subsequently instrumental in student organization and advocacy for social and political reform (until 1969). The Berkeley Free Speech Movement (b) was organized at the University of California at Berkeley by student Mario Savio and others, insisting that the university's administrators remove their ban on campus political activity and recognize students' rights to free speech. The student activism generated by the Free Speech movement continues to this day, albeit not as rampantly as at the movement's inception. In 1968, when first Martin Luther King Jr. and then Robert Kennedy, both major leaders for reform, were assassinated (c), young people were further disaffected. Another reflection of the New Left youth's dissatisfaction with American politics was the occurrence of violent confrontations between protestors and police officers in Chicago's streets outside the 1968 Democratic Convention (d).

105. A: The Supreme Court upheld affirmative action in *Bakke v. University of California*, is not true. In this 1978 case, the Supreme Court actually overturned the earlier affirmative action provision to use quotas for the purpose of attaining racial balance. It is true that when affirmative action began in the 1960s, its aim was to remedy underrepresentation of blacks in higher education and employment by raising the numbers of blacks included until they came closer to being balanced with the numbers of whites (b). Since then, whites opposing affirmative action criticized the ruling insisting that instead of producing the desired goal, affirmative action discriminated against white applicants by pressuring schools and companies to preferentially accept black applicants (c). After the *Bakke v. University of California* decision, additional Supreme Court rulings followed the precedent of that case and further limited what affirmative action could legally do (d).

106. D: The Equal Rights Amendment, though it was approved by Congress in 1972 (c), was not ratified in its deadline year for ratification of 1983, is not correct. The amendment fell short of reaching ratification by just three states' votes. President Reagan did appoint judge Sandra Day O'Connor, the first female justice, to the Supreme Court (a), despite the fact that in general, he and his administration were against feminist agendas (b).

107. D: The statement that the 1986 Immigration Reform and Control Act impeded illegal Mexican immigration is not true. This legislation punished employers with sanctions for hiring undocumented employees, but despite this the illegal immigration of Mexicans to America was largely unaffected by the law. It is true that twice as many people immigrated to America in the 1980s than in the 1970s (a): the number reached over nine million in the 80s. It is true that the majority of immigrants were Latin American (b). In addition to Latin Americans, other large groups of immigrants in the 1980s were Asians and Caribbean inhabitants (c).

108. A: AIDS Cases were not first discovered beginning in 1984, but were found beginning in 1981. The HIV (Human Immunodeficiency Virus) infection that leads to AIDS (Acquired Immune Deficiency Syndrome) spread quickly in users of intravenous drugs (b) as a result of sharing injection needles. Initially, it was also transmitted quickly among male homosexuals (c). It is true

that cases of AIDS multiplied in excess of 8,000 times annually (d). By 1988, more than half of the reported cases of AIDS had resulted in deaths (e).

109. B: Bill Clinton did not receive 47% of the votes but 43.2%, while George Bush received not 35% but 37.7% of the votes. In other words, this was a close election. Although Bush's actions to resolve the Persian Gulf War did earn him high public approval ratings (a), problems with the economy in America weakened his bid for reelection (c). Arkansas Governor Bill Clinton's campaign focusing on his views as a more moderate, less liberal, Democrat appealed to voters (d). Another factor that detracted from Bush's campaign was the third-party candidacy of H. Ross Perot, a billionaire businessman from Texas who received 19% of the votes, diverting enough votes from Bush for Clinton to win (e).

110. C: It is not true that Congress rejected Clinton's health care proposal wholesale (c). Although his motion for universal coverage was denied by Congress, some parts of Clinton's proposal were passed into law, such as the Children's Health Insurance Program (CHIP).

Clinton announced in 1993 that he would suspend the ban on gays in the military. However, due to objections by antigay interests, Clinton changed his policy and reached an agreement with Congress such that military management could not question personnel regarding sexual orientation, and service persons could not offer any information on the subject—the "don't ask-don't tell" policy (a). In 1993, Clinton's administration passed the Family and Medical Leave Act, which required most companies with at least 50 employees to give employees up to 12 weeks of unpaid leave for family bonding and/or to care for an immediate family member who is ill. The act also requires employers to maintain health benefits during that leave. . As the federal deficit continued to grow, Clinton made a financial plan that included raising taxes and lowering federal spending by cutting government jobs and other means. The plan was narrowly passed by Congress (d).

111. B: The "Brady Bill" passed without opposition, is not correct. When John Hinckley Jr. tried to assassinate President Reagan in 1981, he failed, but he severely wounded James Brady, Reagan's Press Secretary, who was riding with him. Brady almost died and suffered permanent disabilities. When the Brady Handgun Violence Prevention Act (1993) was proposed, the National Rifle Association (NRA) lobbied vigorously against it. However, Congress passed the bill over this powerful group's objections. This law mandated a five-day waiting period before a person could buy a handgun (a) and allocated funds towards the design of a computer system that could more quickly and efficiently run background checks (c). Additional crime control legislation proposed by the Clinton administration included a 1994 bill that allocated more than $8 billion to hire an additional 100 000 police officers (d). This bill also provided funds to build more prisons and banned the use of 19 different kinds of assault weapons (e).

112. A: It is not true that the Welfare Reform Act was proposed by President Clinton and modified by Republicans (a). This law was proposed by the Republicans and was then modified by President Clinton. The Welfare Reform Act transferred the responsibility for designing welfare programs from the federal government to the individual states (b). Federal government block grants funded each state's welfare program design (c). In addition to the block grants, another provision of this law was that if heads of households receiving welfare did not get jobs within two years of being awarded benefits, they would lose them (d).

113. E: All of these (e) factors helped the Republicans gain control of both the House and the Senate in 1994 during Clinton's administration. Allegations regarding the President's character, specifically involvement in the Whitewater Development Corporation scandal and allegations of inappropriate sexual advances made by Clinton during his gubernatorial tenure, (a) and (b) were factors that

weakened the Democratic position. Additionally, disagreements regarding healthcare legislation and gays in the military (c) further weakened the President's credibility and strengthened the Republican position. Lastly, Georgia Congressman and Minority Whip, Newt Gingrich's initiative to sign a "Contract with America" (d), a document proposing a more efficient and smaller government, bolster the Republican Party.

114. C: The Senate never voted to impeach Clinton. The grounds for impeachment were perjury and obstruction of justice (a) based upon Clinton's denial of an extramarital relationship with intern Monica Lewinsky. Clinton later admitted to the relationship (d). The House of Representatives voted to impeach the President (b) under the influence of Speaker of the House Newt Gingrich and other Republicans. After a trial in the Senate, the Senate voted against convicting Clinton, and he was acquitted of all charges. As this represented a defeat to the Republicans, Newt Gingrich resigned shortly thereafter (e). Many people agreed with First Lady Hillary Clinton that the entire impeachment episode, regardless of Clinton's actions, was part of a "vast right-wing conspiracy" against Clinton by Republicans, which she stated had gone on since he announced his candidacy for President.

115. D: It is not true that PCs had less impact on businesses than on home users. Businesses had been using mainframe computers since around 1946 (a), after World War II. This use became more frequent as companies found them advantageous to tracking and eventually processing, billing and payroll records. Mainframe computers were so large that they occupied entire rooms. When microprocessors were developed in the 1970s, it became possible to create a much smaller computer, the Personal Computer or PC (b). Due to its much smaller size and price, the PC enabled home computer use for the first time (c). Following the invention of the PC, the Arpanet (Advanced Research Projects Agency Network), a system developed in the 1960s by the Department of Defense and the first packet-switching network in the world, became the model for a similar public system, the Internet (e). The development of the PC, along with that of the Internet and the World Wide Web, had a profound impact on the ways that businesses operated, which is why (d) is incorrect.

116. C: The rates of both productivity and inflation in the US was approximately 2% by 2000. By this time, the US economy was not increasing at a rate of 5% a year (a) but of 4% a year. Almost half of industrial growth contributing to economic prosperity was due to the "information revolution" made possible by the invention of the PC. The rate of unemployment in America at this time had not gone down to 6% (b) but to 4.7%. The stock market in the US had not just doubled in six years (d); it had actually quadrupled from 1992-1998 due to the increase in American households that owned stocks or bonds. Most of this ownership resulted from tax law changes regulating retirement accounts. In the 1998 fiscal year, the federal government did have a surplus, but not of $40 billion (e); the surplus that year was $70 billion, and additional surpluses were predicted for the future.

117. D: It is not true that (d) the Waco siege at the Branch Davidian compound lasted for two weeks. In fact, once the FBI attacked the compound, the resulting siege lasted for 51 days. It is true that the Branch Davidians were a Protestant sect that had split off from the Seventh Day Adventists and lived on a compound near Waco, Texas (a). Following reports of gunfire and weapons caches there, the Bureau of Alcohol, Tobacco and Firearms (ATF) conducted surveillance and obtained a search warrant (b). When ATF attempted to execute the warrant, gunfire was exchanged between the compound and ATF agents, and four agents were killed, whereupon the FBI became involved and attacked the compound (c). Following the 51-day siege, the FBI gassed the main building as Davidians set several fires in the building. Various sources claim the deaths totaled 76-86. One of the fatalities was Branch Davidian leader David Koresh (e), whose original name was Vernon

Wayne Howell. Note: Despite videotaped records, there is still much controversy surrounding this event.

118. B: The GATT countries did agree to abolish or decrease many of their tariffs, but this agreement did not include only 57 countries. It was much larger, including a total of 117 countries. The GATT was approved by Congress in 1994 (a). In addition to having 117 countries agree to increase free trade, the GATT also set up the World Trade Organization (WTO) for the purpose of settling any differences among nations related to trade (c). Another instance of free trade policy established in the 1990s was the Senate's ratification of NAFTA. The negotiation of this agreement was originally made by the first Bush administration, with President Bush and the leaders of Canada and Mexico signing it in 1992 (d), but it still needed to be ratified. When he was elected President following the senior Bush's second term, Bill Clinton also supported NAFTA, and the Senate ratified it in 1994 (e).

119. E: When Gore demanded another recount of votes in Florida during the 2000 election, it yielded the same results, is not true. When Gore demanded another Florida recount, the Supreme Court decided in a vote of 5 to 4 against that recount, so it was not made and there were no more results. It is true that Al Gore did win the majority of popular votes (a). It is also true that votes for Green Party candidate Ralph Nader diverted some votes from Gore (b). Many people admired Nader as a crusader for consumer issues, but there was concern that because he could never attract enough votes to win the election, he would simply hurt Gore's chances by detracting some liberals' votes from Gore. It is true that the electoral vote count from Florida would determine the final outcome of the election (c). It is also true that there was a great deal of confusion in Florida over the way the ballots were designed, the ability of Florida's large population of senior citizen voters to read and fill out the ballots correctly, and whether parts of the ballots had been punched through or not. Controversy also brewed over the numbers of votes, such that the final tally was not even certified until November 27 (d).

120. A: It is not true that the US defeated the Taliban and captured Osama bin Laden shortly after 9/11/2001. Osama bin Laden was killed during a raid on a private compound in Pakistan in 2011, nearly 10 years after the attacks. It is true that Muslim terrorists flew two of the four American airplanes they had hijacked into the twin towers of the World Trade Center in New York City (b). They flew the third of the four planes into the US Department of Defense's headquarters, the Pentagon building in Arlington, Virginia, (c) near Washington, D.C. The fourth plane crashed in a field near Shanksville, Pennsylvania, after some of the passengers on board tried to overtake the terrorists (d). President George W. Bush announced a "war on terrorism" after these attacks killed a total of 2,995 people.

How to Overcome Test Anxiety

Just the thought of taking a test is enough to make most people a little nervous. A test is an important event that can have a long-term impact on your future, so it's important to take it seriously and it's natural to feel anxious about performing well. But just because anxiety is normal, that doesn't mean that it's helpful in test taking, or that you should simply accept it as part of your life. Anxiety can have a variety of effects. These effects can be mild, like making you feel slightly nervous, or severe, like blocking your ability to focus or remember even a simple detail.

If you experience test anxiety—whether severe or mild—it's important to know how to beat it. To discover this, first you need to understand what causes test anxiety.

Causes of Test Anxiety

While we often think of anxiety as an uncontrollable emotional state, it can actually be caused by simple, practical things. One of the most common causes of test anxiety is that a person does not feel adequately prepared for their test. This feeling can be the result of many different issues such as poor study habits or lack of organization, but the most common culprit is time management. Starting to study too late, failing to organize your study time to cover all of the material, or being distracted while you study will mean that you're not well prepared for the test. This may lead to cramming the night before, which will cause you to be physically and mentally exhausted for the test. Poor time management also contributes to feelings of stress, fear, and hopelessness as you realize you are not well prepared but don't know what to do about it.

Other times, test anxiety is not related to your preparation for the test but comes from unresolved fear. This may be a past failure on a test, or poor performance on tests in general. It may come from comparing yourself to others who seem to be performing better or from the stress of living up to expectations. Anxiety may be driven by fears of the future—how failure on this test would affect your educational and career goals. These fears are often completely irrational, but they can still negatively impact your test performance.

Review Video: 3 Reasons You Have Test Anxiety
Visit mometrix.com/academy and enter code: 428468

179

Elements of Test Anxiety

As mentioned earlier, test anxiety is considered to be an emotional state, but it has physical and mental components as well. Sometimes you may not even realize that you are suffering from test anxiety until you notice the physical symptoms. These can include trembling hands, rapid heartbeat, sweating, nausea, and tense muscles. Extreme anxiety may lead to fainting or vomiting. Obviously, any of these symptoms can have a negative impact on testing. It is important to recognize them as soon as they begin to occur so that you can address the problem before it damages your performance.

> **Review Video: 3 Ways to Tell You Have Test Anxiety**
> Visit mometrix.com/academy and enter code: 927847

The mental components of test anxiety include trouble focusing and inability to remember learned information. During a test, your mind is on high alert, which can help you recall information and stay focused for an extended period of time. However, anxiety interferes with your mind's natural processes, causing you to blank out, even on the questions you know well. The strain of testing during anxiety makes it difficult to stay focused, especially on a test that may take several hours. Extreme anxiety can take a huge mental toll, making it difficult not only to recall test information but even to understand the test questions or pull your thoughts together.

> **Review Video: How Test Anxiety Affects Memory**
> Visit mometrix.com/academy and enter code: 609003

Effects of Test Anxiety

Test anxiety is like a disease—if left untreated, it will get progressively worse. Anxiety leads to poor performance, and this reinforces the feelings of fear and failure, which in turn lead to poor performances on subsequent tests. It can grow from a mild nervousness to a crippling condition. If allowed to progress, test anxiety can have a big impact on your schooling, and consequently on your future.

Test anxiety can spread to other parts of your life. Anxiety on tests can become anxiety in any stressful situation, and blanking on a test can turn into panicking in a job situation. But fortunately, you don't have to let anxiety rule your testing and determine your grades. There are a number of relatively simple steps you can take to move past anxiety and function normally on a test and in the rest of life.

> **Review Video: How Test Anxiety Impacts Your Grades**
> Visit mometrix.com/academy and enter code: 939819

Physical Steps for Beating Test Anxiety

While test anxiety is a serious problem, the good news is that it can be overcome. It doesn't have to control your ability to think and remember information. While it may take time, you can begin taking steps today to beat anxiety.

Just as your first hint that you may be struggling with anxiety comes from the physical symptoms, the first step to treating it is also physical. Rest is crucial for having a clear, strong mind. If you are tired, it is much easier to give in to anxiety. But if you establish good sleep habits, your body and mind will be ready to perform optimally, without the strain of exhaustion. Additionally, sleeping well helps you to retain information better, so you're more likely to recall the answers when you see the test questions.

Getting good sleep means more than going to bed on time. It's important to allow your brain time to relax. Take study breaks from time to time so it doesn't get overworked, and don't study right before bed. Take time to rest your mind before trying to rest your body, or you may find it difficult to fall asleep.

Review Video: The Importance of Sleep for Your Brain
Visit mometrix.com/academy and enter code: 319338

Along with sleep, other aspects of physical health are important in preparing for a test. Good nutrition is vital for good brain function. Sugary foods and drinks may give a burst of energy but this burst is followed by a crash, both physically and emotionally. Instead, fuel your body with protein and vitamin-rich foods.

Also, drink plenty of water. Dehydration can lead to headaches and exhaustion, especially if your brain is already under stress from the rigors of the test. Particularly if your test is a long one, drink water during the breaks. And if possible, take an energy-boosting snack to eat between sections.

Review Video: How Diet Can Affect your Mood
Visit mometrix.com/academy and enter code: 624317

Along with sleep and diet, a third important part of physical health is exercise. Maintaining a steady workout schedule is helpful, but even taking 5-minute study breaks to walk can help get your blood pumping faster and clear your head. Exercise also releases endorphins, which contribute to a positive feeling and can help combat test anxiety.

When you nurture your physical health, you are also contributing to your mental health. If your body is healthy, your mind is much more likely to be healthy as well. So take time to rest, nourish your body with healthy food and water, and get moving as much as possible. Taking these physical steps will make you stronger and more able to take the mental steps necessary to overcome test anxiety.

Review Video: How to Stay Healthy and Prevent Test Anxiety
Visit mometrix.com/academy and enter code: 877894

Mental Steps for Beating Test Anxiety

Working on the mental side of test anxiety can be more challenging, but as with the physical side, there are clear steps you can take to overcome it. As mentioned earlier, test anxiety often stems from lack of preparation, so the obvious solution is to prepare for the test. Effective studying may be the most important weapon you have for beating test anxiety, but you can and should employ several other mental tools to combat fear.

First, boost your confidence by reminding yourself of past success—tests or projects that you aced. If you're putting as much effort into preparing for this test as you did for those, there's no reason you should expect to fail here. Work hard to prepare; then trust your preparation.

Second, surround yourself with encouraging people. It can be helpful to find a study group, but be sure that the people you're around will encourage a positive attitude. If you spend time with others who are anxious or cynical, this will only contribute to your own anxiety. Look for others who are motivated to study hard from a desire to succeed, not from a fear of failure.

Third, reward yourself. A test is physically and mentally tiring, even without anxiety, and it can be helpful to have something to look forward to. Plan an activity following the test, regardless of the outcome, such as going to a movie or getting ice cream.

When you are taking the test, if you find yourself beginning to feel anxious, remind yourself that you know the material. Visualize successfully completing the test. Then take a few deep, relaxing breaths and return to it. Work through the questions carefully but with confidence, knowing that you are capable of succeeding.

Developing a healthy mental approach to test taking will also aid in other areas of life. Test anxiety affects more than just the actual test—it can be damaging to your mental health and even contribute to depression. It's important to beat test anxiety before it becomes a problem for more than testing.

Review Video: <u>Test Anxiety and Depression</u>
Visit mometrix.com/academy and enter code: 904704

182

Study Strategy

Being prepared for the test is necessary to combat anxiety, but what does being prepared look like? You may study for hours on end and still not feel prepared. What you need is a strategy for test prep. The next few pages outline our recommended steps to help you plan out and conquer the challenge of preparation.

STEP 1: SCOPE OUT THE TEST

Learn everything you can about the format (multiple choice, essay, etc.) and what will be on the test. Gather any study materials, course outlines, or sample exams that may be available. Not only will this help you to prepare, but knowing what to expect can help to alleviate test anxiety.

STEP 2: MAP OUT THE MATERIAL

Look through the textbook or study guide and make note of how many chapters or sections it has. Then divide these over the time you have. For example, if a book has 15 chapters and you have five days to study, you need to cover three chapters each day. Even better, if you have the time, leave an extra day at the end for overall review after you have gone through the material in depth.

If time is limited, you may need to prioritize the material. Look through it and make note of which sections you think you already have a good grasp on, and which need review. While you are studying, skim quickly through the familiar sections and take more time on the challenging parts. Write out your plan so you don't get lost as you go. Having a written plan also helps you feel more in control of the study, so anxiety is less likely to arise from feeling overwhelmed at the amount to cover.

STEP 3: GATHER YOUR TOOLS

Decide what study method works best for you. Do you prefer to highlight in the book as you study and then go back over the highlighted portions? Or do you type out notes of the important information? Or is it helpful to make flashcards that you can carry with you? Assemble the pens, index cards, highlighters, post-it notes, and any other materials you may need so you won't be distracted by getting up to find things while you study.

If you're having a hard time retaining the information or organizing your notes, experiment with different methods. For example, try color-coding by subject with colored pens, highlighters, or post-it notes. If you learn better by hearing, try recording yourself reading your notes so you can listen while in the car, working out, or simply sitting at your desk. Ask a friend to quiz you from your flashcards, or try teaching someone the material to solidify it in your mind.

STEP 4: CREATE YOUR ENVIRONMENT

It's important to avoid distractions while you study. This includes both the obvious distractions like visitors and the subtle distractions like an uncomfortable chair (or a too-comfortable couch that makes you want to fall asleep). Set up the best study environment possible: good lighting and a comfortable work area. If background music helps you focus, you may want to turn it on, but otherwise keep the room quiet. If you are using a computer to take notes, be sure you don't have any other windows open, especially applications like social media, games, or anything else that could distract you. Silence your phone and turn off notifications. Be sure to keep water close by so you stay hydrated while you study (but avoid unhealthy drinks and snacks).

Also, take into account the best time of day to study. Are you freshest first thing in the morning? Try to set aside some time then to work through the material. Is your mind clearer in the afternoon or evening? Schedule your study session then. Another method is to study at the same time of day that you will take the test, so that your brain gets used to working on the material at that time and will be ready to focus at test time.

STEP 5: STUDY!

Once you have done all the study preparation, it's time to settle into the actual studying. Sit down, take a few moments to settle your mind so you can focus, and begin to follow your study plan. Don't give in to distractions or let yourself procrastinate. This is your time to prepare so you'll be ready to fearlessly approach the test. Make the most of the time and stay focused.

Of course, you don't want to burn out. If you study too long you may find that you're not retaining the information very well. Take regular study breaks. For example, taking five minutes out of every hour to walk briskly, breathing deeply and swinging your arms, can help your mind stay fresh.

As you get to the end of each chapter or section, it's a good idea to do a quick review. Remind yourself of what you learned and work on any difficult parts. When you feel that you've mastered the material, move on to the next part. At the end of your study session, briefly skim through your notes again.

But while review is helpful, cramming last minute is NOT. If at all possible, work ahead so that you won't need to fit all your study into the last day. Cramming overloads your brain with more information than it can process and retain, and your tired mind may struggle to recall even previously learned information when it is overwhelmed with last-minute study. Also, the urgent nature of cramming and the stress placed on your brain contribute to anxiety. You'll be more likely to go to the test feeling unprepared and having trouble thinking clearly.

So don't cram, and don't stay up late before the test, even just to review your notes at a leisurely pace. Your brain needs rest more than it needs to go over the information again. In fact, plan to finish your studies by noon or early afternoon the day before the test. Give your brain the rest of the day to relax or focus on other things, and get a good night's sleep. Then you will be fresh for the test and better able to recall what you've studied.

STEP 6: TAKE A PRACTICE TEST

Many courses offer sample tests, either online or in the study materials. This is an excellent resource to check whether you have mastered the material, as well as to prepare for the test format and environment.

Check the test format ahead of time: the number of questions, the type (multiple choice, free response, etc.), and the time limit. Then create a plan for working through them. For example, if you have 30 minutes to take a 60-question test, your limit is 30 seconds per question. Spend less time on the questions you know well so that you can take more time on the difficult ones.

If you have time to take several practice tests, take the first one open book, with no time limit. Work through the questions at your own pace and make sure you fully understand them. Gradually work up to taking a test under test conditions: sit at a desk with all study materials put away and set a timer. Pace yourself to make sure you finish the test with time to spare and go back to check your answers if you have time.

After each test, check your answers. On the questions you missed, be sure you understand why you missed them. Did you misread the question (tests can use tricky wording)? Did you forget the information? Or was it something you hadn't learned? Go back and study any shaky areas that the practice tests reveal.

Taking these tests not only helps with your grade, but also aids in combating test anxiety. If you're already used to the test conditions, you're less likely to worry about it, and working through tests until you're scoring well gives you a confidence boost. Go through the practice tests until you feel comfortable, and then you can go into the test knowing that you're ready for it.

Test Tips

On test day, you should be confident, knowing that you've prepared well and are ready to answer the questions. But aside from preparation, there are several test day strategies you can employ to maximize your performance.

First, as stated before, get a good night's sleep the night before the test (and for several nights before that, if possible). Go into the test with a fresh, alert mind rather than staying up late to study.

Try not to change too much about your normal routine on the day of the test. It's important to eat a nutritious breakfast, but if you normally don't eat breakfast at all, consider eating just a protein bar. If you're a coffee drinker, go ahead and have your normal coffee. Just make sure you time it so that the caffeine doesn't wear off right in the middle of your test. Avoid sugary beverages, and drink enough water to stay hydrated but not so much that you need a restroom break 10 minutes into the test. If your test isn't first thing in the morning, consider going for a walk or doing a light workout before the test to get your blood flowing.

Allow yourself enough time to get ready, and leave for the test with plenty of time to spare so you won't have the anxiety of scrambling to arrive in time. Another reason to be early is to select a good seat. It's helpful to sit away from doors and windows, which can be distracting. Find a good seat, get out your supplies, and settle your mind before the test begins.

When the test begins, start by going over the instructions carefully, even if you already know what to expect. Make sure you avoid any careless mistakes by following the directions.

Then begin working through the questions, pacing yourself as you've practiced. If you're not sure on an answer, don't spend too much time on it, and don't let it shake your confidence. Either skip it and come back later, or eliminate as many wrong answers as possible and guess among the remaining ones. Don't dwell on these questions as you continue—put them out of your mind and focus on what lies ahead.

Be sure to read all of the answer choices, even if you're sure the first one is the right answer. Sometimes you'll find a better one if you keep reading. But don't second-guess yourself if you do immediately know the answer. Your gut instinct is usually right. Don't let test anxiety rob you of the information you know.

If you have time at the end of the test (and if the test format allows), go back and review your answers. Be cautious about changing any, since your first instinct tends to be correct, but make sure you didn't misread any of the questions or accidentally mark the wrong answer choice. Look over any you skipped and make an educated guess.

At the end, leave the test feeling confident. You've done your best, so don't waste time worrying about your performance or wishing you could change anything. Instead, celebrate the successful

completion of this test. And finally, use this test to learn how to deal with anxiety even better next time.

Important Qualification

Not all anxiety is created equal. If your test anxiety is causing major issues in your life beyond the classroom or testing center, or if you are experiencing troubling physical symptoms related to your anxiety, it may be a sign of a serious physiological or psychological condition. If this sounds like your situation, we strongly encourage you to seek professional help.

How to Overcome Your Fear of Math

The word *math* is enough to strike fear into most hearts. How many of us have memories of sitting through confusing lectures, wrestling over mind-numbing homework, or taking tests that still seem incomprehensible even after hours of study? Years after graduation, many still shudder at these memories.

The fact is, math is not just a classroom subject. It has real-world implications that you face every day, whether you realize it or not. This may be balancing your monthly budget, deciding how many supplies to buy for a project, or simply splitting a meal check with friends. The idea of daily confrontations with math can be so paralyzing that some develop a condition known as *math anxiety*.

But you do NOT need to be paralyzed by this anxiety! In fact, while you may have thought all your life that you're not good at math, or that your brain isn't wired to understand it, the truth is that you may have been conditioned to think this way. From your earliest school days, the way you were taught affected the way you viewed different subjects. And the way math has been taught has changed.

Several decades ago, there was a shift in American math classrooms. The focus changed from traditional problem-solving to a conceptual view of topics, de-emphasizing the importance of learning the basics and building on them. The solid foundation necessary for math progression and confidence was undermined. Math became more of a vague concept than a concrete idea. Today, it is common to think of math, not as a straightforward system, but as a mysterious, complicated method that can't be fully understood unless you're a genius.

This is why you may still have nightmares about being called on to answer a difficult problem in front of the class. Math anxiety is a very real, though unnecessary, fear.

Math anxiety may begin with a single class period. Let's say you missed a day in 6th grade math and never quite understood the concept that was taught while you were gone. Since math is cumulative, with each new concept building on past ones, this could very well affect the rest of your math career. Without that one day's knowledge, it will be difficult to understand any other concepts that link to it. Rather than realizing that you're just missing one key piece, you may begin to believe that you're simply not capable of understanding math.

This belief can change the way you approach other classes, career options, and everyday life experiences, if you become anxious at the thought that math might be required. A student who loves science may choose a different path of study upon realizing that multiple math classes will be required for a degree. An aspiring medical student may hesitate at the thought of going through the necessary math classes. For some this anxiety escalates into a more extreme state known as *math phobia*.

Math anxiety is challenging to address because it is rooted deeply and may come from a variety of causes: an embarrassing moment in class, a teacher who did not explain concepts well and contributed to a shaky foundation, or a failed test that contributed to the belief of math failure.

These causes add up over time, encouraged by society's popular view that math is hard and unpleasant. Eventually a person comes to firmly believe that he or she is simply bad at math. This belief makes it difficult to grasp new concepts or even remember old ones. Homework and test grades begin to slip, which only confirms the belief. The poor performance is not due to lack of ability but is caused by math anxiety.

Math anxiety is an emotional issue, not a lack of intelligence. But when it becomes deeply rooted, it can become more than just an emotional problem. Physical symptoms appear. Blood pressure may rise and heartbeat may quicken at the sight of a math problem – or even the thought of math! This fear leads to a mental block. When someone with math anxiety is asked to perform a calculation, even a basic problem can seem overwhelming and impossible. The emotional and physical response to the thought of math prevents the brain from working through it logically.

The more this happens, the more a person's confidence drops, and the more math anxiety is generated. This vicious cycle must be broken!

The first step in breaking the cycle is to go back to very beginning and make sure you really understand the basics of how math works and why it works. It is not enough to memorize rules for multiplication and division. If you don't know WHY these rules work, your foundation will be shaky and you will be at risk of developing a phobia. Understanding mathematical concepts not only promotes confidence and security, but allows you to build on this understanding for new concepts. Additionally, you can solve unfamiliar problems using familiar concepts and processes.

Why is it that students in other countries regularly outperform American students in math? The answer likely boils down to a couple of things: the foundation of mathematical conceptual understanding and societal perception. While students in the US are not expected to *like* or *get* math, in many other nations, students are expected not only to understand math but also to excel at it.

Changing the American view of math that leads to math anxiety is a monumental task. It requires changing the training of teachers nationwide, from kindergarten through high school, so that they learn to teach the *why* behind math and to combat the wrong math views that students may develop. It also involves changing the stigma associated with math, so that it is no longer viewed as unpleasant and incomprehensible. While these are necessary changes, they are challenging and will take time. But in the meantime, math anxiety is not irreversible—it can be faced and defeated, one person at a time.

False Beliefs

One reason math anxiety has taken such hold is that several false beliefs have been created and shared until they became widely accepted. Some of these unhelpful beliefs include the following:

There is only one way to solve a math problem. In the same way that you can choose from different driving routes and still arrive at the same house, you can solve a math problem using different methods and still find the correct answer. A person who understands the reasoning behind math calculations may be able to look at an unfamiliar concept and find the right answer, just by applying logic to the knowledge they already have. This approach may be different than what is taught in the classroom, but it is still valid. Unfortunately, even many teachers view math as a subject where the best course of action is to memorize the rule or process for each problem rather than as a place for students to exercise logic and creativity in finding a solution.

Many people don't have a mind for math. A person who has struggled due to poor teaching or math anxiety may falsely believe that he or she doesn't have the mental capacity to grasp mathematical concepts. Most of the time, this is false. Many people find that when they are relieved of their math anxiety, they have more than enough brainpower to understand math.

Men are naturally better at math than women. Even though research has shown this to be false, many young women still avoid math careers and classes because of their belief that their math abilities are inferior. Many girls have come to believe that math is a male skill and have given up trying to understand or enjoy it.

Counting aids are bad. Something like counting on your fingers or drawing out a problem to visualize it may be frowned on as childish or a crutch, but these devices can help you get a tangible understanding of a problem or a concept.

Sadly, many students buy into these ideologies at an early age. A young girl who enjoys math class may be conditioned to think that she doesn't actually have the brain for it because math is for boys, and may turn her energies to other pursuits, permanently closing the door on a wide range of opportunities. A child who finds the right answer but doesn't follow the teacher's method may believe that he is doing it wrong and isn't good at math. A student who never had a problem with math before may have a poor teacher and become confused, yet believe that the problem is because she doesn't have a mathematical mind.

Students who have bought into these erroneous beliefs quickly begin to add their own anxieties, adapting them to their own personal situations:

I'll never use this in real life. A huge number of people wrongly believe that math is irrelevant outside the classroom. By adopting this mindset, they are handicapping themselves for a life in a mathematical world, as well as limiting their career choices. When they are inevitably faced with real-world math, they are conditioning themselves to respond with anxiety.

I'm not quick enough. While timed tests and quizzes, or even simply comparing yourself with other students in the class, can lead to this belief, speed is not an indicator of skill level. A person can work very slowly yet understand at a deep level.

If I can understand it, it's too easy. People with a low view of their own abilities tend to think that if they are able to grasp a concept, it must be simple. They cannot accept the idea that they are capable of understanding math. This belief will make it harder to learn, no matter how intelligent they are.

I just can't learn this. An overwhelming number of people think this, from young children to adults, and much of the time it is simply not true. But this mindset can turn into a self-fulfilling prophecy that keeps you from exercising and growing your math ability.

The good news is, each of these myths can be debunked. For most people, they are based on emotion and psychology, NOT on actual ability! It will take time, effort, and the desire to change, but change is possible. Even if you have spent years thinking that you don't have the capability to understand math, it is not too late to uncover your true ability and find relief from the anxiety that surrounds math.

Math Strategies

It is important to have a plan of attack to combat math anxiety. There are many useful strategies for pinpointing the fears or myths and eradicating them:

Go back to the basics. For most people, math anxiety stems from a poor foundation. You may think that you have a complete understanding of addition and subtraction, or even decimals and percentages, but make absolutely sure. Learning math is different from learning other subjects. For example, when you learn history, you study various time periods and places and events. It may be important to memorize dates or find out about the lives of famous people. When you move from US history to world history, there will be some overlap, but a large amount of the information will be new. Mathematical concepts, on the other hand, are very closely linked and highly dependent on each other. It's like climbing a ladder – if a rung is missing from your understanding, it may be difficult or impossible for you to climb any higher, no matter how hard you try. So go back and make sure your math foundation is strong. This may mean taking a remedial math course, going to a tutor to work through the shaky concepts, or just going through your old homework to make sure you really understand it.

Speak the language. Math has a large vocabulary of terms and phrases unique to working problems. Sometimes these are completely new terms, and sometimes they are common words, but are used differently in a math setting. If you can't speak the language, it will be very difficult to get a thorough understanding of the concepts. It's common for students to think that they don't understand math when they simply don't understand the vocabulary. The good news is that this is fairly easy to fix. Brushing up on any terms you aren't quite sure of can help bring the rest of the concepts into focus.

Check your anxiety level. When you think about math, do you feel nervous or uncomfortable? Do you struggle with feelings of inadequacy, even on concepts that you know you've already learned? It's important to understand your specific math anxieties, and what triggers them. When you catch yourself falling back on a false belief, mentally replace it with the truth. Don't let yourself believe that you can't learn, or that struggling with a concept means you'll never understand it. Instead, remind yourself of how much you've already learned and dwell on that past success. Visualize grasping the new concept, linking it to your old knowledge, and moving on to the next challenge. Also, learn how to manage anxiety when it arises. There are many techniques for coping with the irrational fears that rise to the surface when you enter the math classroom. This may include controlled breathing, replacing negative thoughts with positive ones, or visualizing success. Anxiety interferes with your ability to concentrate and absorb information, which in turn contributes to greater anxiety. If you can learn how to regain control of your thinking, you will be better able to pay attention, make progress, and succeed!

Don't go it alone. Like any deeply ingrained belief, math anxiety is not easy to eradicate. And there is no need for you to wrestle through it on your own. It will take time, and many people find that speaking with a counselor or psychiatrist helps. They can help you develop strategies for responding to anxiety and overcoming old ideas. Additionally, it can be very helpful to take a short course or seek out a math tutor to help you find and fix the missing rungs on your ladder and make sure that you're ready to progress to the next level. You can also find a number of math aids online: courses that will teach you mental devices for figuring out problems, how to get the most out of your math classes, etc.

Check your math attitude. No matter how much you want to learn and overcome your anxiety, you'll have trouble if you still have a negative attitude toward math. If you think it's too hard, or just have general feelings of dread about math, it will be hard to learn and to break through the anxiety. Work on cultivating a positive math attitude. Remind yourself that math is not just a hurdle to be cleared, but a valuable asset. When you view math with a positive attitude, you'll be much more likely to understand and even enjoy it. This is something you must do for yourself. You may find it helpful to visit with a counselor. Your tutor, friends, and family may cheer you on in your endeavors. But your greatest asset is yourself. You are inside your own mind – tell yourself what you need to hear. Relive past victories. Remind yourself that you are capable of understanding math. Root out any false beliefs that linger and replace them with positive truths. Even if it doesn't feel true at first, it will begin to affect your thinking and pave the way for a positive, anxiety-free mindset.

Aside from these general strategies, there are a number of specific practical things you can do to begin your journey toward overcoming math anxiety. Something as simple as learning a new note-taking strategy can change the way you approach math and give you more confidence and understanding. New study techniques can also make a huge difference.

Math anxiety leads to bad habits. If it causes you to be afraid of answering a question in class, you may gravitate toward the back row. You may be embarrassed to ask for help. And you may procrastinate on assignments, which leads to rushing through them at the last moment when it's too late to get a better understanding. It's important to identify your negative behaviors and replace them with positive ones:

Prepare ahead of time. Read the lesson before you go to class. Being exposed to the topics that will be covered in class ahead of time, even if you don't understand them perfectly, is extremely helpful in increasing what you retain from the lecture. Do your homework and, if you're still shaky, go over some extra problems. The key to a solid understanding of math is practice.

Sit front and center. When you can easily see and hear, you'll understand more, and you'll avoid the distractions of other students if no one is in front of you. Plus, you're more likely to be sitting with students who are positive and engaged, rather than others with math anxiety. Let their positive math attitude rub off on you.

Ask questions in class and out. If you don't understand something, just ask. If you need a more in-depth explanation, the teacher may need to work with you outside of class, but often it's a simple concept you don't quite understand, and a single question may clear it up. If you wait, you may not be able to follow the rest of the day's lesson. For extra help, most professors have office hours outside of class when you can go over concepts one-on-one to clear up any uncertainties. Additionally, there may be a *math lab* or study session you can attend for homework help. Take advantage of this.

Review. Even if you feel that you've fully mastered a concept, review it periodically to reinforce it. Going over an old lesson has several benefits: solidifying your understanding, giving you a confidence boost, and even giving some new insights into material that you're currently learning! Don't let yourself get rusty. That can lead to problems with learning later concepts.

Mometrix

Teaching Tips

While the math student's mindset is the most crucial to overcoming math anxiety, it is also important for others to adjust their math attitudes. Teachers and parents have an enormous influence on how students relate to math. They can either contribute to math confidence or math anxiety.

As a parent or teacher, it is very important to convey a positive math attitude. Retelling horror stories of your own bad experience with math will contribute to a new generation of math anxiety. Even if you don't share your experiences, others will be able to sense your fears and may begin to believe them.

Even a careless comment can have a big impact, so watch for phrases like *He's not good at math* or *I never liked math*. You are a crucial role model, and your children or students will unconsciously adopt your mindset. Give them a positive example to follow. Rather than teaching them to fear the math world before they even know it, teach them about all its potential and excitement.

Work to present math as an integral, beautiful, and understandable part of life. Encourage creativity in solving problems. Watch for false beliefs and dispel them. Cross the lines between subjects: integrate history, English, and music with math. Show students how math is used every day, and how the entire world is based on mathematical principles, from the pull of gravity to the shape of seashells. Instead of letting students see math as a necessary evil, direct them to view it as an imaginative, beautiful art form – an art form that they are capable of mastering and using.

Don't give too narrow a view of math. It is more than just numbers. Yes, working problems and learning formulas is a large part of classroom math. But don't let the teaching stop there. Teach students about the everyday implications of math. Show them how nature works according to the laws of mathematics, and take them outside to make discoveries of their own. Expose them to math-related careers by inviting visiting speakers, asking students to do research and presentations, and learning students' interests and aptitudes on a personal level.

Demonstrate the importance of math. Many people see math as nothing more than a required stepping stone to their degree, a nuisance with no real usefulness. Teach students that algebra is used every day in managing their bank accounts, in following recipes, and in scheduling the day's events. Show them how learning to do geometric proofs helps them to develop logical thinking, an invaluable life skill. Let them see that math surrounds them and is integrally linked to their daily lives: that weather predictions are based on math, that math was used to design cars and other machines, etc. Most of all, give them the tools to use math to enrich their lives.

Make math as tangible as possible. Use visual aids and objects that can be touched. It is much easier to grasp a concept when you can hold it in your hands and manipulate it, rather than just listening to the lecture. Encourage math outside of the classroom. The real world is full of measuring, counting, and calculating, so let students participate in this. Keep your eyes open for numbers and patterns to discuss. Talk about how scores are calculated in sports games and how far apart plants are placed in a garden row for maximum growth. Build the mindset that math is a normal and interesting part of daily life.

Finally, find math resources that help to build a positive math attitude. There are a number of books that show math as fascinating and exciting while teaching important concepts, for example: *The Math Curse; A Wrinkle in Time; The Phantom Tollbooth;* and *Fractals, Googols and Other Mathematical Tales.* You can also find a number of online resources: math puzzles and games, videos that show math in nature, and communities of math enthusiasts. On a local level, students can compete in a variety of math competitions with other schools or join a math club.

The student who experiences math as exciting and interesting is unlikely to suffer from math anxiety. Going through life without this handicap is an immense advantage and opens many doors that others have closed through their fear.

Self-Check

Whether you suffer from math anxiety or not, chances are that you have been exposed to some of the false beliefs mentioned above. Now is the time to check yourself for any errors you may have accepted. Do you think you're not wired for math? Or that you don't need to understand it since you're not planning on a math career? Do you think math is just too difficult for the average person?

Find the errors you've taken to heart and replace them with positive thinking. Are you capable of learning math? Yes! Can you control your anxiety? Yes! These errors will resurface from time to time, so be watchful. Don't let others with math anxiety influence you or sway your confidence. If you're having trouble with a concept, find help. Don't let it discourage you!

Create a plan of attack for defeating math anxiety and sharpening your skills. Do some research and decide if it would help you to take a class, get a tutor, or find some online resources to fine-tune your knowledge. Make the effort to get good nutrition, hydration, and sleep so that you are operating at full capacity. Remind yourself daily that you are skilled and that anxiety does not control you. Your mind is capable of so much more than you know. Give it the tools it needs to grow and thrive.

Thank You

We at Mometrix would like to extend our heartfelt thanks to you, our friend and patron, for allowing us to play a part in your journey. It is a privilege to serve people from all walks of life who are unified in their commitment to building the best future they can for themselves.

The preparation you devote to these important testing milestones may be the most valuable educational opportunity you have for making a real difference in your life. We encourage you to put your heart into it—that feeling of succeeding, overcoming, and yes, conquering will be well worth the hours you've invested.

We want to hear your story, your struggles and your successes, and if you see any opportunities for us to improve our materials so we can help others even more effectively in the future, please share that with us as well. **The team at Mometrix would be absolutely thrilled to hear from you!** So please, send us an email (support@mometrix.com) and let's stay in touch.

> **If you'd like some additional help, check out these other resources we offer for your exam:**
> **http://mometrixflashcards.com/SATII**

Additional Bonus Material

Due to our efforts to try to keep this book to a manageable length, we've created a link that will give you access to all of your additional bonus material.

Please visit http://www.mometrix.com/bonus948/satushist-11703 to access the information.

Made in the USA
Columbia, SC
10 February 2020